The UNDERCLASS QUESTION

Edited and with an
Introduction by

BILL E. LAWSON

Foreword by
William Julius Wilson

TEMPLE UNIVERSITY PRESS

PHILADELPHIA

Temple University Press, Philadelphia 19122
Copyright © 1992 by Temple University. All rights reserved
Published 1992
Printed in the United States of America

Library of Congress Cataloging-in-Publication Data
The underclass question / edited and with an introduction by Bill E.
   Lawson : foreword by William Julius Wilson.
      p. cm.
   Includes bibliographical references and index.
   ISBN 0-87722-922-8 (alk. paper)
   1. Afro-Americans—Government policy. 2. Afro-Americans—Social
conditions—1975– 3. Afro-Americans—Economic conditions.
4. United States—Social policy—1980– 5. Poor—Government policy—
United States. I. Lawson, Bill E.
E185.86.U49 1992
305.896'073—dc20   91-26421

To the future: my son, William Lance Lawson

To the present: my wife, Barbara Lance Lawson

To the past: my aunt, Bertha Kersey

By 1967, whites could point to the demise of slavery, the decline of illiteracy among Negroes, the legal protection provided by the constitutional amendments and civil rights legislation, and the growing size of the Negro middle class. Whites would call it Negro progress, from slavery to freedom and toward equality.

Negroes could point to the doctrine of white supremacy, its persistence after emancipation and its influence on the definition of the place of Negroes in American life. They could point to their long fight for full citizenship when they had active opposition from most of the white population and little or no support from the Government. They could see progress toward equality accompanied by bitter resistance. Perhaps most of all, they could feel the persistent, pervasive racism that kept them in inferior segregated schools, restricted them to ghettos, barred them from fair employment, provided double standards in courts of justice, inflicted bodily harm on their children and blighted their lives with a sense of hopelessness and despair.

In all of this and in the context of professed ideals, Negroes would find more retrogression than progress, more rejection than acceptance.

Report of the National Advisory Commission on Civil Disorders, 1968

CONTENTS

EPILOGUE: *Back on the Block*

FOREWORD

In *The Truly Disadvantaged* I argued that joblessness exacerbated by increasing social isolation in impoverished neighborhoods is the central problem of the underclass. It is important to be cognizant of the association between attachment to the labor force and the neighborhood context in order to understand the unique position of many inner-city ghetto residents. As sociologist Martha Van Haitsma has observed, poor people who reside in neighborhoods that foster or support strong labor force attachment are in a much different social context than those with similar educational and occupational skills who live in neighborhoods that promote or reinforce weak labor force attachment.

Thus neighborhoods that have few legitimate employment opportunities, inadequate job information networks, and poor schools not only create weak labor force attachments, but also raise the likelihood that people will turn to illegal or deviant activities for income. These activities further weaken the attachment to the legitimate labor market. Also, the behavior, beliefs, orientations, and social perceptions associated with chronic subordination in such neighborhoods are less conducive to employment in legitimate labor markets than are those of most other urban neighborhoods. Indeed, there is a difference between, on the one hand, a jobless family that is held down by the macrostructural constraints in the economy and the larger society but that nonetheless lives in an area with a relatively low rate of poverty and, on the other hand, a jobless family that lives in an inner-city ghetto neighborhood that is influenced not only by these same constraints but by the behavior of other jobless families in the neighborhood as well. To capture this process I used the term "concentration effects," that is, the effects of living in an overwhelmingly impoverished environment.

Members of the underclass are distinguished from those of other economically disadvantaged groups by the strong association between their marginal economic position and their neighborhood or social milieu. The dual problem of marginal economic position and social isolation in highly concentrated poverty areas is not captured in the standard designations of "lower class" or "working class."

The crucial question is whether a complex, theoretically defined concept of underclass will be overshadowed in the long run by usages, as seen in recent journalistic descriptions of inner-city behavior, that become code words or ideological slogans. As I have argued elsewhere, if this proves to be true, research scholars ought to give serious consideration to dropping the term and carefully selecting another to describe and highlight the important theoretical linkage between a disadvantaged group's position in the labor market and its social environment.

After reading the essays in this interesting volume, I see that my concerns may not be justified. Lawson and his colleagues have effectively used the concept of underclass to address a complex set of issues on race, class, values, culture, and social policy. Any serious student of inequality in America ought to consider the points raised in *The Underclass Question*. The combined essays by a group of philosophers provide a fresh perspective on the study of the truly disadvantaged. Although I do not agree with some of the interpretations and criticisms of my work, I am impressed with and take seriously the thoughtful and lively discussion of the issues. *The Underclass Question* is a welcome, important, and unique addition to the growing literature on race, class, and poverty in urban America.

WILLIAM JULIUS WILSON

PREFACE

A NUMBER of events conspired to bring this book into existence. First, I grew up in what is now part of the underclass tract in Philadelphia, Pennsylvania: Sixteenth and Federal streets and the Tasker Homes. Although I left Philly at eighteen, I kept returning to visit my friends Thomas (Tim) Clay, Fred Singletary, Allen Nelson, William Hatch, Reggie Richardson, and the late Ellison ("Butch") Matthews. Over the years these friendships have kept me rooted in the reality that my life was greatly affected by having lived in the "hood." Unfortunately, the past twenty-five years have seen my old neighborhoods decline, and I cannot help but be saddened by the social and economic depression I see there.

Second, on April 4, 1968, Martin Luther King, Jr., was murdered, and two days later I was on an airplane headed to Vietnam as a grunt. When I got to 'Nam, two important events were taking place: The 1968 Tet offensive and the black troops' protest of the murder of Dr. King. The latter event would have the greatest impact on me during my tour and later on my academic scholarship. Over the next eleven months, I had ample opportunity to discuss with black, Hispanic, and white soldiers the "race" problem in America. Much of the debate centered on the question of whether blacks and other minorities had any moral or political obligation to fight for American interests or America. Many white soldiers felt that America offered the best opportunities for racial and ethnic minorities. This feeling was not shared by most of the black and Hispanic soldiers with whom I talked. At that time I had no way of knowing that my Ph.D. dissertation would cover aspects of that debate: What are the political obligations of oppressed minorities in a liberal democratic state?

Third, in graduate school at the University of North Carolina at Chapel Hill, I was fortunate to be able to work with Steve Darwall, Arthur Kuflick, Jane English, Ernest Manasse, and Paul Ziff. These understanding professors allowed me the freedom to pursue the issues I felt important, given my background. I drew on my concerns and wrote on the political obligations of oppressed minorities, a question that still drives part of my present research.

Fourth, I was asked by Norm Bowie and Frank Dilley to hold a conference for the Center for the Study of Values at the University of Delaware. Because of trips to my old neighborhood and the publication of William Julius Wilson's *The Truly Disadvantaged*, I decided to focus on the philosophical issues raised by the advent of what has been called the "underclass." Frank and Norm supported my decision without reservations, and I was able to call on ten fine scholars and friends, who agreed to participate even before my ideas for the conference were completely formed.

Fifth, I had the love of my wife, Barbara, and my son, William. I also received moral strength and inspiration from my parents, Edmond Daniel Lawson and Annie J. Lawson. It is the conjunction of these events and a few more that helped make this volume possible.

Looking at my old neighborhood and reflecting on the issues raised by the existence of pervasive and possibly permanent poverty and hopelessness in America bring to mind the debates of my Vietnam days: What are the political and moral obligations of oppressed minorities in a liberal democratic state?

This book is the result of the June 1989 conference "Meditations on Integration: Philosophy and the Black Underclass," which was sponsored by the Center for the Study of Values and the Department of Philosophy at the University of Delaware. The conference was partially funded by grants from the Delaware Humanities Forum and the Exxon Education Foundation. Additional funding was provided by the following programs at the University of Delaware: Black American Studies, The Center for Black Culture, Commission on the Status of Women, Commission to Promote Racial and Cultural Diversity, Cultural Activities and Public Events, Department of Philosophy, Minority Affairs, Office of the President, Office of the Provost, and Visiting Scholars and Speakers Subcommittee.

I express my appreciation to the ten conference participants; to the co-organizer of the conference, Norm Bowie; and to Sandy Manno, who put all of the parts together. Thanks also go to Frank Dilley, chair of the Department of Philosophy, who has supported all of my academic endeavors; Sandra Harding, for the lunch meetings and advice; Howard McGary and Laurence Thomas, colleagues and friends, for all of their support and guidance; Jane Cullen, Senior Acquisitions Editor in Philosophy at Temple University Press, for being there; James

Newton, chair of Black American Studies at the University of Delaware, for support and patience; Renata Johnson, for being my eyes at the library; Donald and Sharon Baker, for allowing me the use of their home for needed breaks; Donald Baker, for being a friend; Fred and Sylvia Singletary, for keeping me up on news from the "hood"; Harold Hyman, for being my first philosophy teacher; James Davis, for the advice on social science literature; Chuck Tarver, for encouraging me to stay on the case when recording companies did not respond; Kevin Richardson, for being a "rap" master; Claudette Jones, for taping Cornel West's speech; Charlena Lance, for listening; Charlie and Rosa Lee Lance, for watching William those final days; Mary Imperatore and Gail Ross, for helping to put the manuscript together; and Henry Ruf, Henry West, Carol Marks, Kate Rogers, Rod Stewart, John Rubio, Carol Rudisell, Jeff Jordan, Judy Gibson, Andrea Turner, and the members of my department at Delaware, who all supported my efforts in some way. I also wish to acknowledge the support of both Ernst Manasse and Paul Ziff, former professors and longtime friends. For providing a musical background environment at various times, I thank Miles, Trane, Bird, Bobby Watson, Kenny Garrett, Betty Carter, Dianne Reeves, Kool Moe Dee, M. C. Hammer, Digital Underground, Grand Daddy I.U., Public Enemy, Muddy Waters, Bobby Blue Bland, Howlin' Wolf, and Willie Dixon.

Last, but far from least, I want to thank my son, William Lance Lawson, who forced me to take needed breaks.

The Underclass Question

1   MEDITATIONS ON INTEGRATION

Bill E. Lawson

IN 1968, Martin Luther King, Jr., was murdered. Twenty years after his death many people, especially in the print media, assessed the political and social progress black Americans had made.[1] One fact became clear in this assessment: In the years after King's assassination, the social, political, and economic progress of black Americans had been paradoxical.[2]

In a period of the most sweeping antidiscrimination legislation in the history of this country, an ever-increasing number of blacks have been classified as a black "underclass." These poor and mostly urban dwellers are seen as a new social phenomenon. They are unlike poor urban dwellers of the past in that they are described as young, unemployable, and prone to crime and other forms of unestimable behavior. While the number of blacks who can be considered "middle class" has also increased, much of the social debate has been about public policies to alleviate the growing underclass.

One of the more intriguing assessments of the social, political, and economic progress of black Americans is offered by William Julius Wilson in his 1987 work *The Truly Disadvantaged*.[3] Wilson cites what he takes to be a curious paradox: "That whereas economic growth since World War II enabled many blacks to experience occupational mobility, recent structural shifts in the economy have diminished mobility opportunities for others. And whereas antidiscrimination legislation has removed many racial barriers, not all blacks are in a position to benefit from it."[4]

Wilson concludes that the position of some blacks has actually deteriorated during the very period in which the most sweeping antidiscrimination legislation and programs have been enacted and implemented. "The net effect is a growing economic schism between poor and higher-income blacks."[5]

Wilson, of course, was not the first to call attention to the urban

1

poor. As early as the 1830s, researchers noted the existence of a group of blacks that seemed to be mired in poverty. These blacks were called the "rabble." Researchers on poverty and blacks more often used the term "poor" to describe the group and the "culture of poverty" thesis to explain its existence. This thesis postulates that black culture is pathological and that negative social behaviors are passed from one generation to another.

However, it was not until the 1960s that the term *underclass* was applied directly to blacks.[6] In the past decade, the term has come to be used almost exclusively to describe those black persons living in poverty in urban areas.[7]

Despite a great deal of research on the underclass, important questions remain:

1. Is the underclass simply a new label for the poor or does it represent a distinct group?
2. Assuming the two groups are different, is the underclass a subset of the poor, are the poor a subset of the underclass, or do the two groups overlap?
3. What characteristics most distinguish the underclass from the poor: (a) the length of time they remain poor; (b) their geographic concentration and/or isolation; (c) their attitudes; or (d) their behavior?[8]

The social science literature is teeming with answers to these questions.[9] However, social scientists disagree on how the underclass should be defined, and thus on how many individuals should be included in the group. The failure to characterize accurately the group affects the type of governmental policies formulated to deal with urban poverty. Furthermore, Wilson believes that governmental policies have been based on principles that do nothing to help those members of the underclass.

It is now recognized that unless something drastic is done a segment of the black population will never be able to participate fully in the social and political life of America. Wilson thinks that social policies framed around either equality of opportunity or preferential treatment have failed to eliminate the economic or social inequality faced by this group. These approaches fail because they advance advantaged minority members but do not significantly change the position of the truly disadvantaged.

The principle of equality of individual opportunity, according to Wilson, is the bedrock of the old civil rights movement, which emphasized the rights of minority individuals. The old civil rights movement was in line with the basic assumption of liberal democratic thought. It was assumed that the government could best protect the rights of individual members of minority groups not by formally bestowing rewards and punishments based on race or ethnic categories, but by using antidiscrimination legislation to enhance individual choice in education, employment, voting, and public accommodations. This position takes its lead from the Supreme Court rulings that stated that the Fourteenth Amendment was not a black-specific amendment. Equal opportunity was to be applied to individuals and not to groups. The individual, therefore, was the "unit of attribution for equality considerations,"[10] and the ultimate goal was to reward each citizen based on merits and accomplishments. In short, equality of opportunity meant equality for each citizen.

According to Wilson, the major problem with this approach is that it does not address the substantive inequality that the truly disadvantaged had when obstacles based on racial bias were removed. Citing William Rasberry, Wilson adds:

> There are some blacks for whom it is enough to remove the artificial barriers of race. After that, their entry into the American mainstream is virtually automatic. There are others for whom hardly anything would change if, by some magical stroke, racism disappeared from America. Everyone knows this of course. And hardly anyone is willing to say it. And because we don't say it, we wind up confused about how to deal with the explosive problems confronting the American society, confused about what the problem really is.[11]

Programs based on the principle of equal opportunity help those who already have the skills necessary to get employment, not those who most need governmental support. Wilson thinks that any governmental program to end black poverty must include jobs for the hard-core unemployed. Changes in the economic structure have made it impossible for many young black men to find secure employment, and therefore to overcome the inequalities of the past. Employment of young black males will help them to become supporters of their families. Since families are the cultural and value bedrock of society, the social values of the underclass will change, making their integration into the American mainstream easier.[12]

The policy of providing jobs, however, must not be based on race, even if most of the underclass is black. It must be part of a nationwide jobs program. Thus Wilson proposes a program that will benefit all Americans who suffer because of class disabilities. He thinks that such a program will indeed aid members of the black underclass. However, to make the program acceptable to the majority of Americans, the elimination of urban poverty has to be part of the program's hidden agenda. That is, while the primary aim is to address urban poverty, it has to be sold as a policy to address the interests of all Americans. In this manner, the policy will improve the life chances of groups such as the ghetto underclass by emphasizing programs in which the more-advantaged groups of all races positively relate.[13] What we must do, if Wilson is correct, is mask our intent to help truly disadvantaged blacks. Thus Wilson proposes a program that has as its stated aim the economic improvement of the quality of life for all poor Americans. Wilson's goal, it seems, is to devise a strategy that will enable members of the underclass to integrate into the mainstream of American life.

Wilson's analysis has been both praised and attacked by social scientists.[14] His position and the debate it has stirred gives us cause to pause and reflect on the possibility of integrating poor blacks into the American mainstream. This reflection is necessary for a number of reasons. First, Wilson's work has become the focal point for much of the current discussion of the underclass and urban poverty.[15] Second, the term *underclass* has now come to be almost solely identified with urban blacks and Hispanics.[16] While Wilson has come to realize the negative manner in which the term underclass is now used and admits that the negative connotations were never his intention,[17] sociologist Carol Marks notes: "The term's acceptance is so wide, in fact, that the thematic contradictions which lie just below the surface are seldom noted. That the class exists is generally not disputed (though the term is often maligned), but on few other issues is there anything like common agreement."[18] Third, if there is indeed an underclass, what philosophical assumptions underpin programs and policies that push for the integration of poor blacks into the American mainstream? Clearly what we believe about a group will have an important effect on the policies formulated. Thus assumptions about the relationship between poverty, the black American experience, and social policies should be examined.

In the past few years, a cottage industry has been established whose primary aim is to do research on the "underclass." Research is now being carried out by economists, political scientists, educators, and theologians,[19] nearly all of whom are putting forward programs and policies intended to help integrate the underclass.

Philosophers have not been unaware of the growth of what has been termed the "underclass"[20] and have realized that the growth of a politically and economically disadvantaged black group in a period of purported growth of a black middle class raises some interesting philosophical questions regarding (1) conceptualizing poor urban blacks as a class; (2) the relationship between values formation and social progress; (3) affirmative action and the underclass; (4) our conception of the political and legal rights of the underclass; and (5) intragroup values and obligations. It is clear from these concerns that any analysis of the urban poor must include a philosophical approach.[21]

This book presents such an analysis. Like much of the current discussion of the underclass, Wilson's *The Truly Disadvantaged* or some question that arises from his analysis is the focus for most of these papers. The authors, however, share common perspectives on the black urban underclass. The authors generally agree that a segment of the black population may never be able to enjoy the fruits of the American dream (although this group may not be a class) and that this segment is often plagued by those factors that are cited as group characteristics by authors such as Wilson (high incidence of unemployment, welfare dependency, crime, violence, etc.). But they also agree that the existence of this "class" is a by-product of the normal functioning of a capitalist economy and that proposals to eliminate the underclass without addressing fundamental social change are not only doomed to failure, but may reinforce racism and political oppression. In this regard, throughout the authors suggest that far from being dysfunctional, blacks are behaving precisely the way that one should expect them to behave if one takes seriously the problems of race and class discrimination in the United States.

The authors do not try to show that such a social entity as an underclass exists, nor do they attempt to show that the underclass is a special segment of the black urban poor.[22] The authors realize that, unfortunately, attitudes about underclass blacks are used to make judgments about all poor blacks, if not about all blacks. It is unclear whether most Americans make such distinctions between poor blacks and members of the underclass. The failure to make this distinction may prove to be a problem for implementing programs that empower the poor. Given the pervasive use of the term *underclass* and the negative connotations that go along with its use, it seems clear that even if we assume that we can empower some of the urban poor, their empowerment is qualified by their being identified with the underclass. It is also questionable, given some descriptions of the underclass, that social programs meant to empower the poor would have any positive effect on the underclass. Of course, we still need to know what empowering the poor means in the American political and economic context. Empowering the poor is an interesting concept given that these persons are American citizens and, as such, are supposed to have some political power.[23]

Wilson has recently said that he will no longer use the term *under-class* and speaks instead of the "ghetto poor." This pronouncement illustrates the extent to which he sees his ability to direct or focus the tone of the "underclass" debate.[24] Nevertheless, the phrase "ghetto poor" is not without problems. Are all blacks who live in ghetto areas part of the underclass? Without making the necessary distinctions between the status of poor blacks, it is unclear what this change of terms will accomplish in regard to popular conceptions of poor urban blacks. However, Wilson's disavowal of the term *underclass* does not affect the focus of the essays in this book. What we call this segment of the black population is, at this juncture, secondary to many of the points raised in the three sections of this volume.

Social scientists may find this book somewhat uneven because it tends to focus on Wilson's work, with little mention of other social scientists. But it should be remembered that Wilson's analysis is the focal point of much of the current debate, and that most social scientific research on poverty and the underclass carries a strong quantitative approach and usually abstains from dealing with the normative/value question, which philosophers are more proficient to handle. Most of the authors in this volume concern themselves either totally or in large measure with conceptual and normative questions pertaining to the underclass.[25] What is the role of racism in the emergence and maintenance of the so-called underclass? To what extent should public policies be race-based? These questions provide in part both the rationale and focus of this book.

Will Class-Specific Programs Eliminate Urban Poverty?

Can an appeal to class-based programs eliminate urban poverty? What is the role of race in the emergence and maintenance of the underclass? Is the "underclass" a "class"? In Chapter 2, Bernard R. Boxill discusses the problems involved in using class-based programs to eliminate the underclass. Boxill examines Wilson's claim that the underclass can be eliminated through class-based programs that attempt to raise the income level of all Americans. Wilson thinks that helping the underclass has to be part of a social policy that downplays race. Boxill argues that Wilson's position fails to show how these programs will overcome the racial animosity that arises when programs are implemented to help blacks. Racism will be a factor in the acceptance of these programs. Whites, according to Boxill, will still dislike blacks getting better jobs. Boxill thinks that we can admit that the significance of race has declined, but that we still need to be cognizant of the importance of racial animosity as an impediment to social progress.

The main thrust of Boxill's work is to refute Wilson's claim that social policy must be rooted in appeals to the self-interest of the white majority. Boxill argues that Wilson's position is just a restatement of the position of Booker T. Washington, who also thought that the best approach to social change was an appeal to the self-interest of whites.[26] Boxill thinks that this approach is misguided. Social reforms should be justified in terms of their moral correctness: justice. Appeals to self-interest may not get the social programs that one wants.

Boxill thinks that W.E.B. Du Bois, on the other hand, realized that social reform often comes at the expense of self-interest. While Du Bois also thought that it was the moral responsibility of blacks with high moral insight to be role models and teachers to the black masses, he did not show a disdain for the masses. In the end, Boxill wants to expand the moral duties of those persons Du Bois called the "talented tenth" to teach the white majority as well.

In Chapter 3, Leonard Harris examines the questions that arise when a certain segment of poor American citizens are called a "class." Harris agrees with Boxill that it is not necessary to appeal to racism to explain the emergence of the "underclass." However, to call this segment of American poor a "class" raises some interesting questions about what type of social entity it is.

Harris focuses on the use of the term *class* to define the social status of the urban poor and notes that there are minimal criteria for a class to exist as a social entity. One important aspect of class status is class agency. Classes are agents if they have special interests that either the class or its members are, or are potentially, struggling to realize. Harris argues that various descriptions of the urban poor fail to show in what sense they constitute a class. Comparing the underclass to Marx's *lumpenproletariat* fails because, unlike the *lumpenproletariat,* the underclass has no special class characteristics that can be used to better the position of other classes. The *lumpenproletariat* had its ruthlessness, which could be used by the working class to further the ends of both groups. What are the estimable qualities of the underclass?

What are the interests of the underclass? Harris thinks that the manner in which this group has been described shows that it has no class-based interest. As a class it does not have socially redeeming characteristics. All that the members of this class share is the brute fact of social situation. In fact, if we accept what seems to be Wilson's understanding of social agency, the underclass as a class is at the same time impotent as an agent, culpable for its own plight, and lacking socially estimable qualities. Harris concludes by asking: In what sense does this group constitute a class? How can social policy be framed given these assumptions?

Are There Values Unique to Urban Blacks?

Part Two focuses on the values held by some members of the urban poor. Is it the case that urban poor suffer from a pathological value system that fosters a "cycle of poverty"? Can the lack of economic achievement by blacks be totally attributed to their being lazy? What are the obligations of middle-class blacks to the urban poor?

Howard McGary examines one of the negative value claims that is often made against members of the urban poor: Urban blacks do not make it in American society because they are lazy. McGary thinks that motivation to overcome social adversities is reinforced by one's under-standing of both the value of the goal and one's likelihood of success. When we examine the social world of the urban poor, we can under-stand why many of its members would not try to make it in the social marketplace. It is true that if one tries long enough and has the patience of Job, one may make it out of poverty. However, if it takes Herculean effort to overcome some social adversities, one should not be held in moral contempt if one does not try. McGary is not claiming that there are not some lazy individuals among the urban poor; indeed, there are lazy persons in all groups. Nor is he claiming that persons should not attempt Herculean efforts. He is suggesting that negative value claims about the urban poor need to be assessed with an eye toward factors that engender what are taken to be positive social values.

Tommy Lott continues the discussion of value formation and cop-ing from the social pressures of being black and poor in urban America. Lott notes that, while Wilson claims to reject the "culture of poverty" thesis, his position offers no criticism of its advocates' view of black culture. Wilson, according to Lott, acquiesces to the neoconservative contention that the culture of black urban poor people is pathological. Lott argues that an understanding of black urban culture reveals that many of the values of mainstream America have been recoded into the lifestyle and social understanding of urban youth. There is no reason, as McGary notes, to believe that urban blacks have different values than mainstream America. They differ only in their ability to act on those values. However, urban blacks, according to Lott, have found the per-fect vehicle to express their values. The values held and advocated by urban black youths can be found in rap music.

Rappers understand that they have mainstream values without the ability to act on them. Lott thinks that rap music, when properly understood, has been encoded with the necessary messages for political and social resistance. Urban blacks realize that without fundamental structural changes in the social, political, and economic institutions they will also be trapped in poverty. Lott thinks that as long as black urban youth in extreme-poverty neighborhoods see themselves trapped under America's apartheid their cultural expression will continue to exhibit elements of resistance. The culture of urban black America is not pathological.

In Chapter 6, I examine the claim that middle-class blacks are in some sense responsible for the advent and continuation of the urban underclass. Wilson and others have argued that the movement of middle-class and working blacks out of the "ghetto" has caused the decline in the quality of life for urban blacks. Are middle-class blacks obligated to stay in these neighborhoods? I think that if we use the "race as family" model, the answer is yes. However, I think that the "race as family" model fails as a justification for race-based obligations. I admit that there may be race-based obligations, but the moral scope of this type of obligation must be examined. Racism challenges many black Americans not to see their fate tied to the fate of poor blacks. What will it take to free middle-class blacks from an obligation to help poor blacks because of societal racism? I argue that many blacks believe that white Americans will never accept blacks as social equals, partly because of a failure by whites to establish basic trust between the races. I conclude that until blacks think that whites as a group can be trusted, the question of race-based obligations in America will dominate the political and moral landscape of the black community.

What Is the Relationship Between Racism and Social Policy?

What is the relationship between legal rights and social progress? Do affirmative action programs help only undeserving blacks? Anita L. Allen argues that the conception of legal rights embraced in good faith has worked along with racism and brute politics to further black inequality. American law, she notes, has not been a natural ally of the black underclass. From the *Dred Scott* case on, America's legal theorists have shown disdain for blacks as legitimate legal rights claimants. While the understanding of who may have a legal right has been officially broadened to include blacks, the full practical benefits of having rights is still beyond the reach of the black underclass.[27] Lower levels of compliance with the law and ineffective law enforcement in underclass communities may signal the absence of meaningful rights, partially undercutting the sense in which rights and equal legal rights can be meaningfully ascribed.[28]

Allen admits that social problems exist in many urban areas, but these social problems do not by themselves explain the existence of an underclass. One must, she thinks, look at the history of legal and political decisions that have impacted on the legal status of blacks. These decisions give us a clearer understanding of why, coupled with the social problems, there is an underclass. Blacks have had to fight to be seen as persons deserving of legal rights. The lack of enforcement of legal rights has impacted on all areas of black life. Allen concludes that barriers to the elimination of the black underclass include conceptual barriers relating to how society thinks about legal rights and rights holders.

Some black scholars have joined the chorus of those who appeal to the "culture of poverty" thesis to explain the advent and continuation of the so-called underclass. Thomas Sowell and Glenn Loury have been in the forefront of this neoconservative critique of the black urban poor. Sowell and Loury have argued that race-specific policies are inappropriate and ineffective for alleviating the plight of the urban poor. Albert G. Mosley examines their arguments and finds that both Sowell and Loury use rhetorical sleight of hand to misdirect the reader's attention away from the social, political, and economic history of blacks in America.

Sowell, for example, acknowledges the special case of the African American, yet he does not focus on the debilitating effects of slavery, segregation, and unequal treatment justified by racism. Loury, according to Mosley, proposes to shift our focus from the disparities among groups per se to disparities in the rewards to the different types of activities toward which various group members incline. The purpose of Sowell's and Loury's arguments is to show that no matter what the social, political, or economic history of African Americans, they deserve no special consideration. More specifically, affirmative action is not a justified social policy for any group of blacks. Finally, Mosley discusses Wilson's position, which he links with Sowell and Loury. All three of these scholars seem to think that the problems of the so-called underclass can be solved without major changes in the basic structure of America's social and political institutions.

Frank M. Kirkland's essay encapsulates many of the points made throughout the volume.[29] Kirkland examines Wilson's claim that a social policy of universal economic reforms will help the plight of the underclass. The government has to try to ensure that the economic system does not work against members of the underclass by not providing them jobs. Like Boxill, Kirkland notes that a universal jobs program will still possibly engender white worker antagonism. But Kirkland also thinks that Wilson's approach is flawed for a number of reasons. First, Wilson seems to take it on faith that governmental intervention will produce the types of programs needed. Second, given the relationship of the government to the business community, it is unclear that the policies formulated will be rational. Third, Wilson, according to Kirkland, underestimates the role of the government in making the underclass. Although Wilson acknowledges past racism, what Kirkland has in mind is the impact governmental agencies have on the lives of members of the underclass. Kirkland thinks that it is not welfare but the manner in which welfare is administered that helps to keep so many blacks in the underclass. Thus, like Harris, he thinks that the underclass is constantly being remade and shaped by policy makers. This idea is in line with the point made by McGary and Lott that the values expressed by members of the underclass can only be understood in light of their day-to-day existence and how that existence is impacted upon by structural conditions.

Kirkland wants to show how any policy to alleviate urban poverty must focus on economic and structural impediments that erode ethical life for the urban poor. He thinks, like I do, that middle-class blacks have an obligation to establish institutions that help young urban dwellers make the transition to adulthood. Yet the programs designed to alleviate the poverty of the underclass must also be understood in relation to the knowledge that America has, as Allen notes, often failed to take blacks seriously as legal rights holders. Kirkland concludes that any programs that aim at the betterment of the underclass must be bilateral in that they must address cultural and economic concerns, and serial in that programs meant to address cultural concerns cannot be established independently of programs that address political and economic concerns.

In the Epilogue, Cornel West discusses the issues surrounding doing research on the underclass and being a black philosopher. West addresses the concerns of writing on the underclass when one may be a former member of the underclass or have close family members who are part of the underclass. He notes that academia has never shown a great deal of respect for study of the black experience or for the scholarship of blacks. Although for blacks work in academia is frequently stressful, and black scholars often work on these issues with nonsupportive colleges, West argues that blacks, women, and other members of the so-called nonelite have to stay on course and continue to address social justice issues.

In conclusion, the contributors think that the combination of certain attitudes and assumptions about the impact of race, class, the economy, governmental policies, and our conception of citizenship makes it difficult to formulate policies that redress the problems faced by the urban poor. It remains to be seen whether policy makers can work through the maze of conceptual confusion that formulates attitudes about black Americans in general and poor blacks in particular.

This volume will, of course, raise many more questions than it answers. For example, how does the social situation of blacks impact on our understanding of impartiality in ethical theory? Should the fact that a group suffers from race and class discrimination lessen its political obligation to the state? [30] What will it take to make America a racially integrated society? What do we mean by racial integration? [31] How does poverty affect one's status as a citizen? How will American citizenship be defined in the twenty-first century? There are enough ethical issues involving the black American experience to keep philosophers writing for decades to come.

This volume is a work in the classic form of a philosophical meditation, that is, a work in which philosophers explore the conceptual landscape to show how our understanding of certain social problems can be enhanced by reflecting on the underlying philosophical assumptions we hold. As René Descartes noted in the First Meditation regarding long-held and cherished beliefs:

> Already some years ago I have noticed how many false things I, going into my youth, had admitted as true and how dubious were whatever things I have afterwards built upon them, and therefore that once in my life all things are fundamentally to be demolished and that I have to begin again from the first foundations if I were to desire ever to stabilize something firm and lasting in the sciences. But the task seemed to be a huge one, and I waited for that age which would be so mature that none more fit for the disciplines to be pursued would follow. Thus I have delayed so long that I would now be at fault if by deliberating I were to consume that time which remains for what is to be done. Today then I have opportunely rid the mind of all cares and I have procured for myself secure leisure, I am withdrawing alone and I shall at last devote myself seriously and freely to this general demolition of my opinions.[32]

This volume shares certain aspects of Descartes's *Meditations* in that as Descartes's work challenged the prevailing views of epistemological certainty, the writings in this work challenge certain sociological assumptions about how urban poverty and the urban poor should be viewed.[33] For example, it is often believed that poor blacks have not succeeded in America because they are lazy; that black urban culture is pathological; that affirmative action programs help undeserving blacks; that class-based programs will end urban poverty; and that the possession of legal rights by blacks will help eliminate poverty. All of these beliefs are mistaken. Therefore, it is my hope that, like Descartes's work, this volume will give social scientists and those persons interested in achieving social justice reasons to rethink certain assumptions about the relationship between poverty, the black experience in America, and governmental policies.

Finally, the title of this chapter is taken from a musical composition written by Charles Mingus, "Meditations on Integration."[34] One cannot read the voluminous literature on poverty in America and not be moved emotionally. The existence of long-term and possibly permanent poverty coupled with racism, sexism, and classism is a blight on the American liberal ideological landscape. I was tempted, after much reflection on the plight of the urban poor and their prospects to achieve full American citizenship, to use the title of Mingus's autobiography, *Beneath the Underdog*,[35] for this volume.

NOTES

1. See, for example, "The Dream Then and Now," *Life*, April 4, 1988; "The Black Middle Class: Plenty of Gains, But Progress Is Slow," *Business Week*, March 14, 1988, pp. 62–70; "Black and White: How Integrated Is America?" *Newsweek*, March 7, 1988, pp. 18–43; "The Emerging Black Middle Class," *Washington Post: National Weekly Edition*, February 8–14, 1988, pp. 6–8.

2. Ronald Mincy, "Paradoxes in Black Economic Progress: Income, Families and the Underclass," *Journal of Negro Education* 58, no. 3 (Summer 1989): 255–69; and Paul E. Peterson, "The Urban Underclass and the Poverty Paradox," in *The Urban Underclass*, ed. Christopher Jencks and Paul E. Peterson (Washington, D.C.: Brookings Institution, 1991), pp. 3–28.

3. William Julius Wilson, *The Truly Disadvantaged: The Inner City, the Underclass, and Public Policy* (Chicago: University of Chicago Press, 1987), p. 134.

4. Ibid.

5. Ibid.

6. See Leslie Inniss and Joe Feagin, "The Black 'Underclass': Ideology in Race Relations Analysis," *Social Justice* 16, no. 4 (Winter 1989): 13–34.

7. For a discussion of the white underclass see Ronald Mincy, *Is There a White Underclass?* (Washington, D.C.: Urban Institute, 1988).

8. Erol R. Ricketts and Isabel V. Sawhill, "Defining and Measuring the Underclass," *Journal of Policy Analysis and Management* 7, no. 2 (1988): 316–25.

9. See, for example, Jencks and Peterson, *The Urban Underclass*; and *The Ghetto Underclass: Social Science Perspectives*, Special Editor, William Julius Wilson, *The Annals of the American Academy of Political and Social Science* 501 (January 1989).

10. Wilson, *The Truly Disadvantaged*, p. 112.

11. Ibid., p. 113.

12. This section draws on my discussion of Wilson in "Moral Discourse and Slavery," in Bill Lawson and Howard McGary, *Between Slavery and Freedom: Philosophy and American Slavery* (Bloomington: Indiana University Press, forthcoming).

13. Wilson, *The Truly Disadvantaged*, p. 120.

14. Wilson addresses many of the criticisms of his position in "Public Policy Research and *The Truly Disadvantaged*," in *The Urban Underclass*, ed. Jencks and Peterson.

15. William Julius Wilson, "Studying Inner-City Social Dislocation: The Challenge of Public Agenda Research," *American Sociological Review* 56 (February 1991): 1–14.

16. See, for example, Douglas G. Glasgow, *The Black Underclass* (New York: Random House, 1981); Ken Auletta, *The Underclass* (New York: Vintage Books, 1982); Michael Harrington, *The New American Poverty* (New York: Holt, Rinehart and Winston, 1981); and Charles Murray, *Losing Ground* (New York: Basic Books, 1984).

17. Wilson, "Studying Inner-City Social Dislocation."

18. Carol Marks, "The Urban Underclass," *Annual Review of Sociology* 17 (1991): 446.

19. Martha A. Gephart and Robert W. Pearson, "Contemporary Research on the Urban Underclass: A Selected Review of the Research that Underlies a New Council Program," *Social Science Research Council* 42, no. 1/2 (June 1988): 1–10.

20. See, for example, Jennifer L. Hochschild, "The Politics of the Estranged Poor"; Bernard Boxill, "Wilson on the Truly Disadvantaged"; and William Julius Wilson, "The Truly Disadvantaged Revisited: A Response to Hochschild and Boxill," in Symposium on William Julius Wilson, The Truly Disadvantaged, *Ethics* 101 (April 1991): 560–609.

21. William Julius Wilson, "The Truly Disadvantaged Revisited," p. 593.

22. See Christopher Jencks, "Is the American Underclass Growing?" in *The Urban Underclass*, ed. Jencks and Peterson, pp. 28–100.

23. Bill Lawson, "Groups and Individuals in the American Democracy," *Logos* 6, no. 2 (1985): 105–15.

24. Wilson, "Studying Inner-City Dislocation," p. 6.

25. Works with a similar approach include Alan Rosenberg and Gerald E. Myers, eds., *Echoes from the Holocaust: Philosophical Reflection on a Dark Time* (Philadelphia: Temple University Press, 1988); Norm Bowie, ed., *Equal Op-*

portunity (Boulder, Colo.: Westview Press, 1988); William T. Blackstone and Robert Heslep, eds., *Social Justice and Preferential Treatment: Women and Racial Minorities in Education and Business* (Athens: University of Georgia Press, 1977); and Virginia Held, Kai Nielsen, and Charles Parson, eds., *Philosophy and Political Action* (New York: Oxford University Press, 1972).

26. See, for example, Washington's "Atlanta Exposition Address," in *Negro Social and Political Thought 1850–1920*, ed. Howard Brotz (New York: Basic Books, 1966), pp. 356–59.

27. Lawson, "Groups and Individuals in American Democracy."

28. Bill Lawson, "Politically Oppressed Citizens," *Journal of Value Inquiry* 25, no. 4 (October 1991): 335–38.

29. Wilson addresses criticisms of his position in *The Urban Underclass*, ed. Jencks and Peterson. The essays in this book serve as an interesting point of contrast and comparison for the views presented in that volume.

30. Bill Lawson, "Crime, Minorities and the Social Contract," *Criminal Justice Ethics* 9, no. 2 (Summer/Fall 1990): 16–24.

31. Howard McGary, "Racial Integration and Racial Separatism: Conceptual Clarifications," in *Philosophy Born of Struggle*, ed. Leonard Harris (Dubuque, Iowa: Kendall/Hunt, 1983), pp. 199–211.

32. René Descartes, *Meditations on First Philosophy*, trans. George Heffernan (Notre Dame: University of Notre Dame Press, 1990), p. 87.

33. This is not a postmodern critique.

34. Alternative titles for this composition include "Meditation for Integration"; "Meditations on Inner Peace"; "Praying for Eric"; and "Meditation for a Pair of Wire Cutters." The composition can be heard on Charles Mingus, *Music Written for Monterey, 1965, Not Heard . . .* (East Coasting JWL 0013; JWL 0014 mono); Charles Mingus, *Meditation* (France's Corner FCD 102); and James Newton, *Romance and Revolution* (Bluenote BT85134). I also want to suggest the following pieces of music to listen to and enjoy. These compositions, I think, reflect the moods of the different articles: Boxill: Sonny Rollins, "The Freedom Suite," *Freedom Suite* (Riverside Records OJC-067); Harris: Grachan Moncur, "New Africa," *New Africa* (Actuel 21); McGary: Billy Harper, "Destiny Is Yours," *Destiny Is Yours* (Steeplechase SCCD 31260); Lott: Don Pullen, "Endangered Species: African American Youth," *Random Thoughts* (Bluenote 94347); Lawson: Kenny Garrett, "African Exchange Student," *African Exchange Student* (Atlantic AMG A282156); Allen: Gary Thomas, "By Any Means Necessary," *By Any Means Necessary* (Polydor JMT 834 432); Mosley: Max Roach, "It's Time," *It's Time* (Impulse A-16); Kirkland: Geri Allen, "The Nurturer," *The Nurturer* (Bluenote CD 795139-2); and West: Bobby Watson, "In a Sentimental Mood," *Post Motown Bop* (Bluenote CDP 7951482).

35. Charles Mingus, *Beneath the Underdog* (New York: Penguin Books, 1979).

PART *One*

Class Analysis

2 THE UNDERCLASS AND THE RACE/CLASS ISSUE

Bernard R. Boxill

WHICH IS FUNDAMENTAL, race or class? With the advent of the black underclass, this long-debated question once again divides those who try to understand the intertwined problems of race and class in America. In this essay I propose to describe its application to the underclass and to explore its moral implications.

The Race/Class Issue

We must first clarify what the race/class issue is about. It is not about the necessary or sufficient conditions for the existence of an underclass. Racism is not necessary for the existence of an underclass. Marx's description of the *lumpenproletariat* is similar to contemporary descriptions of the underclass, but he accounted for it without appealing to racism. And racism is not sufficient for the existence of an underclass. Not every society debased by racism has an underclass. The issue concerns the necessary conditions for the existence in the present-day United States of an underclass that is overwhelmingly black. All parties agree that one condition is a disproportionately large number of black people with class-related disabilities—for example, a dearth of appropriate work skills—but some maintain that current racism is also among these conditions, while others deny this.

This issue is only the latest manifestation of one of the oldest debates in African-American political thought. From the start some African-American thinkers and reformers—let us call them the race school—tended to put most of the blame on white racism as the main cause of black ills in America, while others—let us call them the class school—tended to put most of the blame on black disabilities.

The class school is not necessarily inspired by Marxism. No doubt a Marxist could subscribe to its main tenet, but so also could a critic

19

of Marxism and an admirer of the free market. Marxists may never-theless suppose that the issue can be decided by their theory that class conflict is the fundamental conflict in society. This is a mistake. Even if the Marxist view were true, it would have no clear implications for the issue before us.

Sometimes the Marxist position is interpreted as the view that capi-talism is the cause of racism. This is quite implausible, and indeed a little absurd, since racism obviously predated capitalism. A more plau-sible view is that, while capitalism exacerbates racism, class conflict is the cause of racism. Since class conflict predates capitalism, this pro-posal cannot be brushed aside like the last one. But it is still clearly inadequate as it stands. Class conflict cannot be the cause of racism in the sense of being *sufficient* for the existence of racism. Since racism involves hostile and contemptuous attitudes between different races, class conflict cannot cause racism unless different races are somehow involved in it.[1] In such a context, the idea that class conflict is likely to exacerbate or even to cause racism is quite plausible. Racism is a for-midable weapon for fighting a racially different opponent. If it did not already exist, classes would invent it to help them fight, subdue, and exploit other racially different classes. But why should only class con-flict engender racism? If classes are likely to invent racism to help them fight and subordinate other classes, why would not other groups—for example, nations—also be likely to invent racism to help them fight other groups or nations?

But suppose that class conflict is in some way necessary for the gen-eration of racism. In that case, if racism is the main cause of black ills, class conflict is a necessary condition for these ills. But this does not amount to a withdrawal of, or even to a qualification of, the claim that racism is the main cause of black ills in America. To cite a necessary condition for racism is not to deny either its existence or its causal efficacy. Let us then set Marxism aside and proceed with our analysis.[2]

While the class school is united in discounting the role of current racism in the genesis of the black underclass, it is divided over the role of past racism. Some scholars, such as Thomas Sowell, seem to accord past racism little importance. Sowell argues that a group's work habits, discipline, and attitude toward education are the product of a long historical evolution and can be changed only very gradually. The implication is that if many blacks have class-related disabilities, this is probably mainly due, not to the group's recent and, in historical terms, relatively brief experience of racism, but to its far longer historical ex-perience reaching back to centuries of rural life in Africa. I do not think that this position is plausible. Probably Sowell does not think so either because he does not hold it consistently, often conceding that black slavery—which I take to involve an extreme form of racial discrimination—had a disastrous effect on the slaves', and their descendants', attitudes toward work.[3] Accordingly, I do not discuss his work in any detail.[4]

Wilson's View of the Underclass

The views of William Julius Wilson are more plausible. Unlike Sowell, Wilson never downplays the effects of past racism. He clearly states that past racism is necessary to explain why the present underclass is overwhelmingly black. According to Wilson it was past racism, continuing for "decades, even centuries," that created "a racial division of labor" confining blacks to the "low-wage sector of the economy" where they were "more adversely affected by impersonal economic shifts in advanced industrial society," eventually becoming the underclass.[5] But he is equally firm in denying that current racism plays a significant role in explaining the genesis of the black underclass. Not that he denies that racism persists; indeed, he denies that he ever suggested that racism has even declined.[6] His point is that although racism persists, there is no need to appeal to it in order to explain why a disproportionate number of blacks fall into the underclass. He feels that class-related disabilities and impersonal shifts in the economy are a sufficient explanation.[7]

Wilson sometimes writes as if he believes that his view that current racism does not play a significant role in explaining the genesis of the black underclass implies that strategies to help the underclass join the mainstream can be color-blind. Thus his own strategy ostensibly consists of what he calls "class specific" rather than "race specific" programs. Class-specific programs are color-blind, that is, available to all who could be "objectively classified as disadvantaged in terms of their economic class background." Among the most important criteria for being classified as disadvantaged would be low income, a broken home, poor education, and linguistic differences. Race and past discrimination would be irrelevant. Wilson maintains that this would not only help the white poor, who are now ignored in programs of reverse discrimination, but would also more effectively help the black poor than the present programs based on race, which mainly help the black middle class.

The most important of Wilson's class-specific programs are income redistribution, compensatory job training, compensatory schooling, and special medical services. The main objective of these programs is to overcome the joblessness of the black underclass, particularly male joblessness. Since he maintains that male joblessness is the main cause of the destruction of black ghetto families, he believes that his strategy will restore these families. Wilson thinks that this is a crucial result because society has traditionally depended on the family to provide children with the basic personal qualities they need to take advantage of education and employment opportunities.

To restore the black ghetto family, however, is not necessarily to solve the problem of the underclass. Historians have demonstrated that the disintegration of the black underclass family is a fairly recent phenomenon. But blacks have always been poor and, according to Wilson, predisposed to becoming an underclass. If so, restoring the black family is consistent with black poverty and, in particular, with conditions predisposing blacks to becoming an underclass.

In the book *Justice, Equal Opportunity, and the Family*, which Wilson cites approvingly, the author, James Fishkin, explains why this is so. According to Fishkin, given background inequalities, different families will differ in how well they prepare their children to succeed. If differential preparation for success generally translates into differential success, this argument implies that children of the poorest families will tend to end up at the bottom of the economic ladder and will be disproportionately confined to the least-skilled, lowest-paying jobs in society. This suggests that if Wilson's strategy succeeded in restoring black ghetto families but left these families in the poorest position in society, their offspring would tend to remain in precarious economic circumstances and—on Wilson's own account—would be likely to reconstitute an underclass as soon as economic progress faltered.

It may be supposed that, despite background inequalities, inequalities in opportunity could be substantially reduced if schools for relatively disadvantaged children were made more equal to schools for relatively advantaged children. Unfortunately, however, there seems to be considerable evidence against this view. Children from relatively advantaged families apparently have a class edge over other children before they ever get to school, and they retain this edge throughout their schooling. Indeed, this class edge may be one of the factors that makes the schools they attend better than the schools attended by children from relatively disadvantaged families. After an exhaustive study of the evidence, for example, Christopher Jencks and colleagues concluded that "the characteristics of a school's output depend on a single input, namely the characteristics of the entering children."[8]

Fishkin's argument may seem to be refuted by the experience of immigrant groups, which have almost routinely climbed from poverty

to affluence in America. But the underclass is different from the immigrant groups that have succeeded in America. Wilson admits that
the underclass has "negative attitudes" toward menial jobs. Immigrant
groups, however, see these jobs as the bottom rung of the ladder to
success. Indeed, in *The Declining Significance of Race* Wilson specifically
claims that these immigrants take jobs the underclass disdains. This
furnishes a possible clue to the success of the immigrant groups: high
motivation. This presumably can outweigh the material advantages of
the advantaged classes and allow the poor to overtake the well-to-do.

Let us reconsider Fishkin's argument. This argument assumes that
the society always awards jobs and places to those who are most qualified for them. However, if the society implemented a program of preferential treatment that reserved a substantial number of desirable jobs
and places to offspring of disadvantaged families, even if they were not
the most qualified for them, these people would have a fighting chance
to overcome their class disadvantages. This suggests that preferential
treatment for underclass blacks would solve the difficulty posed by
Fishkin's argument that children of the poorest families tend to remain
at the bottom of the economic ladder. Wilson seems to acknowledge
this because, despite first appearances and the ostensible reliance on
color-blind "class specific" programs, he includes preferential treatment
for underclass blacks as an essential part of his strategy for helping
them join the mainstream.

People with racist attitudes will probably oppose a policy of preferential treatment for members of the race they despise, even if this
policy is justified. And if they are in a majority and in a democratic
polity, they will probably successfully oppose the policy. This raises a
serious difficulty for Wilson that he would very much like to avoid. As
we have seen, while he includes preferential treatment for underclass
blacks as part of his strategy for helping them join the mainstream,
he insists that racism has not declined. If what I have said is correct,
the majority will successfully oppose his strategy. Of course, he denies
that current racism plays a significant role in explaining the generation
of the black underclass. But even if he is right about this, it does not
follow that a racist majority would not oppose preferential treatment
for underclass blacks. The fact—if it is a fact—that underclass blacks
are so poorly qualified that the majority does not have to indulge its
racist attitudes in order to keep them out of jobs, does not imply that it
would not indulge its racist attitudes and oppose preferential treatment
for them if this were proposed. Wilson himself admits the difficulty,
though only indirectly. For example, no other interpretation can be
placed on his argument that President Reagan managed to introduce

"sweeping tax and budget cuts" by persuading the middle classes that the "drop in their living standards was attributable to the poor (and implicitly minorities)." [9]

More interesting is how Wilson proposes to circumvent the difficulty. One proposal is vigorous economic growth and full employment. Wilson cites Lester Thurow: "In periods of great economic progress when [the incomes of the middle classes] are rising rapidly, they are willing to share some of their income and jobs with those less fortunate than themselves, but they are not willing to reduce their real standard of living to help either minorities or the poor." [10] However, although vigorous economic growth and full employment would certainly make it easier for the majority to accept preferential treatment for underclass blacks, these factors are probably not enough; remember that preferential treatment means preferring blacks over at least equally qualified whites for desirable jobs and positions. Wilson evidently agrees, because he has a second, more unusual stratagem: to camouflage the offending programs so that the majority is unlikely to notice them. Thus he describes his "hidden" agenda for liberal policy makers: to "construct an economic-social reform program in such a way that the universal programs are seen as the dominant and most visible aspects by the general public." [11] In this way the "targeted programs"—by which Wilson means the race-specific programs such as preferential treatment for blacks—would be "less visible" and thereby "indirectly supported and protected." [12] In what follows, I will point to the historical precedents of this strategy of Wilson's and present what I argue are its moral defects.

The Class School

We must go back to the race/class issue. As I noted, the race school shows a marked willingness to blame white racism for black ills, while the class school shows a marked willingness to blame black disabilities. The disagreement is not over a few isolated facts; its sources lie in deep and conflicting views about human nature and philosophy.

The crucial assumption of the class school is that most human beings are overwhelmingly self-interested. This assumption seems commonplace, but it leads the class school to two characteristic, and controversial, claims. The first claim emphasizes the dominance of self-interest over racist attitudes. It says that even when people have racist attitudes, most will resist indulging them when doing so would be seriously detrimental to their interests. The second claim emphasizes the dominance of self-interest over morality. It says that most people will resist the demands of justice or morality when these demands are seriously detrimental to their interests.

The first claim explains why the class school tends to cite black disabilities rather than white racism as the cause of black ills, even while it admits that racism flourishes. If this is true, even racist employers will not generally refuse to hire blacks simply because they are black, since doing so would be detrimental to their interests if blacks are well qualified. Similarly, the claim implies that even a racist public will not generally refuse to patronize black businesses and enterprises simply because they are black, because while doing so would indulge its racist attitudes, it would not be in its interests if those businesses are efficient and productive. On grounds such as these, the class school argues that if blacks were qualified and competent, they would thrive even in the face of racism, so that the root cause of black ills is not white racism but black incompetence.

This diagnosis of the cause of black ills leads naturally to the recommendation that blacks overcome their incompetence and acquire economically valuable skills. The seminal thinker of this line of thought is Booker T. Washington. In its depreciation of the role of racism the class school is ultimately integrationist, although it also has a separatist wing.

The claims I have just sketched suffer from a grave weakness. Their key conclusion, that if blacks were competent they would be invulnerable to the effects of racism, is plausible only in the context of a free market. Outside of that context, or where the market is not free, the claim is demonstrably false. Suppose, for example, that blacks cannot choose their employers. The most dramatic case of this was the European enslavement of Africans. In that context, competence was no protection against the effects of racism. On the contrary, it helped to make blacks victims of racism. Martin Delany saw this very clearly when he argued that Africans were not enslaved because they were inferior, but because they were superior. His point was that Europeans tolerated enslaved Africans precisely because Africans had superior skills and qualities that made enslaving them profitable.

Although Delany's argument thus implied that black competence was one of the main reasons why Europeans enslaved Africans, he did not blame competence for African enslavement. Since competence is generally a desirable quality, this is not surprising. More interestingly, however, although his argument also implied that European self-interest and racism were also among the main reasons why Europeans enslaved Africans, he did not blame these factors for African enslavement either. Presumably, he assumed that racism and self-interest were more or less unalterable features of human nature. Delany blamed African enslavement on the fact that Africans were unable to prevent Europeans from enslaving them. If this had not been the case, the same self-interest that motivated Europeans to enslave Africans would have motivated them to leave Africans in freedom—even if Europeans would have liked to enslave Africans because they had the qualities that would make their enslavement profitable, and even if Europeans had racist attitudes that would have enabled them to enslave Africans with relative equanimity. In thus locating the main cause of black ills in some black disability, Delany showed himself to be a member of the class school. But the precise nature of the disability he cited, black powerlessness, and the recommendation it moved him to make—that blacks should acquire power—led him in a separatist direction.

Let us now consider the second key claim of the class school, namely, that most people will resist the demands of morality when these demands are seriously detrimental to their interests. Because of its adherence to this claim, the class school proposes that reforms should always be presented to the public as serving its interests. Thus, while the class school may admit that reform is demanded by justice, what it always chooses to emphasize is that reform will benefit the public—if not in the short term, then in the long term. This is particularly clear in its integrationist wing. For example, while Booker T. Washington certainly thought that his reforms were just, it was not their justice that he urged on the public, presumably on the assumption that he would otherwise not be heeded. What he emphasized to the public was that his reforms would lead to overall prosperity. This reliance on the public's self-interest rather than its moral sense is also clear in the rhetoric of the separatist wing of the class school, though there is a difference in the way it appeals to that self-interest; whereas the integrationist wing appeals to the majority's self-interest by trying to persuade it of the increased profits and economic advantages reform will bring, the separatist wing appeals to the majority's self-interest by threatening to harm it unless it implements the reforms demanded.

In insisting on the dominance of self-interest over morality, the class school does not mean to imply that moral considerations play no role in human affairs. It does, however, suggest that this role is subsidiary and only supportive. In particular, the class school suggests that, whatever the validity of moral considerations, they will generally have little motivating force unless the relations it recommends obtain. Thus its integrationist wing implies that until blacks acquire skills and competence, and by steady productive work contribute to the markets of the world, they will not respect themselves or be respected by the majority; its separatist wing implies that, until blacks can credibly threaten the white majority, they will not respect themselves or be respected by the majority.

To anyone familiar with Sowell's writings, it should be clear that he writes in the tradition started by Washington.[13] The case of Wilson may not be so clear, but he too writes in that tradition. Note his reticence about mentioning the moral ground of his reforms. Thus, while he allows that past racism is an important cause of the black underclass, he never gives this fact any particular moral significance, denying, for example, that it is any part of the case for special treatment of blacks.[14] Throughout he relies on Washington's practice of emphasizing the advantages reform will bring to the majority. Thus stressing the importance of "how the issues are defined," he argues that "economic and social reforms must be presented as benefitting all groups in the United States not just poor minorities."[15]

Wilson's handling of preferential treatment is especially revealing. He never considers presenting it to the public as a demand for justice. Instead, recognizing that there is no plausible way of persuading the majority that preferential treatment is in its interest, he proposes to camouflage it. As noted earlier, his "hidden agenda" calls for making special programs for blacks "less visible" by mixing them in with universal programs to which the more advantaged groups can "positively relate."[16] Since by "positively relate" Wilson means "benefit," this last point reveals how firmly Wilson is wedded to the idea that the public will tolerate reform only if it can be persuaded that reform serves its self-interest.

Finally, I draw attention to Wilson's apparent reliance on the idea that acquiring skills and good steady work is basically all the moral education people need. The class school's most eloquent defender of this idea is, of course, Washington; however, this idea is implicit in Wilson's firm rejection of the "culture of poverty" theory. Wilson does not deny that the underclass has a specific culture—he calls it the "ghetto-specific culture"—and he does not deny that this culture includes "negative social values." But he denies that these values have any life of their own.[17] He insists that they are the result of external social conditions, especially "joblessness,"[18] and will almost automatically be replaced by more positive values when the underclass gets skills and good jobs.

The class school is right about many things. For example, the view of its separatist wing that groups will not respect each other as moral equals unless they have reason to fear each other is worthy of serious consideration and is quite possibly true. Before dismissing this view, the reader might find it worth recalling that David Hume went considerably further, suggesting that respect may not even be owed to the weak. According to Hume, we "should not, properly speaking, lie under any restraint of justice" with regard to a "species of creatures . . . which, though rational, were possessed of such inferior strength, both of body and mind, that they were incapable of all resistance, and could never, upon the highest provocation, make us feel the effects of their resentment."[19] I also endorse the view of its integrationist wing that acquiring skills and having good, productive work are morally uplifting and conducive to self-respect and the respect of others.[20] Nevertheless, I believe that the class school is deeply mistaken. These mistakes will emerge from a consideration of the race school.

The Race School

Although the race school can hardly dispute the commonplace that most human beings are overwhelmingly self-interested, it rejects the class school's inference that even those with strong racist attitudes will generally resist indulging these attitudes when doing so is seriously detrimental to their interests. Therefore, the race school can disallow the class school's argument that the main cause of black ills is black incompetence rather than white racism. But the race school does not propose to fight racism by persuading the majority that it sets back its interests by indulging its racist attitudes; it sees better than the class school that the majority can often indulge these attitudes without seriously affecting its interests. The race school's attack on racism is more direct and consists in an attempt to persuade the majority that, whether or not indulging its racist attitudes is detrimental to its interests, it ought not indulge these attitudes because doing so is unjust. Accordingly, the race school must also reject the claim of the class school that most people will resist the demands of justice when doing so is seriously detrimental to its interests.

This is clear enough from a consideration of the works of the great exponents of the race school, Frederick Douglass, W.E.B. Du Bois, and Martin Luther King, Jr. These thinkers, unlike those of the class school, never hesitated to state plainly, emphatically, and publicly that the reforms they urged were justified on the moral ground that blacks were seriously wronged and harmed by racism and racial discrimination. I do not mean that they believed that the public is always, or even often, ready to heed moral considerations; Douglass, Du Bois, and King were never so naive. They state as clearly as the exponents of the class school that the public is often ignorant or unheedful of the dictates of justice. But their impassioned protest of injustice and their eloquent and unrelenting appeal to the public's sense of justice implied that they believed that the public could be educated to mend its ways.

In its insistence on moral suasion, the race school announces its conviction that the members of the public must ultimately come to view each other as moral equals. But the class school does not suggest that moral suasion alone is sufficient to achieve this end. Perhaps very early in his career, when he was most under the influence of William Lloyd Garrison, Douglass might have believed this. Soon, however, he began to argue that, at least in the fight against slavery, moral suasion had to be supplemented with slave rebellions. This signaled no deviation from his firm conviction that a belief in moral equality was the foundation of a harmonious society. According to Douglass, violent self-defense on the part of the slave was a means to this belief. He argued that under the circumstances the slave had to fight back, both to believe in his moral equality and to make his master believe in it.

Du Bois also conceded that moral suasion is generally not sufficient for people to accept each other as moral equals. He was clear that acquiring economically valuable skills and good, steady, well-paid work were also essential to achieving that end. But he was equally clear that these were not enough; if they were, skilled, hard-working people would always be just, but we know that they are not. In addition to being skilled and productive, people must also reflect actively, deeply, and honestly on moral issues if they are to understand and accept their moral equality. This was the point Du Bois wanted to make in his famous dispute with Washington. According to Du Bois, "If we make money the object of man-training, we shall develop money-makers but not necessarily men." Thus, he insisted on specifically moral education. "Men we shall have," he wrote, "only if we make manhood the object of the work of the school—intelligence, broad sympathy, knowledge of the world that was and is, and on the relation of men to it. . . . On this foundation we may build breadwinning, skill of hand and quickness of brain with never a fear that the child and man mistake the means of living for the object of life." He concluded that "education must not simply teach work—it must teach Life. The Talented Tenth of the Negro race must be made leaders of thought and missionaries of culture among their people."[21]

The standard objection to this view is that it is elitism. This objection is unjustified. First, Du Bois says that those with the greatest moral insight must *teach* those with less insight. Since this implies that those with less moral insight are teachable, it contains no suggestion that they are impervious to moral instruction and must be manipulated to conform to the right view. On the contrary, it implies that they can and indeed must come to share the moral insights of the "Talented Tenth." Furthermore, Du Bois insisted on equal rights of political participation for everyone, specifically equal voting rights and provisions for protection of freedom of speech. This shows that, while he acknowledged that some had a duty to instruct others, he was aware that this had its dangers and took precautions against it degenerating into indoctrination and manipulation. If this is elitism, it is the unavoidable elitism of John Stuart Mill in his best moments.

Now let us compare Du Bois's alleged elitism with the elitism of the class school, for the class school does involve an elitism, which is all the more dangerous because it is insidious. Consider, for example, Booker T. Washington. Although Washington opposed Du Bois's insistence on protest, he was as clear as Du Bois that what Du Bois protested were injustices. He depreciated protest because he doubted that the public, white as well as black, could fully understand or be moved by the demands of justice, so he saw no point to it. Thus he opposed the public appeals that Du Bois insisted on, preferring to operate behind the scenes with the hidden movers of society who did understand and appreciate the demands of justice, manipulating the masses to achieve the results he thought they were too morally blind to ever see or appreciate. This aspect of Washington's activities has sometimes been offered to extenuate his ostensible concessions to injustice, but I think it reveals a contempt for the moral powers of the average person and an elitism that is far more objectionable than Du Bois's frank view that some people have greater moral insight than others. As I have emphasized, Du Bois also insisted that all people, both the more and the less insightful, should have equal rights to participate in the running of their society. I submit that the same charge of elitism can be leveled at Wilson's strategy, with its "hidden agendas" and elaborate schemes to make needed reform "less visible." Nor does his admiration for the "corporatist democracies" with their associations with fascism and manipulative elites give us reason to withdraw the charge.

Conclusion

If the analysis in this chapter is sound, the philosophy starting with Booker T. Washington and stretching down to Sowell and Wilson must be rejected. The errors of that philosophy stressed in this chapter are the tendency to maintain that reform must always serve the majority's interests and, where this is not plausible—as in the case of preferential treatment—the tendency to conceal its reforms. The first tendency either misunderstands the nature of justice or depreciates its importance. The second tendency is opposed to the spirit and letter of democracy, is elitist, and implies an unjustified contempt for the moral powers of the average person.

I do not mean that the average person is usually ready to give justice, or that we should not try to ease the burden of the costs of reforms by making them part of a total package that includes vigorous economic growth. My objection is the implication that this is enough. I agree with Du Bois that the exclusive emphasis on jobs and money will only bring us money-makers. But a harmonious society cannot be based on money-making. It must be based on mutual respect and a public acknowledgment of the importance of justice. These do not arise spontaneously in a society devoted to money-making. At best, money-making will suffice when there is such vigorous economic growth that everyone can benefit. But what are we to do when the economic growth slows and stops, as inevitably it must and should? Mill expressed more than an opinion when he claimed not to be "charmed with the ideal of life held out by those who think that the normal state of human beings is that of struggling to get on; that the trampling, crushing, elbowing, and treading on each other's heels, which form the existing type of social life, are the most desirable lot of human kind, or anything but the disagreeable symptoms of one of the phases of industrial progress."[22]

In anticipation of the day when we cannot all continue to get richer, the "Talented Tenth" of both races must stimulate the public to reflect on the moral equality of every man and woman, which is the more solid basis of a harmonious society. In particular, even as government uses vigorous economic growth to "lubricate" the passage of reforms necessary to enable the black underclass to join the mainstream, the "Talented Tenth" should always emphasize publicly and without embarrassment that every one of these reforms is demanded by strict justice. I would add only one qualification to Du Bois's recommendation. He stated that the "Talented Tenth" of the black race had a duty to educate the black majority. I would add that it also has a duty to help educate the white majority.

NOTES

1. I set aside the claim that the concept of race is not biologically useful. See Anthony Appiah, "The Uncompleted Argument: Du Bois and the Illusion of Race," *Critical Inquiry* 12 (Autumn 1985). The claim may be true but is

irrelevant to the present issue, which does not imply that the concept of race is useful biologically.

2. For a fuller analysis see my "The Race–Class Questions," in *Philosophy Born of Struggle*, ed. Leonard Harris (Dubuque, Iowa: Kendall/Hunt, 1983), pp. 107–16.

3. Thomas Sowell, *Ethnic America* (New York: Basic Books, 1981), p. 187.

4. I have attempted a much fuller discussion in my *Blacks and Social Justice* (Totowa, N.J.: Rowman and Allanheld, 1984), chap. 2.

5. William Julius Wilson, *The Truly Disadvantaged* (Chicago: University of Chicago Press, 1987), p. 12.

6. One might have inferred this from the title of his earlier book, *The Declining Significance of Race*, 2d ed. (Chicago: University of Chicago Press, 1980).

7. Ibid., pp. 10, 11. See also p. 113.

8. Christopher Jencks, *Inequality* (New York: Harper and Row, 1972), p. 256.

9. Wilson, *The Truly Disadvantaged*, p. 120.

10. Lester Thurow, "Recession Plus Inflation Spells Stasis," *Christianity and Crisis*, March 30, 1981, pp. 91–92.

11. Wilson, *The Truly Disadvantaged*, p. 155.

12. Ibid., p. 163.

13. I have discussed the views of these two thinkers in *Blacks and Social Justice*, chap. 2.

14. Wilson, *The Truly Disadvantaged*, p. 117.

15. Ibid., p. 155.

16. Ibid., p. 165.

17. Wilson, *The Truly Disadvantaged*, pp. 137–39.

18. Ibid., pp. 56, 57.

19. David Hume, "An Enquiry Concerning the Principles of Morals," sec. III, part I, in *Enquiries Concerning Human Understanding and Concerning the Principles of Morals*, ed. L. A. Selby-Bigge and rev. P. H. Nidditch, 3d. ed. (Oxford: Oxford University Press, 1975), p. 190.

20. The philosophical precedents of this idea are numerous. See, for example, Jean-Jacques Rousseau's argument that Emile must have a trade (*Emile*, trans. Allan Bloom [New York: Basic Books, 1979], pp. 195–203); Karl Marx's remarks on work; and Laurence Thomas, "Self-Respect: Theory and Practice," in *Philosophy Born of Struggle*, ed. Leonard Harris (Dubuque, Iowa: Kendall/Hunt, 1983), pp. 174–89.

21. W.E.B. Du Bois, "The Talented Tenth," in *The Seventh Son*, vol. 1, ed. Julius Lester (New York: Random House, 1971), p. 403.

22. John Stuart Mill, *Principles of Political Economy*, ed. W. J. Ashley (New York: A. M. Kelley, 1965 [1848]), p. 748.

3   AGENCY AND THE CONCEPT OF THE UNDERCLASS

Leonard Harris

WHAT THE UNDERCLASS means as a social entity and what it implies for grand social theory are the foci of my comments. I explore the meaning of the underclass as a social entity, for example, class, class sector, and theoretical abstraction, through ontological issues of agency. The meaning of the underclass has been consistent in William Julius Wilson's works. "What distinguishes members of the underclass from those of other economically disadvantaged groups is that their marginal economic position or weak attachment to the labor force is uniquely reinforced by the neighborhood or social milieu. . . . The concept of 'underclass' was used in *The Truly Disadvantaged* to describe the dual problem of marginal economic position and social isolation in highly concentrated poverty areas."[1] He has distanced his meaning from pejorative connotations and unintended inferences by emphasizing the term's technical meaning and practical import for left-liberal social action.[2] Wilson's concept of the underclass and his accompanying analyses have provided a deep understanding of contemporary immiserization.

I argue that individuals are conceived as utility maximizing agents by Wilsonian liberals and conservatives—making it especially difficult for liberals to distance their use of references to the least well off from conservatives—whether the referring concept is underclass, ghetto poor, or simply the poor. On my interpretation, the conception of individuals in the Wilsonian analysis of the underclass is coterminous with a subtle notion of a social entity informing that analysis. The type of social entity that the underclass or ghetto poor stands for raises numerous problems in philosophy and social theory; it may be a strong contribution or an Achilles' heel.

Definition

The underclass, as a social entity, is a "heterogeneous grouping of inner-city families and individuals whose behavior contrasts sharply from that of mainstream America." It also contrasts sharply with the behavior patterns of previous generations of inner city poor. The underclass is distinguishable from the lower class (or low poverty sector) and the working class. The deleterious results of socially limited networks and neighborhood isolation on job potential help distinguish the underclass from other poverty sectors. The concept of underclass as a social entity is not intended to imply that individuals or cultures cause poverty, although debilitating individual and cultural traits may well exacerbate the condition.[3]

The underclass denotes a sharp increase in inner city dislocations. It is "populated almost exclusively by the most disadvantaged segments of the black urban community" who are outside the mainstream of American occupational systems, primarily families below the poverty level, recidivist criminals, second- and third-generation welfare-dependent persons, and homeless persons. The underclass consists of individuals who lack training and skills to match available employment positions within geographical reach. These individuals experience long-term unemployment or are not members of the labor force. They experience long-term spells of poverty and/or welfare dependency. Underclass individuals are often "engaged in street crime and other forms of aberrant behavior." Long-term unemployed, welfare-dependent families are not necessarily street criminals, but they do share the same hyperghettoized community.

The underclass has become increasingly isolated socially from mainstream patterns and norms of behavior. Stable families, networks of friends and relatives, church associations and attendance, and links to educational or skill-training institutions are least secure and developed among the underclass. There is a high degree of alcoholism and substance abuse and a higher rate of teenage pregnancy, single mothering, and absentee fathers than in other sectors of the population. Women in the underclass are twice as likely as men to be jobless; men in the underclass are more likely to be imprisoned than men in any other class. The concept of underclass denotes "a new sociospatial pattern of class and racial domination, recognized by the unprecedented concentration of the most socially excluded and economically marginal members of the dominated racial and economic group."[4] The underclass is thus chronically isolated, disaffected, and disassociated from other classes.

The causes for the existence of the underclass are multifaceted, but stress is placed on changes in economic and social structures. The "interrelated set of phenomena captured by the term 'underclass' is primarily social-structural."[5] Those interrelated phenomena include class composition, welfare trajectory, financial assets, social capital, and residential patterns. The restructuring of American capitalism—primarily the movement of industries outside urban centers; the increase in service work and technological-based production; the exodus of middle-class and working-class blacks; rapid deterioration of housing, schools, businesses, and recreational facilities; and government policies that channeled disproportional shares of federal, state, and municipal resources to more affluent sectors—"converged to undermine the material foundations of the traditional ghetto."[6] The result has been hyperghettoization of blacks into an underclass.

Wilson contends that racism, understood as the belief in the inherent superiority of races, is a historically important factor in shaping social structures. However, he holds that contemporary structural transitions outweigh the impact of racism on the lives of blacks. Explanations that appeal to racist beliefs and policies are less revealing than explanations that take account of social structures and objective economic conditions. Moreover, recent research suggests that there are underclass situations in Western countries such as the Netherlands. This further suggests that underclass situations are not best explained by a strong appeal to racial causes, but to the sorts of structural variables that Wilson generally uses to account for immiseration.

What Type of Social Entity?

Wilson's depiction of the underclass does not make it unreasonable to ask: What type of social entity is the underclass? Passengers on a train, for example, are serial agents. They share several common traits; for example, they can be said to act collectively, without any one passenger having an intention to act or withhold an action. Passengers normally do not have codified knowledge, decision procedures, or internally generated representatives—they nonetheless behave in fairly common ways across lines of culture. The government, train company, or consumer agencies may all claim to aid or represent passengers, but being a passenger or having a unique or generous experience as "passenger" is not an important criterion for acting in this capacity. If X is a passenger, and if for the next three generations X's children are passengers as a function of the fear of driving X has passed on, it does not follow that X and X's children are members of the passenger class. "Passengers" is not a class. Rather, the train company, consumer groups, and government officials define or mandate the existence of the serial "passenger"; they are the abstraction's representative. But there is no solid entity called "passengers," although a great deal can be predicted of persons while existing in the condition of "passenger." The point, contrary to idealists who might claim the class of "passengers" is real just in case train company officials or others decree that it exists, is that the referent of "passengers" is serial even if no one portends to represent "passengers." Moreover, the general character traits of "passengers" may be reasonably associated with, but are definitely not coterminous with, the traits of individual passengers. The collectivity of "passengers" exists as a plurality of individual agents sharing a common condition, but "passengers" as a real collective agent does not exist.

We can theoretically construct a history of "passengers" that may be of great use in understanding contemporary passengers and predicting the behavior of future passengers, but we would be mistaken to suppose that passengers are agents, that is, forging their direction or seeking to actualize their interests. If we find that contemporary passengers are different in important ways from previous generations, their newness may imply a great deal about the total character of society. But we would not be warranted in claiming that this newness is an aberration, violation, corruption, sign of the imminent collapse or of the malfunction of transportation without a separate argument showing that the system as such is in disarray. The reason is that there is no actual coherent history of "passengers," self-consciously pursuing their interest and imbued with a sense of cohesion or identity, any more than there is an actual coherent history of the underclass, the ghetto poor, or the poor.[7]

We can depict passengers in terms of common conditions, experiences, family structure, and so on. This would be treating "passengers" as a theoretical and serial entity, analogous to a theoretical class. A theoretical class consists of individuals occupying "similar positions in social space (that is, in the distribution of powers), [who] are subject to similar conditions of existence and conditioning factors and, as a result, are endowed with similar dispositions which prompt them to develop similar practices."[8] Theoretical classes, like theoretical serials, are useful for predicting behavior and distinguishing behavior between groups, but the reality of collective agency is a different matter. That is, we cannot mutatis mutandis infer that the members of an entity, theoretical, serial, or otherwise, has or will develop a unity of consciousness, sense of community, and representatives that vicariously act in its name, or that it will pursue its own interest. If a social entity has requisite traits for agency—for example, automobile workers or U.S. soldiers stationed in Panama—it may be defensible to treat them as agents of their station, but it is not defensible to approach passengers as if they are representatives of all the riders on a train.

If the underclass were a theoretical class, a serial entity, or both, an inference suggesting it had real agency may not involve the sort of inappropriate inference that Hegel and Marx have been criticized for, namely, taking "the things of logic to be the logic of things." This is because Wilson does not claim that the underclass will act elusively in representing Absolute Spirit (Hegel) or to secure the liberation of the working class (Marx). The underclass, as I will discuss in some detail, is an impotent actor, that is, it is structurally disorganized and its salvation depends on governmental, philanthropic, corporate, or charitable agents. Analogously, "passengers," as a theoretical class, is fruitfully described as a collective entity. "Passengers," as a serial entity, is arguably represented by consumer groups and government agencies, in part because the social entity of "passengers" is incapable of representing itself.

Imagine a study of the "urban rich." Suppose we found twenty-three characteristics that distinguished the "urban rich" from previous generations of "the rich," rural or urban. Suppose that their behavior was unduly helpful to themselves; say they rarely married, had more one-child families, were more likely than previous rich to be sexual libertines practicing safe sex, were health conscious, and were shrewd investors in corporate and ghetto property without moral reflection. We might be hard pressed to show that they acted as a social entity, but if they could be fruitfully described as a social entity by virtue of shared conditions, experiences, and behaviors, it might also be the case that they, the new "urban rich," were an impotent entity, that is, incapable of acting on their own behalf. "The rich are always with us" faces the same sort of construction versus reality problem as "the poor are always with us." Both are theoretical abstractions that mean to refer to a social reality but are at best abstractions with shifting referents. Analogously, "underclass" may describe a new social situation that seems less a class than a seriality; less a coherent entity than a condition of immiserization of disparate persons entrapped in urban-based poverty; less a social reality, in the sense of a collective with self-consciousness, than a part of a continuance of poverty with shifting contours.

If the underclass is considered a class or a class sector, in Marx's sense of class, it may be dependent on a controversial Marxist view of class. If Marx believed that class traits reside or are manifest in class members and that the acts of classes are isomorphic or generally coter-

minous with the acts of individuals, then his view of classes is subject
to critique as a hegemonic conception of agency; for example, it may
over-generalize the character of persons, submerge individual uniqueness, and ignore categories such as gender and race. The concept of the
underclass may not be akin to a hegemonic conception, which over-
generalizes the traits of its members, but instead may unfold itself as
an illusory category. In other words, as a social entity that does not
act—albeit, cannot act precisely because social entities do not act—
individuals act and their collective acts are reified as the actions of a
social entity.[9]

These lines of argument might be fruitful if the underclass were
conceived as a social agent with powers. However, the underclass is not
so conceived. If the concept of the underclass is an illusory entity, its
reification has more to do with how its members are collectively excised
than with how we reify its social agency. If the concept of the underclass is hegemonic, it is hegemonic without being a class conception.
The newness of the underclass may be explained by the tremendous
concentration of the immiserated in cramped urban squalor and by new
attitudes of self-effacement. It may be explained by structural forces
such as industry and middle-class movements. But how is it a class or
a class sector? If it is not a class, class sector, illusory category, serial
entity, or theoretical abstraction, what type of entity is the underclass?
I will first explore the concept of individual agency and then return to
the issue of the type of entity represented by the underclass.

Individual Agency

Wilson's definition of the underclass shares constitutive assumptions
about the nature of individual agency (i.e., individuals as existential
utility maximizers) with conservative views that weigh heavily the importance of cultural and individual traits as causes of poverty. Viewing
individuals as failed utility maximizers is coterminous with the concept
of the underclass as an impotent social agent. Considering Wilson's
view of character traits will allow us to explore individual agency.

Wilson argues that we should abandon policy approaches that
accept people's tastes, values, and character as given attributes. Such
an approach assumes that public policy is to "arrange the incentives
confronting voters, citizens, firms, bureaucrats and politicians so that
they will behave in a socially optimal way." This approach is misguided
according to Wilson because, for one reason, it presupposes a background of common character. Moreover, "this nation has come face to

face with problems that do not seem to respond, or respond enough, to changes in incentives. They do not respond, it seems, because the people whose behavior we wish to change do not have the right 'tastes' or discount the future too heavily. To put it succinctly, they lack character."[10] Wilson rejects those views that claim poverty is caused by character or aberrant cultures: Oscar Lewis's implicit view that pathologies and personal disorders are responsible; George H. Mead's and Lawrence M. Mead's view that the norms of civility and morality are lacking among the underclass; racist views that blacks are inferior; and the Darwinian view held by earlier sociologists that the undeserving poor are responsible and culpable for their condition because of socially inherited natures. (I will refer to Lewis's, Mead's, and Darwinian views as culturalist or culturalism unless otherwise noted, by which I mean specifically the view that aberrant individuals or cultures cause poverty *and* that poor persons bear a significant responsibility for their condition.)

Culturalists and Wilson view the underclass as peopled by persons with defective moral and normative character, with character traits inimical to success in the mainstream. For Wilson, however, character traits are facets of coping mechanisms; for the culturalist, they are misguided choices and cultural beliefs. The existence of certain welfare programs, for example, is not an adequate explanation for changes in the normative character of the poor from previous generations. We must rather look to structural changes and, by implication, coping responses to those changes. Wilson suggests, as did the pragmatists and utilitarians of earlier ages, careful experimentation in social policy formation that involves direct government interventions in transforming the character of the poor, especially through well-directed opportunities to join the mainstream. Rhonda M. Williams, in "Culture as Human Capital: Methodological and Policy Implications,"[11] offers two strong arguments against Wilson's view of underclass character.

The first argument is that the poor may very well be utility maximizers under their condition; thus "racial and class differences in the payoff to human capital affect investment decisions."[12] For example, if college education results in blacks receiving less income than whites, the investment in or valuing of college education has less utility and attraction.

The second argument is that government policies to alter character involve a problem of individual freedom. "The insiders—an administrative, intellectual, and technical elite—will determine and transmit the appropriate values. The outsiders—presumably everyone else—will be the objects of managerial coercion and behavior modification."[13] Further, as Williams notes, values and behavior are presumed to coincide perfectly such that if the poor or anyone else held the right values then they would ipso facto behave in utility-maximizing ways.

Even if character traits of the underclass and mainstream society are identical, as Wilson notes, they are nonetheless inimical to success for members of the underclass. There is, however, another argument that I wish to offer.

The description of the underclass, as a social entity, and description of persons in that class, I contend, are coterminous in Wilson's works. The coterminous character warrants a perception of individual agency that is not incompatible with public policies intended to focus on changing individual character traits as the primary solution, although this is not what Wilson and most liberals intend. Welfare dependency, for example, is coterminous with the character trait of low self-esteem and an evaluative judgment of dependent persons as unaccomplished. A person on welfare is not ipso facto undeserving of public support, nor are such persons necessarily lacking in self-respect. Self-esteem, however, has to do with a sense of self-regard or regard by others because of accomplishments. In William James's sense, as well as Laurence Thomas's sense, it is the relationship of aspiration to success, that is, a degree of correlation between the two.[14]

Dependency on public funds bespeaks a lack of accomplishments, particularly since persons do not normally aspire to be poor. From a third-person standpoint, dependency is not estimable, particularly if the social order is perceived as something other than a zero-sum game offering the possibility of achieving estimable goods. It is not unreasonable to believe, consequently, with or without controversial empirical data, that the dependent have low self-esteem—or at least that the goods held estimable by the mainstream are not held in the same regard by the poor. As Wilson and others point out, the poor no longer consider it embarrassing to receive transfer payments through welfare, but rather often consider it a right or entitlement. This trait of ungrateful consumption of public funds is presented as an example of why the poor are not maximizing on their scarce resources. It is not that such traits cause poverty. They are considered, however, as contributory factors in sustaining or restricting both the bootstrap improvement of the poor and the utility of public policies intended to improve the condition of the poor.

Wilson argues that it is difficult "to entertain the idea that unemployment, underemployment, low income, a persistent shortage of cash, and crowded living conditions directly stem from cultural learning."[15] Rather, cultural transmissions are coping norms that people learn in trying to cope with poverty—not explanations for poverty but symptoms of poverty. Thus, by implication, individuals are effectuating agents (i.e., influencing their environment through their action-choices) in so far as they cope and can thereby be said to manifest or partake in the attributes associated with individual agency (desiring, willing, choosing, thinking, creating, etc.). If, however, they manifest the traits of agency by desiring or choosing dysfunctional attitudes or aberrant character traits, then it is not clear that underclass persons are exculpable for their own immiseration. This follows if we conceive of persons fundamentally as utility maximizers who either cope poorly and fail or calculate risks and benefits well and flourish in a non-zero-sum game.

The notion of a utility maximizer is predicated on a view that considers genuine persons as possessing codified reasoning powers that allow them to make calculated judgments of risk and benefits. Consequently, because underclass persons cannot in all probability actualize themselves, given the impossible odds they face due to low income, crowded living conditions, and so forth, they are conceptually either netherworld beings and nonagents or impotent. That is, if they are not responsible and culpable for their condition (which is different from having caused that condition), then they are nonagents, empty vassals —not just failed utility maximizers, but devoid of the traits that make maximizing possible (desiring, willing, choosing, etc.), or they are responsible but impotent. Utility maximizers cannot be both impotent and without responsibility for their actions over time because choosing between options presupposes an existentially or primordially rooted power of decision-making capacity, a capacity poorly or well used to make calculated decisions. As impotent persons, consequently, it is not unreasonable to conceive of underclass persons as responsible and culpable for their normative traits—but not the cause of the situations that condition their options.

Moral responsibility can be attributed to a random collection of individuals, on Virginia Held's account, because of their individual acts or failures to act.[16] This account, however, as I believe any defensible account of this sort would, requires that the individuals are reasonable agents. They must be assumed to be able to evaluate, weigh, and consider a variety of alternative actions. "Passengers," for example, can be held morally responsible for acting, such as trampling over a child in a rush to leave the train in order to reach work on time, or for not acting, such as not warning against rushing off the train. By analogy, the underclass can be held to some degree, possibly a lesser degree than passengers, responsible for reprehensible actions. Assuming that the underclass is powerless, the degree to which it should be held accountable will be exaggerated and the real culprits of their immiseration relieved.

Even if the underclass is endowed with features that are not reducible to or neatly coherent with the features of individuals, the conditions of unemployment, underemployment, or welfare dependency are suggestive of a low-level, bottom, staid, nonproductive, social impotency conditionality. At least a loose association of class position and individual character is defensible. However, the individual agency of underclass persons is treated as coterminous with its social agency in terms of the traits used to define its character. It is therefore not unreasonable to morally criticize underclass persons by virtue of membership in the underclass. Culturalists may consider individuals and cultures more responsible for immiseration than liberals do, but the basis for both ascriptions of responsibility is identical.

A class, I believe, need not be a historical or effectuating agent, but its individual members must have agency. A class may be on the decline or simply powerless to do anything about its situation, yet individuals of such classes have agency. A class, for example, has an interest by virtue of its relation to production; an individual of that class may or may not choose to promote that interest. A class may not be empowered to actualize its interest, but a normal person always has an irreducible power to choose (unless, of course, individuals are perceived as strictly determined). We may be able to predict, with near-perfect accuracy, that individuals of a given class will select to promote the interest indigenous to their class, but that does not defeat the idea of personhood that views individuals as primordially empowered to choose, only the probability that they are subject to make a choice different from their class affiliation.

My argument relies, in part, on a concept of persons as empowered existential choosers and therefore to some degree responsible. Whether that responsibility warrants policies that focus on changing individual choices heavily depends, in this context, on whether persons are also conceived as utility maximizers. It also depends on whether their primordial reasoning powers are not essentially of the utility-maximizing sort or, if they are, whether other factors are taken into account in their calculations besides how to join the mainstream.[17] If underclass persons are perceived as degraded, dominated, and exploited, for example, and thereby manifesting aberrant behavior in their pursuit to actualize their potentials, they are certainly not failed coping agents, defective calculators, or bereft of intrinsic worth. Enslaved black women, for example, if considered as a class, had agency without having the power as a class to change their position. To perceive them as only responding to their conditions as victims—shrewdly calculating choices in pursuit of the same life as their master; adopting the coping traits of alcoholism, submissiveness, prostitution, or promiscuity as integral to their personhood—is to perceive them from the standpoint of sympathetic masters, male-centered biographers, or conservative social psychologists, but not from the standpoint of actors under conditions of duress pursuing various functional and dysfunctional forms of sustaining senses of self-worth or resistance.[18] Analogously, Wilson does not conceptualize underclass persons as individuals engaged in resisting ruthless material, racial, and cultural onslaughts of their sense of self-worth through aberrant behavior or resistance; rather, they respond or cope. Their methods are dysfunctional and their character defective. The agents that profit from the underclass are, by implication, normal, reasonable, successful, and functional utility maximizers.

It is important to note that utility maximizers may be considered worthy of regard and emulation in success by liberals, but they are not necessarily considered morally good persons by virtue of being successful. One model of a successful utility maximizer and coping agent is, ironically, a college-educated slumlord; one model of an underclass person successful in overcoming the structural constraints that almost absolutely prevent her from escaping the isolation of the underclass is a welfare-dependent mother who comes to live in the suburbs and owns slum rental property. Both count as utility maximizers; neither counts as an agent of change. Nothing is inherently wrong with the way the owners manifest personhood on the utility-maximizer conception of personhood, even if something is wrong with their neglect and superexploitation of their slum property.

Perceiving persons in the underclass as coping may help explain why people behave the way they do as failed or successful utility maximizers within a domain of extremely limited options, but the explanation is inadequate to delimit criticism of underclass persons as such.

My point is not that underclass persons, or anyone else, should be treated or perceived as innocent actors, nor is my point that there are no persons in the underclass with irredeemable or morally reprobate characters. Rather, the concept of personhood as defined by an existential utility-maximizing character constitutes a view of normal personhood shared by Wilson and culturalists. Because the traits of individuals are coterminous with the powerless social traits of the underclass, and because individuals necessarily have agency, it is not inferentially unreasonable to do what Wilson rejects—to hold underclass persons responsible for their condition, a view promoted by culturalists.

The argument against culturalism by Wilson and most liberals is straightforward: The overwhelming array of structural constraints and conditions, such as limited cash flow, social isolation, and overcrowding, increase the probability of defective and dysfunctional character traits. That is, the underclass aspires to the norms of civility and the American dream of a stable family, secure job, credit, home ownership, corporate ownership, and upward mobility. However, its constituting traits are variously described by Wilson as pathological; lacking social skills; burdened with low expectations; lacking moderation, regard for others, and concern for future consequences of immediate action. Persons are normal and reasonable on a utility-maximizing view if, for example, they tend to maximize return on available opportunities and cope with exigencies by using, in the long run, strategies of personal management that generate the greatest return. Generating the greatest return with the least risk requires following laws, avoiding confrontations, maintaining good credit, seeking and maintaining job contacts, accepting without defiance underpaid work, saving diligently, and pursuing supplemental education—all traits that the condition "underclass" itself militates against.

Wilson's argument against culturalism's causal account succeeds because of the evidence showing conditions that make self-effacing behavior probable among the underclass, and thus a symptom of the condition and not its cause; but the argument does not defeat culturalism's central inference—that responsibility and culpability are attributable to individuals and cultural practices. To negate this inference requires a different conception of agency, one that is not bounded by considering individuals as utility maximizers, impotent agents, and nihilists. Unless there are some reasons to revalue our perspective of normality, it is not unreasonable to treat character traits as existentially free or culturally bound choices. Qualitative analyses may help explain their structural arrangement (such as average age of marriage, type of employment, etc.), but they cannot strictly absolve individuals of responsibility.

There is a tremendous difference between conceiving of self-effacing behavior as aberrant primarily because of the social conditions of impoverishment and conceiving it primarily in terms of degradation, domination, and exploitation whether or not it is accompanied by impoverishment. Freedom, for the former, is a matter of joining the mainstream; freedom, for the latter, is a matter of the negation of structural oppression.[19]

The debate between liberals and conservatives concerning the character traits of the underclass is thus analogous to a hermeneutic circle —the liberal description of structural social reality, which stands in opposition to conservative culturalist descriptions, does not make it unreasonable to conceive of persons in the same way as conservatives. It is to Wilson's credit that he has fought vigorously against culturalism on theoretical and practical grounds. However, that fight is made more difficult by intertwining common conceptions of personhood.

Concept of Agency

Social entities can be agents if they act or can be shown to help explain acts; if they affect, or can help explain effects. Social entities need not be reducible to a closed set of individual properties without remainder. In addition, a social entity is not necessarily bound by strict geographical parameters. I assume that the properties of a social entity are relational ("French" is the name for someone who is a national of France) and that it is intended to be referential (it picks out a substance or state of affairs). The members of a social entity possess intentional or unintentional commitments, and the attitudes and beliefs associated with the entity are at best generalizations but are not reducible to all the traits of individuals.[20]

There are minimal criteria for a class, as a social entity, to be an agent. The notion of class "is inseparable from the ambition to describe and classify agents and their conditions of existence in such a way that the cutting-up of social space [the distribution of powers] into classes might account for variations in practices."[21] Classes are agents if they have interests or a group of special interests that the class or its members are, or are potentially, struggling to realize. Such interests are analogous to benefits that help the situation of the class, by virtue of what defines its situation and is endogenous to its being.

A "class" is intended as a designation of an objective social entity. In this sense, it is referential and not a theoretical abstraction. However, it is arguable that classes can be made, or groups motivated to act as a class, in the sense that a given "class" identity is a symbolic representation through which individuals and groups pursue interests or legitimize behavior. Public policy makers, for example, who believe that there is an underclass and make policies to influence that class participate in its creation. Thus, whether Wilson is a realist or an idealist, a class is, or can be, treated as a social being. As an objective substance with properties or as a subjective construction with imagined and symbolic properties (more or less reducible or irreducible to individuals), a class functions as an entity.

A class's homogeneity is usually defined by its relationship to production, common statuses and status symbols, and/or type of product or goods and services it performs or generates. In this sense, classes are to some degree the creative sources or bearers of goods, services, and social standings. It is arguable whether they are differentiated by their homogeneity or relation to production, or whether they are differentiated by the character of their heterogeneity, fragmentation, and bevy of always transitory features.[22] In either case, some boundaries, powers, shared conditions, and life activities distinguish classes and situate their relatedness and position in society.

There are usually norms common to each class. The shared norms instill or potentially instill, in addition to other factors, a sense of unity or identity. The identity of members of the class is constituted, or potentially constituted, in relation to the contours that define the class. Its members may or may not see themselves as representatives of the class, but they are nonetheless best explained in terms of the distinguishable characteristics that separate one class from another.

If the underclass is a social entity, and not simply theoretical or serial, it is an entity encoded with agency. That is, its members must be perceived as having wills, desires, wants, and power to choose, even if it does not act as a collective.

Whether or not classes are agents of history compelled to perform certain functions; whether there is a logic structuring their relationships and futures; whether the interests of a class are realizable or are a subcategory of some larger interest; whether or not what a class tends to create is a superfluous product or service; whether the homogeneity of a class is weak or strong, organized or diffuse, represented or ignored—these are all controversial facets but are not integral to minimal criteria for a class to be an agent. The primary reason for this, relevant to this argument, is that the concept of class entails agency. In order for a category to be a class (rather than group, strata, or association), the collective displays an array of traits roughly analogous to important traits that define individual agency: Special interests, desires, creative acts, powers, objective standing, distinctiveness, relatedness, and norms.

I have intentionally used very broad and general features that define social agency in order to specify a few of the criteria that are most often taken into account in radically different conceptions of social agency. If America, the working class, the middle class, women, the ecology movement, or a battalion of U.S. soldiers stationed in Panama count as social agents, it is by virtue of some of the above criteria. These criteria form a loose and incomplete account of the minimal criteria for a group to count as a social agent. However, the criteria are not without controversial features. Whether social entities exist, whether it makes sense to talk about a social entity effecting change independent of individuals or groups, and to what degree and in what form the characteristics that define a social entity are necessarily reducible to characteristics definitive of individuals—these are a few of the more striking controversies that these criteria do not address. The criteria do, however, give us some basis to see if the concept of the underclass reasonably can be considered as one with a defensible view of agency.

Agency and the Underclass

The underclass, it has been argued, lacks a stake in the political arena.[23] As a class, its social and structural situation makes political involvement unlikely. Rather than the practical question of how the underclass or others intending to represent the underclass might become involved in political processes inclined to improve its condition, I will address what interests are endogenous to it as a class. Although it has been argued that poverty-level families, recidivist criminals, and welfare-dependent persons should not be lumped together in the same class, the interests I will consider are central to what the underclass means even if poverty-level households, recidivist criminals, and welfare-dependent persons are not its members.[24]

Unlike the concepts of bourgeoisie, working class, proletariat, *lumpenproletariat*—and unlike the concepts of upper, middle, and lower class—the concept of underclass does not suggest that it or its members have a special positive interest other than escape and negation. By a special positive interest I mean a good that would benefit a group far more than others but would arguably benefit other groups that do not share its position. In Weberian terms, for example, the lower class is identified with persons of lesser income than others, of humbler origins than others, of simpler home furnishings, less sophisticated moral attitudes, and comparatively crude mannerisms. In one sense, they are close to Rousseau's primitives; in another, they are diligent, if simple and poor, potential Horatio Algers. For example, if the lower class constitutes primarily domestic servants, garbage collectors, and ditch diggers, it is plausible that society as a whole, but especially lower class persons, has an interest in promoting employer civility and free health services. The interest of the lower class is estimable, even if it does generate only low prestige, in the sense that it creates or is responsible for a service. It thereby accomplishes.

The *lumpenproletariat,* on Marx's account, is without effectuating agency, but its interest, actions, conditions, and definition are a function of the interest, actions, conditions, and definition of the working class. The *lumpenproletariat* lacks a position in society that allows it to force others to adhere to its demands. It will, like all other classes, be negated. It can ally with other classes to do what Marx views as necessary for human liberation—destroy capitalism. Its ruthlessness, an attribute needed by the working class, was for Mao Tse-tung as well as Frantz Fanon a beneficial attribute potentially of use by the working class. What interests are associated with the underclass as a function of its condition? What estimable qualities does it possess? What role can it play in its own negation?

Every good, such as affordable housing, health care, or fulfilling and well-paying employment, is an interest a society of flourishing persons has as a whole, but the underclass has a greater need for every good that contributes to flourishing. The underclass's interest is thus nefarious and nonspecific in relation to such goods. Its interest is universal, not in the sense that the whole of humanity would be liberated if the underclass were liberated, but in the sense that any good that benefits humanity is a benefit that the underclass has a greater need for within American capitalism.[25] If a homogeneous group is without a particular interest as a function of its condition, which distinguishes it as a class, and without arguably estimable qualities engendered by the way it makes a living or lives otherwise, in what sense is it a class?

An interest in self-negation and escape is an antithetical interest; that is, it is not a benefit as such, but an ending. It is not something that the class as such receives. Once it is accomplished, its members and their station in life no longer exist. The underclass is defined as the negation of beneficial interest—not in the sense that if everyone becomes underclass the underclass as a distinguishable group disappears, not in the sense that if everyone in the underclass secured and maintained gainful employment the class would cease to be distinguishable, nor in the sense that its interest is in opposition to the interest of all other classes—but in the sense that suicide is not an interest a person or class can have after death. It is not a benefit that is gained, but a means to an ending of the condition for the receipt of benefit. A person can conceivably maintain personal memories after death and thereby a sense of identity. For the underclass, its character traits and structural situation seem of little use to gain it liberation or of any value if liberation were achieved. Its living interest is therefore absolute death. Its identity as such must be negated without remainder.

It may be, however, that the nefarious, antithetical interest and lack of estimable qualities of the underclass is what distinguish it as a class or class sector. If so, then the character of its social agency in other forms is due special attention.

The underclass is bound together, on Wilson's account, as an entity, not by a sense of imagined community or a culture its members seek to promote, nor by a heritage, race, language or religion, but by situation. The degree to which its members feel bound together as an imagined community is in part a function of their isolation. The binding links, such as teens fathering children as a sign of empowerment, function to generate status within the underclass. That activity is disadvantageous. Sharing drug needles or cooperating to sell drugs binds people together, but again that binding is a disadvantageous activity. Many, if not most, of the binding activities are harmful. The helpful norms, such as networking to find gainful employment or sharing parenting responsibilities, are insufficiently practiced to outweigh the deleterious results of the binding norms that promote death, imprisonment, unemployment, underemployment, rape, beatings, and child abuse. The normative homogeneity of the underclass is thus a homogeneity of norms that stand in opposition to the possibility of beneficial bindings. Its homogeneity is one of temporality, impermanence, and narcissism; it is antithetical in that the characteristics that define it are excruciatingly disadvantageous to binding.

Given harmful and inadequate binding norms, does the underclass as a social agent create any material benefits? In what form, if any, is the underclass involved in creating wealth—for example, wealth for real estate owners of inner-city ghetto property through rent payments on deteriorated housing; tax deductions on deteriorated property; chemical, pharmaceutical, boat, airplane, and communication companies by virtue of the illegal drugs consumed by the underclass?

Wilson has noted in numerous publications that the underclass is superexploited. However, it is arguable that the underclass is not sufficiently defined in terms of what it is responsible for creating. Its homogeneity is defined in terms of conditions of impotency, social and economic influences shaping its existence that occur outside of its realm of involvement, intuitively repulsive norms, isolation, forms of dependency, and types of marginal and temporary underemployment or unemployment. Dependency, marginality, or destitution does not suggest individual or social agency through creation and transactions. A social entity that lacks a perspective of agency through transaction is an entity that seems to be either a theoretical abstraction or peopled by severely impotent or less than fully reasonable individuals.

The lack of notions of transaction suggestive of accomplishment, or of transactive relations that suggest the underclass has contributed some arguable good, leaves the underclass as an entity apparently without traits that convey or create status through transaction. An exploited worker, for example, has status or can be conceived as having status as a producer, whether poor or not; a family that is homeless not by choice but from a lack of affordable child care services and rewarding work has status, not because of its destitution but because rents, child care costs, and its resources have forced it to be expelled from transactions beneficial to the family. The reasonable possibility of the family's choosing a different life style has been subverted through no fault of its own. We would be hard pressed, for example, to show that some of America's largest wealth-creating industries, such as pharmaceutical and illegal drugs, are not dependent and enriched by their active trade with poor workers and destitute families. But if poor workers or destitute families are not conceptualized in some form of positive activity, then the character of their status as reasoning agents is an open question—a question that culturalists are quick to answer by heavily weighing the responsibility underclass persons bear for their immiseration.

It is conceivable that the underclass does not, as an entity, create or represent a status, but rather it creates or represents antithetical status; it stands as the negation of esteem, privilege, and persons due deference because it is not an agent of creativity or transaction. It is conceivable that as a class it does not seek even to create the nihilism of status because its members procreate alarmingly often, and frequently out of wedlock, most often sustaining impermanent families generation after generation. Its members too often gain status through narcissistic activity such as drug and alcohol addiction, wife- or mate-beating, and criminal actions of a high degree of failure while simultaneously seeking status through traditional mechanisms of communal involvement, mating, child-rearing, and maximizing income through capitalist ventures popular in the mainstream (inclusive of the drug trade). If its status were so conceived, it would be antithetical to status as such. The underclass is treated, however, as the result of structurally impervious or misdirected forces, but it is not treated as an agent that can effect those forces on its own behalf.

As Wilson and others note, there is an asymmetry between the mainstream and the underclass. If the economy falters, the underclass is the most affected; if the economy booms, the underclass does not necessarily improve its standing. Since the underclass is a part of the same economic domain as all other classes, it seems as if the structure of the domain itself may stand in opposition to the well-being of the underclass. It is therefore not the antithesis of forces shaping its own making. The Hegelian master–slave dialectic consequently would be inapplicable to the underclass because the master is not identified with any particular individual or opposing class. The class contradiction of traditional Marxism is mute because the working class and the bourgeoisie stand outside of the underclass. Whose class interest the underclass can conceivably contribute to is not clear. The possibility of the underclass participating in a postmodern revolution appears mute because the conditions often treated as ushering in a postmodern era (technology, service industry, mobility, temporary relationships, etc.) are also conditions that help create, and presumably help perpetuate, the underclass's isolation. The underclass seems to be an entity without power and without potential power.

Conclusion

The underclass, as a social entity, is arguably serial; neither a class nor a class sector. It is not an agent of creativity or transaction, and it lacks estimable qualities or an interest it can be said to be actively trying to actualize. Williams may be right in noting that the underclass "will be the objects of managerial coercion and behavior modification" if their freedom is dependent on external agents. However, as constructed, it would seem that the situation is unavoidable if utility maximizing defines individual agency.

It is lamentable that some liberals and conservatives have joined to promote a "reciprocal responsibilities" approach to welfare. The idea is to offer underclass persons incentives to "reform the assumed habits of the apathetic, deviant, and destructive individuals that supposedly make up the 'underclass.'"[26] However, the concept of personhood, which makes incentives and reciprocal responsibilities seem viable because people are viewed as essentially utility maximizers, is also the concept of personhood encoded in the critique of culturalism. If people are or must become utility maximizers, is the possibility of underclass persons manifesting that potential neutered if they are described as essentially nihilistic? If a social entity is constructed through notions of destitution, dependency, isolation, entrapment, and homelessness, and if it is not unreasonable to infer that its individual members characteristically manifest a defective agency, is it a concept of a social entity that denudes its members of status? The existence of the underclass may bespeak a new era in capitalist exploitation—an era that has created a slave quarter without creating structural malfunction.

My speculations on the type of social agency the underclass represents hopefully will encourage research and theoretical debate about the way social entities are constructed and their members described. The concept of the underclass and Wilson's contributions to social theory and public policy considerations certainly raise hard questions for grand theories about social agency, and even harder questions for well-meaning persons seeking radical social transformation.

NOTES

Acknowledgment: An early version of this paper was presented at the University of Delaware, Conference on Philosophy and the Underclass, June 1989.

1. William Julius Wilson, "Response to Hochschild and Boxill," *Ethics* 101 (April 1991): 601.
2. William Julius Wilson, *The Truly Disadvantaged* (Chicago: University of Chicago Press, 1987), pp. 6–8.
3. William Julius Wilson, "The American Underclass: Inner-City Ghettos and the Norms of Citizenship" (Godkin Lecture, Harvard University, April 26, 1989). Also see "The Ghetto Underclass and the Social Transformation of the Inner City" (Plenary Lecture, American Association for the Advancement of Science, Chicago, February 15, 1987); and Richard P. Nathan, "Will the Underclass Always Be with Us?" *Society* 24 (March–April 1987): 57–62. For the liberal genealogy of "underclass," see Wilson, *The Truly Disadvantaged*, p. 6; William Kornblum, "Lumping the Poor: What Is the 'Underclass'?" *Dissent* 31, no. 3 (Summer 1984): 275–302; Richard McGahey, "Poverty's Voguish Stigma," *New York Times*, March 12, 1982, p. 29; and Michael B. Katz, *In the Shadow of the Poorhouse* (New York: Basic Books, 1986), pp. 274–75. For an example of an operational definition of the underclass, see E. R. Ricketts and I. Sawhill, "Defining and Measuring the Underclass," *Journal of Policy Analysis and Management* 7, no. 2 (1988): 316–25. For an example of an approach that includes the wit, tenacity, strategies for survival, resistance, and the devastating role played by the mainstream, see Douglas G. Glasgow, *The Black Underclass* (New York: Vintage Books, 1981).
4. William Julius Wilson and Loïc J. D. Wacquant, "The Cost of Racial and Class Exclusion in the Inner City," *Annals of the American Academy of Political and Social Science* 501 (January 1989): 25. Also see William Julius Wilson, "Studying the Inner-City Social Dislocation: The Challenge of Public Agenda Research," *American Sociological Review* 56 (February 1991): 1–14.
5. Wilson, "Studying the Inner-City Social Dislocation," p. 8.
6. Ibid., p. 11.
7. Russian serfs and African-American slaves were both poor, for example, and we can treat their condition as historically rooted in certain world situations, common conditions of unfree labor, and service to masters, but their actual realities were different in crucial ways; they did not act as a connected collective, and their common interests were pursued by each separately. Their designation as "poor" tells us comparatively little. See Peter Kolchin, *Unfree Labor* (Cambridge, Mass.: Harvard University Press, 1987).

8. For this distinction, although used in another context, see Pierre Bourdieu, "What Makes a Social Class? On the Theoretical and Practical Existence of Groups," *Berkeley Journal of Sociology* 32 (1987): 1–6.

9. As examples of these lines of argument by contemporary authors, see André Gorz, *Farewell to the Working Class* (Boston: South End Press, 1980); and C. Mouffe and E. Laclau, *Hegemony and Socialist Strategy* (London: Verso, 1985).

10. For an example of these concerns, see Wilson, "The American Underclass."

11. Rhonda M. Williams, "Culture as Human Capital: Methodological and Policy Implications," *Praxis International* 7, no. 2 (July 1987): 152–63. Also see William A. Darity, Jr., "The Human Capital Approach to Black–White Earnings Inequality—Some Unsettled Questions," *Journal of Human Resources* 17, no. 1 (1982): 72–93; and Gary Becker, *Human Capital* (New York: National Bureau of Economic Research, 1964).

12. Williams, "Culture as Human Capital," p. 156. Also see Jennifer L. Hochschild, "The Politics of the Estranged Poor," *Ethics* 101 (April 1991): 563–70; Bernard Boxill, "Wilson on the Truly Disadvantaged," *Ethics* 101 (April 1991): 587.

13. Williams, "Culture as Human Capital," p. 162.

14. See William James, "The Consciousness of Self," in *Principles of Psychology*, vol. 1 (New York: Henry Holt, 1893), pp. 291–401. Also see Laurence Thomas, "Self-Respect: Theory and Practice," in *Philosophy Born of Struggle*, ed. Leonard Harris (Dubuque, Iowa: Kendall/Hunt, 1983), pp. 174–89.

15. William Julius Wilson, "The Underclass: Issues, Perspectives and Public Policy," *Annals of the American Academy of Political and Social Science* 501 (January 1989): 185.

16. See Virginia Held, "Can a Random Collection of Individuals Be Morally Responsible," in *The Spectrum of Responsibility*, ed. Peter A. French (New York: St. Martin's Press, 1991), pp. 265–74.

17. There are certainly other options besides the sort of naturalist conception of personhood I offer, which sees personhood in terms of existentially rooted capacities to choose; primordial reasoning that weighs self-esteem through empowerment, for example, transforming nature in one's own self image as distinct from transforming nature for the interst of others; and self-creative cultural acts rather than pedantic imitations of the culture of the ruling class without its material or psychological rewards. The idea is to suggest a different concept of personhood than the utility-maximizing approach.

18. See Hazel V. Carby, *Reconstructing Womanhood* (Oxford: Oxford University Press, 1987); Harriet Jacob, *Incidents in the Life of a Slave Girl* (Cambridge, Mass.: Harvard University Press, 1987); Mary Prince, *The History of Mary Prince, a West Indian Slave* (New York: Routledge, Chapman and Hall, 1987).

19. See, for example, the difference between Frantz Fanon and the comparatively conservative Sigmund Freud, Carl Jung, and Alfred Adler, in Hussein A. Buham, *Frantz Fanon and the Psychology of Oppression* (New York: Plenum Press, 1985).

20. See David-Hillil Ruben, "The Existence of Social Entities," *Philosophical Quarterly* 32, no. 129 (October 1982): 295–310.

21. Bourdieu, "What Makes a Social Class?" p. 6.

22. As contra Bourdieu, see John B. Thompson, *Studies in the Theory of Ideology* (Berkeley: University of California Press, 1984), pp. 62–63.

23. Jennifer L. Hochschild, "Equal Opportunity and the Estranged Poor," *Annals of the American Academy of Political and Social Science* 501 (January 1989): 143–55.

24. Kornblum, "Lumping the Poor," pp. 295–302.

25. Unlike Marx's or Weber's conception of the working class, the underclass is not in a position to control goods and services crucial to society as a whole. Rather than the question, Who needs the Negro? we might ask, Who needs the underclass?

26. See the argument against the reciprocal responsibility approach by Loïc J. D. Wacquant, "The Ghetto, the State, and the Capitalist Economy," *Dissent* 36, no. 4 (Fall 1989): 508–20.

PART *Two*

Urban Values

4 THE BLACK UNDERCLASS AND THE QUESTION OF VALUES
Howard McGary

THE BLACK UNDERCLASS is said to be poor, badly educated, directly related to crime either as perpetrators or victims, and typically young. Data indicate that, unlike the black urban poor in the recent past, the underclass also appears to be locked into a cycle of poverty. If these data are accurate, then the crucial question is "Why are members of the underclass locked into their underclass status?" A debate rages between conservatives and liberals about how to answer this question. Conservatives maintain that the key to solving the problem is altering the values of the black underclass so that it might better participate in the capitalist market economy.[1] Conservatives also typically add that the state should eliminate many of the burdensome regulations that they believe work to the detriment of people at the bottom rungs of the socioeconomic ladder, for example, minimum wage laws. Liberals, on the other hand, assert that the state must play an active role in solving the problems of the black underclass. The state, in their view, should create laws and programs that provide state funds to educate and house those who are said to be locked into the black underclass.

The dispute between conservatives and liberals over the black underclass often occurs in the political arena, but it occurs in academic circles as well. William Julius Wilson in his book *The Truly Disadvantaged*[2] argues that liberals have failed to keep up their side of the debate in the dispute over the black underclass. He attributes this to a reluctance by liberals to examine some of the controversial data about members of the black underclass. Wilson believes that the sensitive nature of these data causes liberals to believe that if they examine the data they will be accused of "blaming the victims." They also fear that focusing on the inadequacies of this class will allow some to intensify the racism that exists in American society. Refusing to focus on the personal shortcomings of the members of the underclass, the liberals find fault instead with the design of social institutions.

In my view, both the conservative and liberal solutions involve doctrinaire commitments that blind each approach to the virtues of the other's solution. Conservatives are right to focus on the mindset of members of the underclass, and liberals are correct when they maintain that we must focus on the social structure—but what they both fail to appreciate is just how much the design of social institutions influences the way people think. I argue that members of the underclass do suffer from an understandable but crippling resentment that is fostered by the unjust design of the basic structure of society.

My aim in this discussion is modest. I wish to suggest a possible reason why both conservatives and liberals miss the point. In doing so, I take it as a postulate that it is possible to solve the problems of the black underclass without rejecting the capitalist mode of production. This is a big assumption, but one that conservatives and liberals usually accept. First, I describe what prominent liberal theorists have meant by full citizenship, especially in modern democratic societies. Second, I explain the kinds of things that can count as evidence that one has full citizenship. Third, I argue that members of the black underclass have good reason to doubt that they have full citizenship. I conclude by showing what effects having reasonable doubts about one's political status can have on persons considered to be in the "underclass."

In Wilson's recent work he chooses to distance himself from the term "underclass."[3] According to Wilson, the term has taken on too many meanings and has become the subject of heated debates between those on the right, who believe that members of the underclass cause their own predicament because of their unwillingness to work due to poor values, and by liberals, who claim that the underclass is caused by structural weaknesses in the economy. Wilson believes that the controversy surrounding this term may discourage serious scholars from doing conceptual and theoretical work on this group out of fear of becoming embroiled in a media and political controversy. In order not to discourage research in this area, Wilson suggests that the term "underclass" be replaced by the expression "ghetto poor."

However, Wilson fails to see that it is not the name that causes the controversy, but the phenomenon itself. Even if we substitute the term "ghetto poor" for the term "underclass," people who believe that the behavior patterns of poor ghetto dwellers are caused by bad values will continue to do so in spite of the name change. Likewise, those who believe that the behavior patterns of this group are due to structural problems will continue to do so. Changing the name of those who are experiencing prolonged poverty and joblessness will do little to halt the political debate over what causes this phenomenon and how to remedy it. Wilson is correct in asserting that both sides of the debate have committed a fallacy by attempting to derive evaluative conclusions from his factual premises. However, I do not think that changing the name of the subjects of this debate will prevent people on both sides from making such invalid inferences. Nor will it assure timid scholars who are reluctant to become a party to political controversy.

The Nature of Full Citizenship

Individuals join together to form civil society for a variety of reasons, many of which have been discussed by political theorists. Some say that the only valid ground for state authority is the protection of the individual. Others maintain that it is for the promotion of the interests of those who form the social union. Those of a more collectivist sort claim that the promotion of the common good is the basis for civil society. I do not want to enter into this debate. My point is that in the liberal tradition a person who is said to be a citizen has the same basic rights as any other citizen. Of course, this does not mean everyone within the liberal tradition has defined the consequences of equal citizenship in the same way. For instance, some have been strong supporters of individual rights, while others have focused on the common good and have supported the rights of individuals only when doing so promotes the common good. However, the U.S. Constitution vests rights in individuals, and modern theorists—be they contractarians, human rights theorists, or utilitarians—have been leery of any proposal that denies equal protection under the law to any citizen.

As Ronald Dworkin has said, equal citizenship requires each citizen to be treated with "equal concern and respect."[4] The belief that one is treated with equal concern and respect has an important impact on one's self-concept and plays a vital role in the formula for flourishing in a social context. By flourishing, I have in mind being able to construct one's life plan consistent with one's abilities and talents. Citizenship, in the liberal tradition, is thought to provide one with the opportunity to flourish by arranging society such that its basic structure does not unfairly inhibit or prohibit one's pursuit of a chosen plan of life. The belief that one has a full citizenship also allows one to feel comfortable in supporting and defending what John Rawls has called the "basic structure of society." By basic structure Rawls means "the way in which the major social institutions distribute fundamental rights and duties and determine the division of advantages from social cooperation." Rawls goes on to define major social institutions as "the political constitution and the principal economic and social arrangements." The major institutions "define people's rights and duties and influence their life prospects."[5] Full citizenship certainly does not entail that one will get whatever one wants, but it does say that one will have the opportunity to satisfy one's needs and desires. When these things cannot be satisfied, it cannot be blamed on the basic structure of society.

In this view, citizens are competitors in a game of life in which rules are not rigged in favor of any of the competitors. However, this view does not assume that people cannot be treated unfairly because of the unjust actions of individuals; it is clearly understood that the unfairness is not the result of the design of the basic structure of society. Persons who feel that they are full citizens believe that their rights are recognized and protected and that their failings can be traced to some personal shortcoming, individual act of injustice, or poor fate, but not to the design of the basic structure of society.

Evidence of Full Citizenship

What things count as evidence in modern liberal democratic societies that one has full citizenship? The following list is not inclusive, but it does include many important indicators of full citizenship. Citizens have the right to participate in the political process. They have the right to earn a living without being forced to engage in activities that are degrading or exploitative. Citizens are not denied opportunities simply because of their race, sex, or religious affiliations. Citizens also have legal due process. Notice that I have not included in this list a right to a certain income. Liberals have disagreed over whether citizens' basic rights include welfare rights. However, citizens who languish in a permanent condition of poverty in a society that has plenty have to wonder about their equal citizenship status.

Having the secure conviction that one has the aforementioned rights and opportunities helps to foster the belief that one can succeed, but just as important, it allows one to believe that one is a legitimate member of a social community, and that the community interprets the common good in a manner that is consistent with one's own good. Of course, this does not mean that everything always goes one's way. Nor does it mean that some individuals cannot have more of society's good than others. However, to use Rawlsian terminology, it does mean that even the least-advantaged members of society will have a secure conviction that the basic structure of society is just.

Laziness and the Black Underclass

Wilson and others have defined the black underclass as young, poorly educated, intimately connected to crime either as perpetrators or as victims, and locked into a cycle of poverty. The important question is "Why is a certain segment of society plagued by these problems?" I said that both conservatives and liberals have their fingers on part of the answer. The liberals are correct in maintaining that there is still work to be done to guarantee equal opportunity to certain groups, particularly blacks. They are also correct in contending that the state must play some active role in this process. For example, because of their race blacks are still severely restricted when it comes to finding decent, inexpensive housing. This is true even for blacks who have been able to acquire middle-class status, but it is an especially acute problem for blacks who are members of the lower classes. A persistent worry for these people is finding and keeping a place to live.[6] As psychological studies have shown, this type of insecurity is very debilitating, especially for the young.

Conservatives, of course, argue that we have equal housing legislation on the books, so adding additional legislation will not solve the problem. Conservatives may be right that equal housing laws are on the books, but they are wrong if they mean that these laws are being enforced. In fact, during the Reagan years, in which we have seen the emergence of the black underclass, the enforcement of equal housing laws has been virtually nonexistent. Therefore, I think the liberals are right that there is more work for the state to do, even if it is primarily the enforcement of civil rights laws already on the books.

But liberals may be wrong if they believe that at this point in the process enforcement of civil rights laws will solve the problems facing the underclass. Of course, few liberals have said that legislation alone will solve the problems. This is just a caricature of the liberal view advanced by some conservatives. However, I think it is fair to say that liberals have been reluctant publicly to declare that something about the persons who make up the underclass may contribute to their underclass status.

Here we can learn from the conservatives, but they are not the only persons who have asked blacks to examine themselves for a solution to their predicament. Black Muslims, for example, have consistently urged black people to examine their commitments, habits, and values and to fashion their own remedy to their problems rather than waiting for whites to solve them.[7] But, unlike the conservatives, the Muslims are quick to warn that the initial cause of black people's problems is white people. Black Muslims have attempted to provide an economic and social structure for blacks to enhance their self-esteem while providing them with the necessary resources for putting their life plans into action. Booker T. Washington also asked blacks to do some critical self-evaluation before fashioning their own programs for economic and social improvement.[8]

Clearly there has been progress over the years when it comes to race relations, and it is probably true that the significance of race is declining. Nonetheless, race is still an important defining characteristic of persons in our society. It is my contention that blacks in the underclass have been placed in an untenable position that makes it extremely difficult for them to evaluate their personal successes and failures. They have been told that racism no longer exists, and wealthy and middle-class blacks are pointed to as support for this claim. So, when poor blacks fail people are quick to say that it is because of personal shortcomings and not systemic failings. Some black scholars recently have claimed that the values of the black underclass are the source of its predicament.[9] In other words, opportunities exist for these poor blacks, but the members of the underclass fail to take advantage of these opportunities because they are lazy, undisciplined, and too prone to satisfying their immediate desires. This view has become quite popular in some quarters.

Let us now examine this harsh critique of members of the black underclass. Being lazy means being resistant to work or disposed to idleness. Are all or most members of the black underclass lazy? I think not. First, it is not at all clear that blacks in the underclass are resistant to work. In order for someone to be properly described as being lazy, there must be a genuine opportunity for that person to engage in meaningful and nonexploitative work. For example, it would be wrong to call slaves lazy because they refused to work in the slavemaster's cotton fields. And it would be wrong to label as lazy someone who refused to prostitute his or her body for a wage. One thing is certainly clear. Blacks in the underclass are not turning down good-paying, safe, and non-dead-end jobs. It is questionable whether enough gainful employment exists to successfully integrate members of the underclass into the broader economy. In fact, some economists have argued that integration of the underclass would require a rapid growth of the economy.[10] There is no guarantee that such growth will occur. Another question is whether it is rational for mothers heading single-family households to accept jobs that do not have health plans and child care services. Given the tremendous costs of health care and child care, the welfare system may be the only viable alternative for many underclass families.

But what about those women who do work their way off of the welfare system? Typically, these are people who have family to draw upon. Of course, a few women manage to secure low-paying entry-level jobs that do provide some modest health coverage; however, such jobs are the exception rather than the rule.

Those who criticize the members of the black underclass for lacking in values will sometimes admit that members of the black underclass face harsh conditions, but they quickly add that these persons have to be tough and do those things that will allow them to flourish. Is it fair to expect members of the black underclass to fight through these adversities? I do not deny that some do, but should this be expected of all members of this group? For example, suppose a person loses both legs because of some unjust act, and that the injustice goes uncompensated. Suppose further that this person goes on to accomplish a great deal in spite of her handicap. Should anyone in her circumstances be expected to act as she does? I think not. This person receives high praise because she stands apart from the norm. If her accomplishments were what the average person could be expected to do, then we would not hold her in such high regard. So, it would seem to be wrong or at least insensitive to condemn people for not being exceptional at overcoming serious adversities. However, I think this is just what is being expected of members of the black underclass.

I have attempted thus far to cast doubt on the claim that members of the black underclass are lazy. Now I would like to buttress my rejection of this claim by looking carefully at the claim that members of this class are poorly motivated due to laziness. Such a view overlooks the relationship between being motivated and having the secure conviction that the rules or structure of society are not stacked against one. Living in a society in which one has good reason to believe that the basic structure is just does a lot for enhancing or at least sustaining one's motivational level. Members of the underclass lack good evidence that they live in such a society. When they look around their community, they see that its members lack the material things and opportunities that many other communities take for granted. This is especially devastating when we note that a large segment of the underclass are children. It is extremely difficult for children to understand that they must use modest opportunities and resources to fight against awful odds if they are to succeed, especially when they know that children in other communities do not face such an uphill struggle. They often see this as too much to ask of them, and this belief works against their being highly motivated. Is this a reasonable conclusion? I think so. Rawls has persuasively argued that people do not deserve the benefits that result from the luck of the natural lottery.[11] Therefore, children in the black underclass do not deserve to be poor, nor do children born into affluent families deserve to be rich. The large number of children in the black underclass have a good reason for thinking that their situation is not something that they deserve. They are born into poor families and must work harder than people from more affluent families if they are to succeed. These beliefs have a negative impact on their motivational levels.

If what I have argued for so far is sound, then we can see several reasons for doubting that members of the black underclass are lazy. Similar arguments would also seem to apply to the criticism that members of the black underclass are undisciplined and unable to defer gratification. Being disciplined and deferring gratification both depend upon having good evidence that the cards are not stacked against one. Exit studies for female and black students who have dropped out of graduate programs point to the difficulty of being disciplined when the environment in which one must operate is tainted by racism or sexism. Students in these studies report that it is difficult to separate their inadequacies from biased or unfair expectations. This uncertainty serves to impact negatively on their ability to gain strength through training. While in the process of growing and acquiring new skills, a time that is generally filled with self-doubt, they find it extremely taxing to separate the anguish and paranoia associated with a rigorous graduate program from the subtle forms of racism and sexism that still exist in institutions of higher learning. The underclass faces the same problem, but in more drastic circumstances. So, one should be cautious in such circumstances in condemning those who must deal with covert racism as suffering from a lack of discipline.

Of course, one could object that my argument is unsound because blacks in the past had to deal with racism and its effects, but nonetheless they were motivated to succeed and clearly did not suffer from "poor" values. However, such a response does not succeed when examined closely. First, the claim that blacks suffer because of poor values has existed since slavery. In fact, it was even offered as a justification for slavery. So, the idea that the downtrodden position of underclass blacks can be attributed to their poor values or lack of values is not new. What is new, though, is that we now have a chorus of black voices singing this tune. Unlike in the past, the increase in violent crime and the drug problem have caused many, including blacks, to search frantically for answers that may help to eliminate social problems that touch all of our lives. However, many critics might agree that the appeal to poor values was once a smoke screen, but that now this position has credibility.

Another explanation exists for why the effects of racism severely hamper members of the black underclass to a degree not experienced by blacks up until the 1960s. Several commentators, discussing the impact of integration on black communities in the United States, have pointed out that middle-class blacks have left these communities and taken with them the tax base and many of the things associated with stable communities. Large, urban black communities are now pretty much populated by blacks from the bottom rung of the economic ladder. Major institutions in these communities have been either destroyed or severely weakened by the flight of the black middle class. One consequence of this flight is that people do not have the resources at their disposal to address many day-to-day problems. This may seem like a small point, but I assure you that it is not. It is one thing for a person from the outside to say that you can make it and another for someone who is struggling with the inadequate resources to do so. At one time, "making it" meant rising to the top in one's community, and as individuals progressed, so did the community. However, since the integration movement "making it" has meant escaping from one's community. This has the consequence of intensifying any antagonisms that exist between poor blacks and those who are better off. Members of the so-called black underclass now face a society in which the basic structure is not just, intense competition for scarce resources, and abandonment by those best able to help ward off the effects of living in a society that is still plagued by racism.

Some may find my conclusion about laziness and the black underclass disturbing because they believe that it provides a convenient rationale for underclass blacks to acquiesce in their downtrodden position. Others may conclude that it supports the more disturbing position that black people (especially healthy black males) should be excused for failing to do what is necessary in order to provide for their families. However, neither of these things follow from anything that I have said. It is not my contention that blacks should not go beyond what is expected of whites if they are to overcome the adversities that are so much a part of their daily lives. What I do say, however, is that those who cannot muster this strength should not be described as lazy. Many people in the black underclass are putting forth a gallant effort against bad odds to secure a living for their families. We must draw a line between what people are required to do as a matter of moral duty and supererogatory acts. People should not have to sacrifice their sense of self completely, even if doing so would serve some noble end, such as providing for the well-being of one's family. Of course, the morally good person is willing to make some sacrifice; however, at some point we must draw the line. When we fail to do so, then we are too willing to accept false accusations, such as that all the members of the black underclass are lazy, because such accusations wrongly shift the focus from institutional design and social structure to the individual.

The line of argument advanced here does not deny that some members of the underclass are lazy. However, all classes within our society have some lazy members. But for the argument that attributes underclass status to laziness to succeed, it must be the case that all, many, or most of the black underclass is lazy. There is no evidence available to support this strong evaluative claim.

A Final Objection and Reply

One possible objection to the line of reasoning developed in this chapter can be stated as follows: past racism against blacks was so consuming and debilitating that it caused a segment of the black population to be unmotivated even in the face of opportunities. Supporters of this position might contend that these blacks have been reduced to this state by racism and deprivation. They could argue that they should not be accused of blaming the victims, because they are merely stating a psychological fact. They might go on to add that this is an unfortunate consequence of racism, but a consequence nonetheless. According to this view, denying or ignoring this consequence of racism will impede efforts to eliminate the so-called black underclass.

I would respond to such criticism in three ways. First, these critics are correct to think that blacks or any group who experienced systematic wrongdoing would be scared by the process. To think otherwise would be either to underestimate the horrors of racism or to romanticize the strength of black people. But one should be clear about what one takes to be the negative consequences of racism on the motivational structures of blacks. Second, it is one thing to say that genuine opportunities exist for blacks in the underclass and another thing to demonstrate their existence. It is extremely important to be precise about the nature of these opportunities. Third, even if we grant that in the face of opportunities some members of the underclass are unmotivated due to racism, it is not clear that these people should be characterized as having poor values.

When we scratch the surface of my first point, we will see that it is important to be as clear as possible about what the consequences of racism have been on the motivational levels of blacks. All too often people fail to realize that racism affected blacks in very different ways. (This is not to minimize or downplay the harmful effects by saying that they are different.) Undoubtedly, some people used the damaging effects of racism to become stronger persons. It made them have tough skins in the best sense of the term. On the other hand, others were consumed or destroyed by it. And, of course, there are various degrees in between these two extremes. If by scared my critics mean that most or many blacks in the underclass had their motivational structures completely destroyed, then of course laziness would be an issue. But black conservatives such as Glenn Loury, Shelby Steele,[12] and Thomas Sowell, who might identify with this line of criticism, cannot mean that the motivational structures of a large segment of the underclass have been destroyed. If this were true, their proposals for eliminating this class would not make sense. They do not think that these people are incapable of being motivated, but rather that they are not sufficiently motivated because they have become accustomed to handouts and because they fail to recognize viable opportunities for advancement.

This leads to my second point. When black conservatives talk about opportunities, they typically mean that there are jobs available. They claim that certain jobs are crying out to be filled, particularly jobs requiring highly specialized skills or those in the service industries that require minimal skills. This may be true, but a further question has to be asked: If employers are in such desperate need of these employees, why are they not doing more to train and recruit these people? Their lack of effort in these areas may cast some doubt on how desperate they are to fill these jobs.

However, putting this issue aside, there is a more fundamental problem with the contention by black conservatives that ample opportunities exist for those who are willing to work. As we know, being positioned to take advantage of opportunities is conditioned by a number of things, for example, being properly educated or trained and having a work ethic. But several other things impinge on these two factors, for example, health care. All too often members of the underclass lack proper health care—not just health care in the narrow sense of being able to go to a doctor when one is very sick, but health care to the extent that pregnant women in this class can receive the proper prenatal care that is so crucial in preventing infants from experiencing physical and mental problems that will hamper their ability to learn. We also have to focus on environmental impediments such as the disproportionate number of persons from the underclass who are exposed to lead contamination, which can have disastrous effects on a developing child's ability to learn.

What these conservatives fail to see is that legitimate opportunities must be understood as more than whether or not there are jobs available. For example, in a number of large cities, such as Milwaukee, a number of jobs that underclass residents are qualified to fill have moved out of the inner cities to the suburbs, making transportation a major obstacle for people who would like to fill these positions. Furthermore, the cost of housing in the suburbs and housing discrimination prevent them from moving to where the jobs are. Once we see the obstacles that stand in the way of people who have few resources at their disposal, people who appear to lack motivation in the face of opportunity might really require motivational levels that would far exceed those of persons who we think are our most productive and successful citizens.

In light of this, is "lazy" or some other derogatory term the proper way to characterize members of the underclass? I think not. A number of people, including some liberals, are uneasy with my answer. They worry that such a response is a way of coddling people, of encouraging people to acquiesce in their misery. Very often these people will respond, "Surely you are not encouraging members of the underclass to prefer public assistance to earning their own living?" Nothing I have said so far commits me to the view that members of the underclass should not attempt to help themselves. What I have tried to point out are some of the difficulties they encounter in trying to do so. However, if this question is posed to a member of the underclass who has had her motivational level damaged by racial discrimination and injustice, it is not clear that it would be unreasonable or immoral for such a person to prefer public assistance (which includes medical benefits) to a menial, low-paying, dead-end job without medical benefits. At first, this seems ridiculous because the model job we tend to use when analyzing such cases is one that draws on our abilities and talents in ways that we consider to be interesting or, if not, at least compensates such that the job is desirable even if it is uninteresting. If the job is low-paying and uninteresting, we might see it as a viable opportunity if it leads to a job that pays well or does draw on our abilities and talents in interesting ways. However, the question we must ask is, Are members of the underclass being offered jobs that satisfy these conditions? If the answer is yes, then clearly they should prefer working to public assistance. If the answer is no, I do not think that it is clearly rational to prefer a low-paying, uninteresting, dead-end job without medical benefits to public assistance that would provide one with the same income plus medical care.

Of course my critics would argue that I have excluded an important consideration, namely, the joy and satisfaction that a person receives from being self-reliant. In fact, Booker T. Washington, who some see as the father of the black conservative position, stressed the value of self-help in his famous "Atlanta Exposition Address." In this speech, Washington urged blacks to "Cast down your buckets where you are." [13] By this he meant that blacks should take any job, no matter how menial, as a first step on the road toward advancement. Clearly, self-reliance in most cases is a good thing, but even good things can be taken too far. It is clear that in some cases self-reliance can clash with rationality. Are the members of the underclass asked to be self-reliant at the expense of rationality?

Unfortunately, I think that in a large number of cases it is irrational for members of the underclass to choose self-reliance over public assistance. As I said earlier, adequate health care is an important component of any realistic appraisal of the opportunities available to members of the underclass. The United States is one of very few countries that does not provide some form of national health care. Health care in the United States is tied to certain jobs in the form of employee medical benefits. Given the high costs of medical care and the medical problems that correlate highly with poor black people, adequate health care has to be a weighty consideration in the deliberations of members of the black underclass. Surely self-reliance ought to be given some weight by members of this class, but even if it is, it will lose out in their deliberations because being self-reliant would have the undesirable consequence of denying them adequate health care. In order to make self-reliance a rational choice for members of this group, there would have to be structural changes in the current welfare and health care systems.

To think that we can eliminate the problems faced by members of the underclass without altering some of our basic institutions and social policies is to look at the problem through rose-colored glasses.

NOTES

1. See Thomas Sowell, *Race and Economics* (New York: David McKay, 1975).

2. William Julius Wilson, "Studying Inner-City Social Dislocations: The Challenge of Public Agenda Research," *American Sociological Review* 56, no. 1 (1991): 1–14.

3. William Julius Wilson, *The Truly Disadvantaged* (Chicago: University of Chicago Press, 1987).

4. Ronald Dworkin, *Taking Rights Seriously* (Cambridge, Mass.: Harvard University Press, 1977), pp. 180–83.

5. John Rawls, *A Theory of Justice* (Cambridge, Mass.: Harvard University Press, 1971), sec. 2, pp. 7–11.

6. See Herb Boyd, "The Crises in Affordable Housing," *Crisis Magazine* 96, no. 5 (May 1989): 10–15.

7. Elijah Muhammad, *Message to the Black Man in America* (Chicago: Muhammad Mosque of Islam No. 2, 1965).

8. Booker T. Washington, "The Intellectuals and the Boston Mob," in *Negro Social and Political Thought, 1850–1920*, ed. Howard Brotz (New York: Basic Books, 1966).

9. See Glenn Loury, "The Moral Quandary of the Black Community," *Public Interest* 79 (Spring 1985): 9–22.

10. William A. Lewis, *Racial Conflict and Economic Development* (Cambridge, Mass.: Harvard University Press, 1985).

11. Rawls, *A Theory of Justice*, p. 12.

12. Shelby Steele, *The Content of Our Characters: A New Vision of Race in America* (New York: St. Martin's Press, 1990), especially chaps. 3 and 4.

13. Booker T. Washington, "Atlanta Exposition Address," in *Negro Social and Political Thought, 1850–1920*, ed. Brotz, p. 357.

5 MAROONED IN AMERICA: BLACK URBAN YOUTH CULTURE AND SOCIAL PATHOLOGY

Tommy Lott

IN HIS MID-1960s study of the plight of the black family, Daniel Moynihan drew the rather untoward conclusion that "it would be troubling indeed to learn that until several years ago employment opportunity made a great deal of difference in the rate of Negro dependency and family disorganization, but that the situation has so deteriorated that the problem is now feeding on itself—that measures which once would have worked will henceforth not work so well, or work at all."[1] Although Moynihan's speculation emerged from a liberal perspective, ironically, his pessimistic concern has since become a cornerstone of the neoconservative opposition to liberal-sponsored government intervention on behalf of black urban poor people.[2] It is with this realization in mind that William Julius Wilson's recent discussion of the problems faced by the black urban poor has attempted to salvage liberal public policy from this hoisting by its own petards.[3] In keeping with Moynihan's rather bleak assessment, neoconservatives have employed a culture of poverty thesis according to which the black urban poor are conceived of as an isolated group of individuals whose behavior is aberrant and dominated by pathological cultural values. Although on Wilson's account so-called "ghetto" culture is to be viewed as a by-product of socioeconomic conditions in extreme-poverty neighborhoods, his rejoinder to the neoconservative culture of poverty thesis offers no criticism of their view of black culture. Instead, he maintains that changes in the oft-cited destructive aspects of so-called "ghetto" culture can be brought about by addressing more fundamental economic problems.

Wilson rightly wants to connect policies designed to ameliorate the problems of the black urban poor with policies that address broader issues of socioeconomic organization, but it is unfortunate that he needlessly acquiesces to the neoconservative contention that the culture of black urban poor people is pathological.[4] I want to call into

71

question the claim that the culture of black urban poor people is pathological and as such is somehow responsible for the perpetuation of
their plight. Unlike his neoconservative detractors, Wilson is less inclined to draw this conclusion; nonetheless, many of his remarks about
the Moynihanian tangle of pathology lend credence to their viewpoint
and, further, suggest that he has not given sufficient attention to the
conceptual scheme embedded in the expressive culture of black urban
poor people.[5] I aim to rectify this shortcoming in Wilson's account to
some extent by examining the social and political orientation of the
popular culture of black urban youth.

Debates about the so-called black underclass typically presuppose
the legitimacy of the American capitalist social order and employ the
notion of a pathological black "underclass" culture to reiterate the
hegemony of the dominant group's one-way assimilationist ideology.[6]
I present an analysis of the social and political consciousness reflected
in the music and practices of rap artists and their audiences, to show
that some of these cultural manifestations fit into a system of meanings
around which political action and struggle can be organized. On the
basis of criteria that indicate the manner in which certain cultural practices of black urban youth attempt to valorize notions of affirmation
and resistance, a distinction can be drawn between the pathological
social conditions under which the black urban poor live and the culture
they have created to help cope with those conditions. I will argue that,
contrary to the prevailing image of black urban youth as pathological,
black popular culture is understandably in many ways a recoding of
various elements of mainstream culture that have been adapted to fit
the circumstances of extreme-poverty urban neighborhoods.

The Elevation of Black People

Wilson's rather narrow focus on the social conditions of the black
urban poor since the mid-1960s is undoubtedly motivated by his
polemic with neoconservatives. As Moynihan's successor, he is concerned primarily with explanations of the recent deterioration of socioeconomic conditions in extreme-poverty neighborhoods at a time of
increased government-funded poverty programs and civil rights legislation. Of course, this limited concern justifies his use of the term
"underclass" so as to only remotely connect the problem of jobless
black urban youth in the 1980s with the fact that large numbers of
unemployed black people have never been fully absorbed into the labor
force since emancipation from slavery.[7] But if the term "underclass" is

meant to refer to the group of black people who have been permanently on the fringe of the job market, the question of what to do about their plight simply cannot be limited to the scope of Wilson's study. In fact, this question has long been a major preoccupation in black social thought.

In the nineteenth century there were several quite different ideologies about how best to address the socioeconomic plight of black people. I will refer to these views categorically as race uplift theory because, despite their differences, in every case advocates were chiefly concerned with the elevation of black people as a group. Interestingly, some of the most influential notions of race uplift involved various suggestions regarding the role of culture. I want to note a competing tendency to either reject or affirm the intrinsic worth of African-American culture in several versions of race uplift theory.

The prominence of a bootstrap version of race uplift theory in nineteenth-century black intellectual thought is hardly surprising, given its appropriateness as a theory of social change well suited to meet the needs of a large group of ex-slaves. What is surprising, however, is the persistence of this notion into the late twentieth century.[8] Perhaps, as I shall suggest, this is because the conditions to which race uplift theory initially applied have also persisted. Whatever the reason for the notion's longevity, I question the account its recent neoconservative advocates want to offer for its relative inefficaciousness as a theory of social change.

When Martin Delany wrote about the elevation of black people in the mid-1800s, he proposed emigration as the best option.[9] He spoke of black people escaping class oppression in America by finding a place that would permit their socioeconomic development. Edward Blyden added to Delany's argument for emigration the idea of slavery being a manifestation of divine providence.[10] Unlike Delany, who was not especially committed to any particular place, Blyden emphasized a missionary role for black Americans in Africa. Through enslavement Africans would become westernized, and through recolonization they would be returned to their homeland to impart this newly acquired culture to their African brethren. According to Blyden, slavery was to be viewed as part of God's plan to civilize Africa. Although Delany and Blyden shared a similar nationalistic diaspora consciousness regarding the fate and destiny of black Americans as a group, Blyden wanted black Americans to work to elevate Africans, whereas Delany, with little emphasis on culture, wanted to find someplace where conditions would permit the elevation of black Americans. Despite their ideological differences with regard to culture, for both Delany and Blyden the notion of elevation meant, for the most part, escape from the socioeconomic conditions under which black people were oppressed in America.

Blyden's talk of a civilizing mission for black Americans in Africa seems to presuppose that African culture was less valuable than that which had been acquired by slaves in America.[11] This conception of the positive influence of Western culture on African slaves can appear a bit odd when we consider that Frederick Douglass was much more deeply concerned with the deleterious effects of slavery than with its alleged benefits. He believed that through its dehumanizing effects slavery destroyed black people's sense of self-worth and dignity and that, once slavery ended, a period of rehabilitation would be required to rectify this. Needless to say, Douglass wholeheartedly believed that assimilation into the American mainstream would someday be possible once black people were educated and allowed to demonstrate their social equality with whites. Consequently, he vigorously opposed emigration as a policy for elevating black people because he saw ex-slaves as Americans. For Douglass, then, the notion of elevation meant the acculturation of black people into the American mainstream.[12]

What about the fact that the legal segregation that followed slavery would prevent the mass acculturation of black people? Faced with this question, Douglass's assimilationist view found a new expression in the philosophy of Booker T. Washington. Assimilationism required a strategy for changing the socioeconomic conditions of black people. By appealing to the self-interest of whites, Washington advocated economic development as a key to the elevation of black people as a group.[13] Unlike Douglass, he believed (or at least preached) that social equality was not a priority and that black people should not demand it. Rather, it would come eventually with the economic progress of the group.[14]

Washington's emphasis on group economic development as a means to achieve social equality provides the classic formulation of the bootstrap version of race uplift theory. His strategy involved the incremental transformation of the black Southern peasantry into a working class that several generations later would be superseded by a group of entrepreneurs who would comprise a full-fledged middle class ready for assimilation.[15] Although Washington was well known for his commitment to political accommodationism, the most interesting aspect of his bootstrap social philosophy was the role he assigned to the working class in the process of elevating the group. By following his dictum, "Cast down your bucket where you are," the black middle class would develop from that segment of the working class who managed to gain a foothold in the economy. Hence, Washington's political accommodationism was a social philosophy that reiterated the ideals of the American class system.[16]

Despite the much-heralded disagreement between W.E.B. Du Bois and Washington over the role of political agitation, Du Bois seems to have accepted certain fundamental tenets of Washington's social philosophy. For instance, they both advocated separation from whites as a means of self-development.[17] Regarding the cultural integrity of black people, Du Bois asserted, "No people that laughs at itself, and ridicules itself, and wishes to God it was anything but itself ever wrote its name in history."[18] This seems to echo Washington's statement regarding economic development: "No race that has anything to contribute to the markets of the world is long, in any degree, ostracized."[19] Both claims reflect Douglass's earlier concern with the self-esteem of black people as a group. Unlike Washington, however, Du Bois placed a greater emphasis on the cultural status of black people. He argued against "a servile imitation of Anglo-Saxon culture" on the ground that black people have a unique cultural contribution to make and that to accomplish this they must not assimilate.[20] Hence, for Du Bois, social equality would be achieved through the distinctive cultural achievements of black people.

The idea of black people gaining social equality by means of their cultural achievements had already been articulated in the context of the earlier New Negro literary movement. Anna Julia Cooper proclaimed that the political orientation of black literature was "to give the character of beauty and power to the literary utterance of the race."[21] Hence, the much-celebrated Washington–Du Bois exchange should be understood to have emanated from a social context that included a history of ideas about the role of culture in the elevation of black people as a group. When Alain Locke appropriated the concept of the New Negro in the 1920s and spearheaded the so-called Negro Renaissance Movement in Harlem, he seems to have followed through on Du Bois's agenda of developing a talented tenth to produce a black American culture that would be on par with European cultures. For Locke, this meant that the Southern black folk culture that was brought to Northern urban centers at the turn of the century would be rehabilitated and transformed by a vanguard group of artists who would give it expression in higher art forms.[22] Paradoxically, Locke's New Negro emerged as an assimilated black person who proudly displayed the Southern folk heritage of black people.[23]

By examining the history of black American social thought, we can see that, under the banner of race uplift, the idea of social equality for black Americans is quite ambiguous with regard to whether black people ought to pursue a path of maintaining a distinct culture, or whether they ought to acculturate into the mainstream. But even when assimilationism is rejected, the theory often assumes that black American culture figures into elevating the race only as something that itself has to be elevated.

The Black Middle Class's Obligation to Contribute to Group Progress

Many of the turn-of-the-century black writers I have mentioned argued that black people have a duty to perpetuate black culture, albeit face-lifted to meet European standards. Their arguments aimed largely at sustaining the moral imperative of race uplift, namely, that all black Americans are under some (perhaps different) obligation to endeavor to elevate the group. This special obligation derives from sharing a cultural heritage. The specific nature of this obligation depends, of course, on what it means to speak of "elevating" the group, but also on what it means to speak of preserving one's culture.

Although they can be clearly distinguished, there is a tandem relationship between the duty to perpetuate black culture and the duty to seek to elevate the group. For instance, when black writers such as Frances Ellen Watkins Harper and Pauline Elizabeth Hopkins employed their literary output in the service of race uplift their focus was primarily on the obligation of a certain group of black people, namely, mulattoes, to refrain from marrying whites, or passing, and instead to devote themselves to the betterment of the masses of black people.[24] In this case, there was a special duty requiring a sacrifice of social privilege by some members of the group in order to devote themselves more fully to elevating other members of the group. This norm proscribing intermarriage emerged from a social context, namely, legal segregation, in which the biological boundaries of race were understood to be necessary for group identity. Harper and Hopkins explicitly raised the issue of race uplift as a duty and, within the context of their fiction, attempted to shed light on the nature of the educated black elite's special obligation. While Harper and Hopkins focused more on the role of literature in shaping the consciousness of the black middle class to be more receptive to assuming responsibility for various family, educational, and occupational endeavors that would benefit black people as a group, Du Bois and Locke tended to emphasize the uplift of black cultural practices. They seem to have been more concerned with the duty of an educated black elite to elevate various expressions of black folk culture to the status of high art.[25] Taken together, these turn-of-the-century views of race uplift imply that the black middle class has a special obligation not to assimilate into the American mainstream, but as an educated elite seek to transform black cultural expression into some European equivalent.

Proponents of the culture of poverty thesis who maintain that only significant change in the culture of the black urban poor will improve their economic opportunities seem to have adopted Washington's accommodationist view of politics. Despite both thinkers' adherence to a doctrine of social separation, Du Bois was at times antiassimilationist in a sense that Washington was not.[26] Du Bois's notion of social equality entailed a cultural pluralism that he thought could be realized only through political agitation. Unlike Washington, whose focus was on economic development, Du Bois called into question the existing social order that excluded black culture. Hence, for Du Bois culture was a means of gaining social equality.[27]

What happens, however, when bootstrap uplift is combined with social protest? Where neoconservatives err in their criticisms of the civil rights vision is with the supposition that a self-help philosophy precludes a denunciation of America's racism.[28] Marcus Garvey, a self-proclaimed disciple of Washington, keenly recognized that black people were being systematically subordinated to the bottom of the American social order with no chance of eventual assimilation. His emigrationist philosophy explicitly acknowledged that black people would never achieve social equality under America's apartheid.[29]

The reason bootstrap uplift, as a theory of social change, has not produced the desired results is because it is a very misleading success myth. Its advocates present their arguments on the assumption that the existence of what some Marxists refer to as a reserve army of unemployed workers has nothing to do with the nature of capitalism.[30] But if Marxists are right that unemployment is inherent to an advanced industrial capitalist economic arrangement, and if Garvey is right that institutionalized racism operates to keep as many black people as possible in the group of unemployed workers, the creation of the so-called black "underclass" can be viewed as a matter of economically structured racism. Although quite different in many respects, these radical perspectives suggest an alternative framework from which to question the fundamental assumption of Washington's theory of social change, namely, that America's existing socioeconomic arrangement can be made to work such that black people as a group will gain social equality.

These radical perspectives imply that, regarding black middle class's obligation to contribute to group progress, a certain kind of assimilationist role-modeling can be objected to on political grounds. When the black middle class deliberately role-models its economic success, as if to suggest that the masses of black people would also be assimilated into the American mainstream if only they were, in some sense, more acculturated, this practice fosters a social myth regarding what is required for group progress.[31] To what extent would the mere possession of mainstream cultural attributes solve the problem of large numbers of black urban poor people inhabiting the ranks of the unemployed? Neoconservative advocates of bootstrap uplift, who denounce the culture of black urban poor people, cannot draw upon its historical appeal as a theory of social change because, among a group of twentieth-century maroons, there is by now a common understanding of how, as ideology, bootstrap uplift utilizes token models of success to rationalize the exclusion of the masses of black people.

The Concept of the Underclass and Mass Media

The neoconservative critique of liberal social policy is based on the idea that the problems of the urban poor are cultural rather than socioeconomic in origin. By emphasizing "socially dysfunctional behavior," neoconservatives have used the culture of poverty thesis to frame the debate with liberals such that the socioeconomic structure of American society is not at issue. We are constantly reminded that, given the new black prosperity and the ability of the class system to deliver on its promise of opportunity for everyone, the system itself is no longer to blame. Responsibility for their plight must be placed more squarely on the poor themselves. Hence, Wilson's structural argument regarding the erosion of the industrial base, as well as other concentration effects on extreme-poverty neighborhoods, has begun to appear to the American public less salient than the cultural explanations offered by neoconservatives. I suspect that this development has a lot to do with the influence of mass media on the prevailing mainstream conception of black urban poor people. As the site of the debate about the underclass shifts from the academic arena into mass media, structural accounts such as Wilson's have lost ground.[32] Consequently, even Wilson now believes he must argue within a culture of poverty framework.[33]

Mass media operate at many levels to influence public opinion about the plight of black urban poor people, most often with a characteristic ideological posture of subordination.[34] The social construction of the "underclass" concept has been profoundly influenced, not only by the presentation of various notions by social scientists, including Wilson, in popular print media, but also by television programs such as Bill Moyer's documentary "The Vanishing Family" and Bill Cosby's weekly situation comedy. The ideological framing of issues in terms of the culture of poverty thesis is especially emphasized in electronic media.

A recent survey of popular new journals appearing over the past ten years or so revealed that between 1977 and 1988 the prevailing definitions of the underclass moved from a general reference to poverty that included whites to an exclusive emphasis on the behavioral, cultural, and moral characteristics of black urban poor people.[35] This conception of the underclass as exclusively black has become an assumption that is regularly reinforced by television. "The Bill Cosby Show," for example, indirectly displays the culture of poverty frame by role-modeling mainstream corporate values. In this case, the underclass is represented in the program's subtext; that is, the program's images indirectly speak to issues that have been presented in nonentertainment sources such as daily newscasts. By contrast, documentaries such as Bill Moyer's "The Vanishing Family" have more blatantly argued the culture of poverty thesis, making a grandstand effort to establish it with visual proof. These television images of the culture of black urban poor people as pathological have been among the more powerful validations of neoconservative bootstrap ideology. But what about the culture of black urban poor people as viewed from their own perspective?

The Crime Metaphor in Rap Music

The voice of black urban poor people is best represented in black culture through rap music.[36] As a dominant influence on black urban youth, rap music articulates the perspective of a black *lumpenproletariat*. For this reason, class lines have been drawn around it within the black community.[37] This "underclass" status of rap, however, tends to conceal the fact that it has certain social and political dimensions that suggest that something other than pathology is occurring in black youth culture.[38] Unless one listens to rap music regularly, it is extremely difficult to resist the temptation to view black urban poor people through the eyes of the mainstream, which has been unduly influenced by mass media. In mass media, black urban males have been depicted as the number one criminal threat to America. For instance, in the last presidential campaign, Willie Horton was used as a cultural signifier by Republicans to perpetuate the time-honored myth of the black male rapist who deserved to be lynched.[39] The social and political function

of mass media's image of the so-called underclass is to routinely validate this claim, a practice that reached a pinnacle at the time of the
Central Park gang rape when the demand for a lynching was published
by Donald Trump in a full-page ad in the *New York Times*. Trump's ad
is a noticeable manifestation of the mass media's general tendency to
employ a Girardian script when dealing with such potent racial fears.[40]
News reporting of incidents such as the Central Park rape and the
Charles Stuart murder case were cultural spectacles that validated the
consciousness responsible for racist lynchings, a consciousness already
prepared by history. The mass media's labeling black men as criminals serves in the consciousness of many whites as a justification of the
Bernard Goetz–style slayings that have begun to proliferate, including
the recent police beating of Rodney King.[41]

The response of the black community to this media onslaught has
been divided along class lines. The black middle class denounces as a
negative image any association of black people with crime by media. In
rap culture, however, crime as a metaphor for resistance is quite influential. Unfortunately, the generation of this new meaning frequently
has been misunderstood.[42] The point of the rap artist embracing the
image of crime is to recode this powerful mainstream representation.

In their reflections on the social and political significance of their
music, rap artists have sometimes likened their cultural practice to a
kind of alternative media, that is, "black America's TV station."[43] What
they mean is that rap music is a cultural reaction to the hegemony of
television's image of black people. The crime metaphor in rap culture
serves notice on mass media's ideological victimization of black men.
Rap artists have declared war against the dominant ideological apparatus. Their purpose is to invalidate, on a constant basis, the images of
black men in mass media with various recoding techniques that convey
other meanings to their largely black audience.

Scholars who are steeped in cultural studies have begun to take note
of how the deconstructive aspects of rap music lay bare the anatomy of
other black music that has been mediated by the record industry and
transform it through reorganization.[44] Deconstructionism as applied to
rap culture means literally to take on every aspect of the record industry
from production to marketing. The techniques involved in the production of rap music are inherently oppositional because not only do
they aim to dismantle the record industry by scratching, sampling, and
remixing records to create new meanings, but they threaten the very
legitimacy of claiming ownership of black music through copyright
laws. Television ad agencies have appropriated black 1960s and 1970s
soul music to sell their products as a result of their power to purchase

copyrights.[45] On the other hand, when rap artists use sampling devices to reappropriate the same music, they are accused of copyright violations. In response, they have ingeniously claimed to be engaged in the African custom of ancestor worship, thereby rebutting this legal charge from the self-consciously adopted perspective of a diaspora people who desire to retain their African identity.

This exchange reflects the dialectical relationship between black popular culture and mainstream society. The outlawing of rap music in certain places, as well as its exclusion from radio, has only helped it to flourish in an underground market, much in the same way as other illegal goods are bought and sold in that segment of the economy. The political implication of this is that rap artists are subject to the political constraints imposed by the mainstream culture industries only to the extent that they participate in mainstream media. For better or worse, control and censorship of the messages in rap music are limited.

The crowning achievement of rap culture is that within the American system of apartheid the victims have restructured their reality with quite deliberate opposition to mass media's representations. Rap culture is the basis of an authentic public sphere that counterposes itself to the dominant alternative from which black urban youth have been excluded. Middle-class social uplift has been exposed by rap artists as inauthentic role modeling. Such role models lack validity among black urban youth, who are fully aware that they face structurally based unemployment. This is poignantly illustrated in a song by the very popular rap group NWA, who offer their critical assessment of middle-class role models by giving advice to a black male child: they straightforwardly inform him that the name of the game is "bitches and money." I submit that NWA's characterization of success in these terms is a black male *lumpenproletarian* reading of "The Bill Cosby Show." As inhabitants of extreme-poverty neighborhoods, many rap artists and their audiences are entrenched in a street life filled with crime, drugs, and violence. Being criminal-minded and having street values are much more suitable for living in their environment.[46] Without either glorifying or condemning this attitude toward the mainstream, I want to draw attention to the sense in which rap music has shown the potential to engender a liberating consciousness in black urban youth.[47]

Although rap artists appear to be totally free to say whatever they please, in practice this is not entirely so. They must demonstrate through their music that they "know what time it is." This knowledge can only come from one's experience on the streets. Although, at its worst, this knowledge is manifested through egotistical sexual boasting, the core meaning of the rapper's use of the term "knowledge" is to be *politically* astute, that is, to have a full understanding of the conditions under which black urban youth must survive. In many cases rap artists are exchanging largely *inspirational* messages to reinforce self-respect, a measure that is an essential means of coping with their oppression.

Cultural Resistance and Social Pathology

As long as black urban youth in extreme-poverty neighborhoods see themselves trapped under America's apartheid, their cultural expressions will continue to exhibit elements of resistance. The role of the black middle class in helping to alleviate the pathological conditions under which black urban youth must live by seeking to eliminate their cultural practices, especially when these practices provide a means of coping cannot be condoned. Moreover, it is futile for the black middle class to role-model bootstrap uplift in a system of apartheid. Instead, what is needed is a strong black middle-class leadership engaged in the dismantling of this system.

The social isolation Wilson speaks of involves more than just the geographic relocation of black working- and middle-class families. As the economic gap has widened, there has been a psychological distancing by members of the black upper strata from other black people living in extreme-poverty neighborhoods that violates the historically determined cultural imperative to contribute to the elevation of the group.[48] What seems to facilitate this tendency toward class division is the perception that many middle-class black people have of black urban poor people. They frequently adopt the mainstream view, namely, the culture of poverty frame, and see the black urban poor as lacking the cultural attributes that middle-class blacks have had to acquire in order to succeed. But to what extent do black urban youth lack mainstream values?

The culture of poverty frame prevents us from seeing that many of the values held by black urban youth are quite similar to those held by mainstream society. In white America social mores have progressed to the point where childbearing out of wedlock and female-headed households are no longer stigmatized, where involvement with drugs and drug trafficking is quite widespread, where in both foreign and domestic affairs violence is regularly espoused by political leadership as a ready-made approach to conflict resolution, and where criminality runs rampant from Wall Street right through Congress and the White House. Hence, there should be little surprise in discovering that these mores have been replicated in other echelons of American society.

To see the drug trade that has devastated so many black neighbor-hoods as anything other than illegitimate capitalists operating under the auspices of a multinational cartel is to blindly follow the hypoc-risy of mass media's racial hype.[49] As an equal opportunity employer, the drug business is an essential part of the infrastructure of black neighborhoods that have been wrecked by economic dislocation. Black youth who enter the drug trade are frequently as ambitious and as highly motivated as any prep school graduate entering Harvard Busi-ness School.[50] From a mainstream perspective, the mere illegality of drug dealing is sufficient to warrant its condemnation, but that perspec-tive is clearly influenced by the fact that those in the mainstream have access to options not available to black youth living in extreme-poverty neighborhoods.

Given the multinational status of the drug trade, when we speak of pathology there is a need to distinguish between the social con-ditions that induce black teenagers to get involved with drugs and the cultural practices they have developed to cope with their sense of oppression. With regard to drug abuse, as with any other aspect of the social conditions that define the material existence of black urban youth, we must be able to condemn the pathology without condemn-ing the culture.[51] So-called criminal behavior as such is not necessarily pathological.[52] Mainstream observers of black urban youth tend naively to overlook the fact that under the conditions of anarchy that prevail in most extreme-poverty neighborhoods the role of law enforcement is quite dubious with regard to crime.[53] It is simply a fact of daily life that any black man is subject to police harassment and brutality, whether he is criminal or not. This point is vividly captured in N.W.A.'s revenge fantasy "Fuck the Police," which engendered a campaign by the FBI to get authorities to prohibit their concerts. The politically oppressive function of police departments in the black community is a common theme in much rap music, including Boogie Down Production's "Who Protects Us from You?" L. L. Cool J's "Illegal Search," M. C. Trouble's "Got to Get a Grip," and Public Enemy's "Anti-Nigga Machine." Black youth share a widely held view that police departments are simply regu-lating the drug traffic and often profiting from it. This is some of the "knowledge" that rap artists speak of when they extol the virtues of being criminal-minded.

The destructive aspects of drug dealing and drug-related lifestyles has not been overlooked in rap culture. Even some of the most nihilis-tic rap artists have urged their listeners to see where drugs will lead them. In the music of more prominent artists such as Ice-T, Ice Cube, and The Geto Boys, the woes of addiction, violence, and prison life, all of which accompany drug dealing, have been well touted. Contrary to the prevailing mainstream perception, rap artists sometimes quite consciously recode mainstream values by employing so-called "negative images" to communicate very powerful messages to each other about issues of self-respect.[54]

Despite their status as a group of maroons in America's urban centers, ironically, black urban youth, through their culture, have had a major impact on mainstream popular culture. The idea of black urban youth being intelligent users of nonstandard English can no longer be doubted—the large-scale infusion of black street language into mainstream culture is a clear testament to its powerful appeal. By paying attention to the tenacity of rap culture to withstand ostracism, as well as legal condemnation, we can better understand why the retention of a distinctive black identity has it over assimilation for many black youth. The principles of music-making that have been passed on through generations of black musicians, from blues and bebop to contemporary rap, attest to the perpetuation of a syncretic African culture.[55]

The Neoconservative's Dilemma

The duty of black people to maintain their cultural heritage was an integral part of Du Bois's version of race uplift theory. He assigned to the black middle class the role of propagating the cultural ideals of the group. But there are other reasons, apart from the dictates of a race uplift theory, for thinking that black people ought to retain their cultural heritage and not assimilate.

In a classic study E. Franklin Frazier presented a portrait of a black middle class that had degenerated into social pathology.[56] According to Frazier, their particular malaise involved gross self-deception and the fabrication of a world of make-believe largely derived from inauthentic cultural values. Frazier's black bourgeoisie were presented as the epitome of a group of people who have developed a false consciousness because they rejected their cultural heritage. Although Frazier never spells out what he would have considered a more authentic black culture, I suggest on his behalf that the idea of eliminating black culture altogether to pursue assimilation seems to be at odds with the fundamental human right of self-determination. Hence, no theory of social change can justifiably require black people to do this.

Some neoconservatives seem only to be regurgitating a bootstrap version of race uplift when they maintain that an assimilated middle class is necessary for the socioeconomic progress of black people as a group.[57] A dilemma can be posed, however, for subscribers to the culture of poverty thesis who have insisted that the culture of black urban poor people is pathological. On the one hand, given the alleged pathology of so-called ghetto culture, we are led to believe that the black middle class *ought* to assimilate and in some way help the "underclass" by doing so. On the other hand, given Du Bois's argument about propagating black cultural ideals, as well as Frazier's observations regarding the pathology of a black middle class that has failed to do this, there is some reason to suppose that the black middle class *ought not* to assimilate.

This dilemma arises from the presupposition of bootstrap uplift that the problems faced by the black urban poor, as well as the success of the black middle class, is somehow connected with their different levels of acculturation. According to bootstrap uplift, the role of the black middle class in the elevation of the black urban poor is to transmit mainstream culture to them. This suggests, of course, that America's capitalist social order need not be changed and that the problems of the black urban poor are a result of their own cultural maladaptation.

Neoconservatives who have adopted the culture of poverty frame to condemn black culture as pathological have failed to realize the nature of the cultural imperative that obligates the black middle class to endeavor to elevate the masses of black people. In the late twentieth century this imperative must be understood to allow the masses of black people to assimilate with their culture intact, that is, without rehabilitating it to meet the standards imposed by the mainstream society.

NOTES

Acknowledgments: My research for this article was partially supported by a grant from the College of Urban, Labor, and Metropolitan Affairs, Wayne State University, Detroit, Michigan. I gratefully acknowledge helpful comments from Laurence Blum and Adrian Piper on an earlier draft of this chapter.

1. Daniel P. Moynihan, "Employment, Income, and the Ordeal of the Negro Family," in *The Negro American*, ed. Talcott Parsons and Kenneth B. Clark (Boston: Beacon Press, 1965), p. 157.

2. For an incisive analysis of the rise of neoconservative thought regarding race and social policy, see Cornel West, "Race and Social Theory: Towards a Genealogical Materialist Analysis," in *The Year Left 2: An American Socialist Yearbook*, ed. Mike Davis, Manning Marable, Fred Pfeil, and Michael Sprinker (London: Verso, 1987).

3. William Julius Wilson, *The Truly Disadvantaged* (Chicago: University of Chicago Press, 1987).

4. Leonard Harris, "Agency and the Concept of the Underclass," Chapter 3 of the present volume.

5. Some of Wilson's more recent overtures in this direction are plagued by his use of misguided concepts such as "hyperghettoization." William Julius Wilson and Loïc J. D. Wacquant, "The Cost of Racial and Class Exclusion in the Inner City," *Annals of the American Academy of Political and Social Science* 501 (January 1989): 8–25. In response to criticisms of his use of the term "underclass," Wilson reluctantly proposed to substitute the term "ghetto poor," although he professed a preference for the "subtle theoretical meaning" of the former. The term "ghetto," however, has become a post-1960s media reference term for the black community that is equally pejorative, if not overtly racist. Clearly the problem stems from a major shortcoming of Wilson's theoretical orientation, namely, his failure to provide an analysis of culture. See his "Studying the Inner-City Social Dislocation: The Challenge of Public Agenda Research," *American Sociological Review* 56 (February 1991): 1–14. In this regard Paul Gilroy has introduced a much more fruitful methodology for understanding the conceptual scheme embedded in black expressive cultures. See his *Ain't No Black in the Union Jack* (London: Hutchinson, 1986), chap. 5.

6. I use the term *assimilation* to refer specifically to the claim that black people ought to acquire the values, that is, cultural practices, of the dominant European group at the expense of retaining any such values (cultural practices) that are derived from their own African heritage. For a discussion of the variety of meanings attached to this notion see Milton M. Gordon, *Assimilation in American Life* (New York: Oxford University Press, 1964).

7. Orlando Patterson denounces recent scholarship for overlooking the historical persistence since slavery of the so-called "underclass" problem. See his "Toward a Study of Black America," *Dissent* 36, no. 4 (Fall 1989): 477.

8. See, for example, Thomas Sowell, *Ethnic America: A History* (New York: Basic Books, 1981); and Walter Williams, *The State Against Blacks* (New York: McGraw-Hill, 1982).

9. Martin Delany, "The Condition, Elevation, Emigration and Destiny of the Colored People of the United States" (1852?), in *Negro Social and Political Thought, 1850–1920*, ed. Howard Brotz (New York: Basic Books, 1966), pp. 37–101.

10. Edward Blyden, "The Call of Providence to the Descendants of Africa in America" (1862), in ibid., pp. 112–26.

11. See Valentin Y. Mudimbe, *The Invention of Africa* (Bloomington: Indiana University Press, 1988), chap. 4.

12. Frederick Douglass, "The Present and Future of the Colored Race in America" (1863), in *Negro Social and Political Thought, 1850–1920*, ed. Brotz, pp. 267–77.

13. Booker T. Washington, "Atlanta Exposition Address" (September 18, 1895?) and "Address Delivered at Hampton Institute" (November 15, 1895), in ibid., p. 357.

14. Laurence Thomas explores the ethical implications of Washington's

social philosophy in his "Rawlsian Self-Respect and the Black Consciousness Movement," *Philosophical Forum* 9 (1978): 303–14.

15. Washington, "Address Delivered at Hampton Institute," p. 372.

16. Louis R. Harlan, "Booker T. Washington and the Politics of Accommodation," in *Black Leaders of the Twentieth Century*, ed. John Hope Franklin and August Meier (Chicago: University of Illinois Press, 1982).

17. See Bernard R. Boxill, *Blacks and Social Justice* (Totowa, N.J.: Rowman and Allanheld, 1984), chaps. 2 and 8.

18. W. E. B. Du Bois, "The Conservation of Races," in *Negro Social and Political Thought, 1850–1920*, ed. Brotz, p. 489.

19. Washington, "Atlanta Exposition Address," p. 359.

20. Du Bois, "The Conservation of Races," p. 488.

21. W. H. A. Moore, "The New Negro Literary Movement," *AME Church Review* 21 (1904): 52.

22. Nathan Huggins, *Voices from the Harlem Renaissance* (New York: Oxford University Press, 1976).

23. Alain Locke, "The New Negro," in *The New Negro*, ed. Alain Locke (New York: Albert and Charles Boni, 1925).

24. See, for example, Hazel Carby, *Reconstructing Womanhood* (New York: Oxford University Press, 1987), chaps. 4 and 5; and Mary Helen Washington, *Invented Lives* (Garden City, N.J.: Doubleday, 1987), part 2.

25. See Huggins, *Voices from the Harlem Renaissance*; and John Brown Childs, "Concepts of Culture in Afro-American Political Thought, 1890–1920," *Social Texts* 4, no. 28 (1982): 28–43.

26. Du Bois's strongest antiassimilationist views were expressed around the turn of the century, especially in "The Conservation of Races." His position was modified considerably in later writings. See, for instance, his *Dusk of Dawn: An Essay Toward an Autobiography of a Race Concept* (1940; reprint, New York: Schocken, 1968).

27. Henry Louis Gates, Jr., has questioned the arbitrariness of this alleged connection between cultural production as a sign of civilization and the elimination of race prejudice. See his *Figures in Black* (New York: Oxford University Press, 1987), p. xxiii.

28. See Williams, *The State Against Blacks*; and Thomas Sowell, *Civil Rights: Rhetoric or Reality?* (New York: William Morrow, 1984).

29. Marcus Garvey, "Race Assimilation" (1922), in *Negro Social and Political Thought, 1850–1920*, ed. Brotz, pp. 553–54.

30. Julianne Malveaux, "Race, Class and Black Poverty," *Black Scholar* 19, no. 3 (May/June, 1988): 19.

31. Stephen Steinberg, *The Ethnic Myth*, 2d ed. (Boston: Beacon Press, 1989).

32. In his much-neglected book *The Black Underclass* (San Francisco: Jossey-Bass, 1980), Douglas G. Glasgow argues for structural change that would address chronic unemployment in black neighborhoods.

33. James Jennings, "Escaping from the Poorhouse of Ideas," *In These Times*, February 17–23, 1988.

34. Jack L. Daniel and Anita L. Allen, "Newsmagazines, Public Policy,

and the Black Agenda," in *Discrimination and Discourse*, ed. Geneva Smitherman-Donaldson and Teun A. Van Dijk (Detroit: Wayne State University Press, 1988).

35. See Herman Gray, "The Reemergence of 'Culture' in Public Discourse about Racial Inequality and Poverty: The Instance of Media Coverage of the Urban Underclass," paper presented at the Annual Meeting of The Society for the Study of Social Problems, Berkeley, California, August, 1989; and Steinberg, *The Ethnic Myth*.

36. Several black independent filmmakers, such as Haile Gerima, Billy Woodberry, and Charles Burnett, are devoted to presenting the perspective of black urban poor people. Unfortunately, however, their films have not been widely distributed and, consequently, are relatively unknown to either black or white audiences.

37. The class status of rap is indicated most significantly by the linguistic style and behavior of rap artists. Although there are many middle-class suburban rappers, as well as a growing number of white artists, they must be viewed as participating in a black urban art form.

38. Playthell Benjamin refers to rap artists as "cultural deviates, sociopaths who are leading the way to self-destruction" ("Miles of Heart?" *Village Voice*, November 6, 1990, p. 85). See also Nathan Hare and Julia Hare, *Bringing the Black Boy to Manhood: The Passage* (San Francisco: Black Think Tank, 1985), p. 17.

39. For a penetrating analysis of the historical significance of this myth, see Angela Y. Davis, *Women, Race and Class* (New York: Random House, 1981), chap. 11.

40. See René Girard, "Generative Scapegoating," in *Violent Origins: Ritual Killing and Cultural Formation*, ed. Walter Burkert, René Girard, and Jonathan Z. Smith (Stanford: Stanford University Press, 1987), pp. 73–105.

41. In a recent editorial supporting the police against a public outcry over the Rodney King beating, Christopher Matthews asks us, "Who separates the innocent from the guys with the automatic weapons? Who must stalk and restalk the murderers and muggers the courts cannot hold? Who keeps the underclass under control? The cops. Sometimes it's difficult, but support your local police!" *San Francisco Examiner*, March 24, 1991, p. A-25.

42. This suggestion has been rejected by Frank Owen, who maintains that "criminal imagery in rap does not oppose the mainstream at all. It instead creates a vicious, supercilious caricature of mainstream values, with all the liberal cant about honesty and fair play, truth and justice, brutally shorn off" (*Spin* 4, no. 7 [October 1988]: 52). Similarly, Kevin Mattson has argued that rap artists "take up the tradition of black protest not as politics but as style" ("The Dialectic of Powerlessness: Black Identity Culture and Affirmative Action," *Telos*, Summer 1990, p. 178). But if rap was only a matter of style and not politics, why would it provoke various authorities to engage the state apparatus to suppress it, as in the state of Florida's prosecution of 2 Live Crew and the FBI's investigative report to Congress on rap music and its effect on national security? See Lisa Jones, "The Signifying Monkees," *Village Voice*,

November 6, 1990, pp. 43–47, 171; and Houston A. Baker, Jr., "Handling 'Crisis,'" *Callaloo* 13, no. 2 (Spring 1990): 177.

43. A remark made by Chuck D of Public Enemy in an interview with John Leland, "Armageddon in Effect," *Spin* 4, no. 6 (September 1988): 48. Brand Nubian's Derek X claimed: "It's our mass media for getting our message across" ("Brand Nubian," in *Rap Masters Presents Wanted: Rap's 25 Most Hardcore*, April 1991, p. 48). See also Jon Pareles, "How Rap Moves to Television's Beat," *New York Times*, January 14, 1990, sec. 2, p. 1.

44. See Gilroy, *Ain't No Black in the Union Jack*, chap. 5.

45. Robin Hoffman, "Digital Sampling—Lawyers Debate the Legal Realities of an Emerging New Art Form," *Backstage*, October 27, 1989, p. 34.

46. The expression "criminal minded" was coined by KRS-One as an album title and discussed at length on the liner notes of Boogie Down Production's *By All Means Necessary* album.

47. Nancy Guevara arrives at a similar conclusion. See her article "Women Writin' Rappin' Breakin'," in *The Year Left 2*, ed. Davis, Marable, Pfeil, and Sprinker, p. 173. Since the publication of Guevara's article a more widespread radical black consciousness movement has developed among rap artists. Tragedy, Brand Nubian, Paris, and many other younger-generation rappers have begun to exert considerable influence on the political content of music by older-generation rappers such as Big Daddy Kane and Kool Moe Dee.

48. Jack Beatty attributes to Glenn Loury the claim that the success of the black middle class "lies precisely in their euthanasia of the memory of the ghetto" ("The Self-Discovery of the Black Middle Class," *Boston Globe Magazine*, November 17, 1985, p. 49).

49. See, for instance, Louis Kraar, "The Drug Trade," *Fortune* 117, no. 13 (June 20, 1988): 26–38; and Peter T. White, "Coca—An Ancient Herb Turns Deadly," *National Geographic* 175, no. 1 (January 1989): 3–47.

50. Terry Williams, *The Cocaine Kids* (Reading, Mass.: Addison-Wesley, 1988).

51. Patterson insists that there is a distinction between problems that are cultural continuities and those that are socioeconomically conditioned persistences ("Study of Black America," p. 477).

52. Michel Foucault, *Discipline and Punish* (New York: Pantheon, 1977).

53. Bill Lawson, "Crime, Minorities and the Social Contract," *Criminal Justice Ethics* 9, no. 2 (Summer/Fall 1990): 16–24.

54. This recoding of negative images is reflected in many of the names adopted by rap artists, such as Intelligent Hoodlum, Public Enemy, Special Ed, Hoes with Attitude, Bitches with Problems, and Niggas with Attitude.

55. The stringent measure taken to suppress rap music cannot but remind us of the earlier slave codes that aimed to outlaw African drum practices.

56. E. Franklin Frazier, *Black Bourgeoisie* (New York: Free Press, 1957).

57. Thomas Sowell, *Race and Economics* (New York: Longman, 1975).

6　Uplifting the Race: Middle-Class Blacks and the Truly Disadvantaged

Bill E. Lawson

AS ONE READS the literature on the origins of what has been called the "urban underclass," one is immediately struck by the claim that a contributing factor to the emergence of this group is middle-class blacks fleeing the "ghetto" and thereby causing the quality of life to decline for those blacks who remain.

William Julius Wilson, in *The Truly Disadvantaged*, believes "that the exodus of middle- and working-class families from many ghetto neighborhoods removes an important 'social buffer.'" The loss of this "social buffer" reduces the effectiveness of those institutions—churches, schools, stores, and recreational facilities—needed to sustain the community in tense economic times. The presence of middle-class blacks in these areas also helps to keep "alive the perception that education is meaningful, that steady employment is a viable alternative to welfare, and that family stability is the norm, not the exception."[1] This view of the origins of the underclass is echoed by Nicholas Lemann,[2] Pete Hamill,[3] and Kenneth L. Karst.[4]

These writers all point to the movement of middle-class blacks out of the ghetto as quickening the decline of the quality of life of less-advantaged blacks. By implication, middle-class blacks are in part responsible for the advent of the "underclass." If this claim is true, the movement out of urban areas by middle-class blacks harms those blacks who remain. It is not as if those blacks who leave do not realize that their leaving will cause the continual downward slide of the community. In fact, they see the effects of the exodus of middle-class blacks firsthand, and they realize that the community will be harmed if this exodus continues. Since it is generally thought that it is part of our moral duty not to intentionally do harm, are middle-class blacks morally obligated to stay in those neighborhoods to prevent harm?

In Philadelphia, the Healthy Neighborhood Program is addressing the issue of middle-class and working-class blacks leaving the traditionally black communities. Members of this program see the community as a place of strength and a cultural haven that must be protected. They feel that middle-class blacks are morally obligated to do whatever is necessary to preserve the community, even if it means staying when one can leave.

The idea that middle-class blacks are obligated to help those less well off is not new. But are they morally obligated to stay in less-advantaged urban neighborhoods? Is staying in urban neighborhoods part of the obligation of middle-class blacks to their brothers and sisters? Alvin F. Poussaint, associate professor of psychiatry at Harvard, has noted that of all groups, middle-class blacks have been pressured to remain concerned with the fate of the brothers and sisters they have left behind. Because the oppression of blacks has been as a group, success is now viewed in group terms. "The concept that if one is free, all should be free has been extended with less compelling logic, to the conviction that if one achieves, all should be achieving." This pressure comes from whites, poor blacks, and middle-class black activists.[5]

Educational sociologist Signithia Fordham has cited a major change in the manner in which blacks view group progress. The achievements of, for example, Thurgood Marshall, Lena Horne, and Jackie Robinson were once taken for signs of the group's "making it." Today many blacks reject this conception of progress. No longer are the achievements of one black evidence of the advancement of all. "In other words, contemporary Black Americans are opting for a more inclusive view of success."[6]

This reasoning may seem odd because many persons, black and white, believe that the passage of civil rights legislation makes each person individually responsible for his or her own success. Blacks are now, it has been argued, in the same social and political position as white Americans. Furthermore, to think that group success should be inclusive of all members of the group seems to be a great leap of logic. Does anyone really believe that in a capitalistic system all blacks will be able to live a middle-class lifestyle, if, indeed, that is the goal?

We can nevertheless understand why there is pressure placed on middle-class blacks to help less-advantaged blacks. Many persons, both black and white, now realize that the passage of the Civil Rights Bill was not enough. The winning of political rights did nothing to erase the lingering effects of a history of political oppression and racism.[7] Blacks, it is argued, are still subject to acts with racist intent. Prevailing racism is seen as keeping many blacks from succeeding in America.[8] The original goals of equal opportunity, respect for the race, and full citizenship remain unreached. Much work remains to be done to ensure that those blacks who want to achieve can. This conviction that racism is the major cause of black subordination continues to put pressure on middle-class blacks to help disadvantaged blacks after the passage of civil rights legislation. Blacks, and particularly middle-class blacks, are pressured to see themselves as obligated to help other blacks. Middle-class blacks are told not to forget their brothers and sisters as they succeed.[9]

To what extent are middle-class blacks obligated to help those who are less advantaged? Many middle-class blacks are morally torn between their feelings of obligation to other blacks and their desire to take advantage of the social progress of the past forty years.[10]

In 1947, W.E.B. Du Bois stated what he took to be a dilemma for middle-class blacks: "The group has long been internally divided by the dilemma as to whether its strivings upward be aimed at strengthening its inner cultural and group bonds, both for intrinsic progress and for offensive power against caste; or whether it should seek escape wherever and however possible into surrounding American culture."[11] Du Bois, at least the early Du Bois, argued that middle-class blacks should not escape into white American culture and should work to uplift less-advantaged blacks. Today this means that if middle-class blacks are serious about helping the truly disadvantaged, some more affluent blacks must stay in or move into neighborhoods with a large population of economically disadvantaged blacks. Let me be clear here—not all black communities are slums and thus my comments are only meant to address issues concerning those communities with a large population of socially and economically disadvantaged blacks. These are the communities Wilson thinks are socially isolated.[12]

Race and Group Obligations

The obligation to work to uplift other blacks is taken and given as a collective group obligation.[13] Primarily, uplifting the race means the elevation of black people as a group. There are various versions of uplift theory, but only two need concern us here. First, there is Booker T. Washington's view of racial uplift. Washington thought that the elevation of the race depended on economic development of the working poor. That is, poor blacks should develop the skills necessary to become the needed laborers of American society and take on the white middle-class values of hard work and moral restraint. Washington thought that by taking on these values the race would be elevated and that whites would come to see the value of having a hard-working, morally straight group (blacks) in America. Therefore, it was through a rejection of black culture that the race would be elevated.

Du Bois, on the other hand, did not think that a rejection of black culture was necessary for race advancement. As a matter of fact, the culture of blacks was to be the lifeblood of the race's gift to the cultures of the world. The advancement of the race depended upon black culture being preserved and elevated. Once black culture was accepted as being on a par with European culture, the race would be elevated.

Both Washington and Du Bois agreed that it was the duty of better educated and situated members of the race to work for the elevation of the group. This obligation is presented as a moral imperative. Yet this notion of group obligation is not without its problems. How does one come to be under the force of this moral imperative? That is, how does the obligation to support the black community arise?

Clearly, given the racism of American society, blacks are forced to identify with other blacks. However, identifying with a group does not necessarily lead to a moral obligation to help the members of that group. Some blacks probably worked for the betterment of all blacks out of a feeling of self-interest. Blacks not born in America but living there may think that their support of American blacks is out of self-interest. Black leaders have been aware of this and have prodded all blacks to see themselves as morally obligated to help other blacks.[14]

The most common answer to the question about the genesis of race obligations is that one becomes obligated by being born into a racial family. The obligations of blacks to other blacks can best be described as nonvoluntary. These obligations arise in the same manner that obligations to immediate families arise.[15] Being born black, in this case, is similar to being born into a large family. One is born a member of the family and cannot just leave. For many persons, the fact that I am born into a family obligates me to that family, and family membership carries certain obligations and duties.

Familial obligations are often felt very strongly. If I had to choose between saving the life of my son, William, and the life of some other child, I would without hesitation save the life of my son. I feel this way because I see the obligations I have to him arising out of our relationship: father to son. I feel the same way about other close familial relationships, for example, my wife, my mother, my siblings, and, because of marriage, the mother, father, and siblings of my wife. I would to some extent be willing to make sacrifices for them. But what about cousins I have never seen or those immediate family members who wrong me? Am I obligated to help them no matter what?

Here we should note that how one comes to be obligated can be seen in at least two ways. First, one can only be obligated if one voluntarily takes on the particular obligation. For example, I state that I will take care of my neighbor's dogs while she is away on vacation. I have willingly taken on this responsibility and thus am obligated. Of course, my duty to feed her pet can be overridden if some other pressing matter arises, for example, if my son is injured and must be taken to the hospital.

Second, there are obligations that are thought to arise solely because of the nature of the relationship one has with another person or group, for example, obligations that come with being a father. These obligations include, but are not limited to, child care, nurturing, and support of the child and his or her mother. The obligations of fatherhood in this position are not voluntary. A father can choose not to live up to his obligations, but he can be held morally culpable if he does not live up to his expected duties.

It is often thought that the relationship between members of the same race can be modeled on the "relationship model" of obligations. Thus members of a race are often said to belong to a large family. The use of the terms "brother" and "sister" are examples of attempts to make this model part of the value system of black Americans. Most of us have strong emotional and moral identification with our immediate families. It is argued that the same identification exists (or should exist) with our racial group. As members of a large racial family, all blacks must be concerned with the impact of racism and oppression on the other family members.

Does the claim that blacks are part of a great family make it easier to fulfill one's obligations? You help members of your family because they are members of your family, not out of charity or self-interest. The family model plays nicely with the notion that all members of the race should be achieving if one achieves. We want all the members of our family to achieve. In this conception of morality, your family always comes first. But are races analogous to families?

Race as Family

Philosopher Anthony Appiah has examined the "race as family" metaphor and found it lacking as a justification for race-based obligations.[16] Appiah first distinguishes what is meant by "race." He thinks that at least three distinct doctrines might be held to express the theoretical content of what we call "racism": racialism, extrinsic racism, and intrinsic racism.[17] Racialism is the view that members of each race share traits that are not shared with the members of others races.[18] These traits are thought to constitute a sort of racial essence. Although this position was at the heart of most nineteenth-century attempts to develop an account of the races of man, Appiah has argued that racialism is false.[19] However, he thinks that it is not in itself a doctrine that must be dangerous. It is, however, a presupposition of those doctrines that have been called "racism." These other doctrines, "extrinsic racism" and "intrinsic racism," have in the past few centuries been the basis of a great deal of human suffering and the source of a great deal of moral error.[20]

For Appiah, extrinsic racists make "the moral distinction between members of different races." They believe that each race has a racial essence that entails certain morally relevant qualities. The extrinsic racist discriminates on the basis of the belief that different races differ in respects that "warrant the differential treatment, respect—such as honesty or courage or intelligence—that are uncontroversially held (at least in most contemporary cultures) to be acceptable as a basis for treating people differently."[21] One would think that when evidence is produced to the contrary—for example, that blacks do not necessarily lack intellectual capacities, or that Jews are not especially avaricious—an extrinsic racist would give up this position. But as we know, such evidence often fails to change an extrinsic racist's attitude. Appiah thinks that a sincere extrinsic racist suffers from a cognitive incapacity.

Intrinsic racists, on the other hand, are people who differentiate morally between members of different races. Intrinsic racists believe that "each race has a different moral status, quite independent of the moral characteristics entailed by its racial essence. . . . Just as, for example, many people assume that the fact that they are biologically related to another person—a brother, an aunt, a cousin—gives them a moral interest in that person, so an intrinsic racist holds that the bare fact of being of the same race is a reason for preferring one person to another."[22] For an intrinsic racist, no amount of evidence that a member of another race is capable of great moral, intellectual, or cultural achievements, or has characteristics that would make members of one's own race admirable or attractive, offers any grounds for treating that person as one would treat similarly endowed members of one's own race.[23]

Appiah readily admits that many may find his discussion of racism off the mark. Racists are really irrational, it will be argued. Appiah thinks that extrinsic racists do suffer from cognitive incapacity, that is, a failure to take seriously evidence that threatens or undermines one's own interest or self-image. Appiah, however, is concerned with the use of racist doctrines as a justification for moral positions.

The Holocaust and the system of apartheid in South Africa are examples of racist doctrines becoming the basis for the unethical treat-ment of other races. While those in political power have used race as a focal point for politically oppressive and genocidal policies, those groups subject to racist policies have also had to draw on the ideology of race for their own self-image, group survival, and moral solidarity. The two major uses of race as a base for moral solidarity that are most familiar in the West are varieties of Pan-Africanism and Zionism. In each case it is presupposed that a "people," blacks or Jews, has the basis for shared political life in the fact of being of the same race.[24]

Appiah thinks that Jews, through Judaism, have a realistic candi-date for a common and nonracial focus for nationality. However, the people of Africa have a good deal less in common culturally than is usually assumed. What blacks in the West, like secularized Jews, have most in common is that they are perceived—by both themselves and others—as belonging to the same race, and that this common race is used by others as the basis for discriminating against them. The black nationalists, like some Zionists, responded to their experience of racial discrimination by accepting the racialism it presupposed.[25] In black nationalist discourse, it is the fact of a shared race, not the fact of a shared racial characteristic, that provides the basis for solidarity.[26]

Where racism is implicated in the basis for national solidarity, it is intrinsic, not (or not only) extrinsic. Therefore, the idea of fraternity is naturally applied in nationalist discourse. As Appiah observes, the moral status of close family members is not normally thought of in most cultures as depending on qualities of character; we are supposed to love our brothers and sisters in spite of their faults, not because of their virtues.[27]

Appiah cites what he takes to be a classic statement of the "race as family" metaphor by Alexander Crummell, one of the founding fathers of black nationalism: "Races, like families, are the organisms and ordi-nances of God; and race feeling, like family feeling, is of divine origin. The extinction of race feeling is just as possible as the extinction of family feeling. Indeed, a race is a family."[28] The equating of race feel-ing with family feeling has made intrinsic racism less objectionable than extrinsic racism. This metaphorical identification reflects the fact that, in the modern world (unlike the nineteenth century), intrinsic racism is acknowledged almost exclusively as the basis of the feeling of community.[29]

While many would not think of this position as racist, Appiah thinks that it is. "The racism here is the basis for acts of supereroga-tion, the treatment of others better than we otherwise might, better than moral duty demands of us."[30] However, he thinks that intrinsic racism is a moral error. Even if racialism were correct, the bare fact that someone is of another race would be no reason to treat that person worse—or better—than someone of my race.

Drawing on Kant's moral theory, Appiah thinks that in our public lives race should not be a consideration for our treatment of individuals. Persons are owed respect independently of their biological character: if they are to be treated differently there must be some morally relevant differences between them.[31] We can, of course, have aesthetic preferences between people in our private lives; but once our treatment of them raises moral issues, we may not make arbitrary distinctions.[32] Intrinsic racism is a failure to apply the Kantian injunction to universalize our moral judgments.[33]

It is often thought that intrinsic racism can be defended along the same lines that defend the family as a center of moral interests. The possibility of a defense of family relations as morally relevant—or, more precisely, of the claim that one may be morally entitled (or even obliged) to make distinctions between two otherwise morally indistinguishable people because one is related to one and not to the other—is theoretically important for the prospects of a philosophical defense of intrinsic racism. This is because such a defense of the family involves—like intrinsic racism—a denial of the basic claim, expressed so clearly by Kant, that from the perspective of morality, it is as rational agents simpliciter that we are to assess and be assessed.[34] Intrinsic racism denies this claim and runs against the mainstream of Western moral theory.

Appiah thinks that people often fail to distinguish between their private lives, of which the family is of great importance, and their public lives. A nuclear family has, of course, a substantial body of shared experiences, shared attitudes, and beliefs. There is a mutual psychological investment in this group that gives meaning to most of our lives. It is a natural enough confusion—which we find again and again in discussions of adoption in the popular media—that identifies the relevant groups with the biological unit of genitor, genetrix, and offspring rather than with the social unit of those who share a common domestic life.[35] The family model is best suited for those relationships that develop between parents and children. It is not suited, according to Appiah, to account for the moral relationship between biological siblings and half-siblings.

A rational defense of the family ought to appeal to the causal responsibility of the biological parent and the common life of the domestic unit and not to the brute fact of biological relatedness, even if the former pair of considerations defines groups that are often coextensive with the group generated by the latter. Brute biological relatedness bears no necessary connection to the sorts of human purposes that seem likely to be relevant at the most basic level of ethical thought.[36]

Thus members of the black middle class should not feel as if they are letting down their family if they try to make the best possible life for themselves in America. As a matter of fact, if they fail to promote their own interest, they are failing to give due moral weight to the ends of persons who deserve respect as moral agents: themselves.

Yet, even if Appiah is correct and the family model fails to account for obligations based on a biological notion of race, we still must acknowledge that this position has deep psychological roots. It is difficult for many successful blacks to escape the feeling that they owe something to significantly less fortunate blacks as members of a racial family.

Appiah argues against the biological conception of race.[37] However, a view of race that does not draw on the fact of biological relatedness is the position that what race means is lineage. This view of race predates the biological view, and the race-as-lineage proponent can agree with Appiah's skepticism about there being subspecies of human beings. It may be this conception of race that motivates some to see other blacks as members of a racial family.

I will present another challenge to the use of the "race as family" sentiment as a basis for moral action, which presents a problem for either conception. But first, let us assume that the conception of "race as family" does give rise to special obligations to one's race. What are the obligations of middle-class blacks to their family members in poor urban areas?

The Urban Community and Racial Obligations

The past twenty-five years clearly have played havoc with the social and political stability of many traditionally black communities. It is claimed that these years have seen an exodus from the black community by many middle-class and working-class blacks. There are ample examples of what can happen to a black community when the middle class and working class leave. A community that at one time consisted of the full range of social types—the affluent, the poor, the criminal, and the working-class man and woman—now contain just three types: those working to get out, those too poor to ever get out, and the criminal element. Thus, as American society opened up, those who could afford to move left behind the poor and the criminal element and the community deteriorated.[38]

Wilson thinks these poor urban communities have been deprived of their role models, political clout, and economic base. It is thought that if some of those blacks who have money, political clout, and social status stayed in the community, blacks who are less fortunate would benefit through better police protection, better public services, and more political clout. There would also be positive role models in the community. All of these things the community loses when those blacks who can afford to move do so.

Are those more affluent blacks obligated to stay in the less well-off community? Should those blacks who can move stay? Does staying in the community help social progress? If we take seriously the notion of blacks helping to uplift other blacks as members of a family, the answer to these questions would appear to be yes.[39]

The obligation to the race as family entails a general obligation to help preserve a culturally and economically sound black community. It is generally agreed that a healthy, strong black community is necessary for the political, emotional, cultural, and social survival of black people.[40] A strong black community is the lifeblood of black people. It keeps alive the reality of black culture.[41] The lifeblood of black culture must remain intact somewhere. In a strange sense, the positions of Du Bois and Washington have fused. Blacks are now pushed to save and promote black culture, while at the same time acting as middle-class role models. It appears, at first glance anyway, that if middle-class blacks are truly committed to the survival of the black community as a vital entity, some middle-class blacks who can afford to move will have to make the sacrifice and stay in the community.[42]

Many blacks feel a deep commitment to the general black community and want that community to flourish, and yet they believe that to stay in decaying and crime-ridden communities is over and beyond what is owed to the black community. It would be a supererogatory act; one is not obligated to do it, and in certain cases it would be foolhardy if one did.[43] But if the community is to survive, some of those blacks who can afford to leave must stay.

Why can't more-fortunate blacks just give money or set up, for example, a health clinic or financially support events and projects in the community? This was part of Hamill's challenge to middle-class blacks. He wanted to see the black middle class return in "great waves to urban ghettos." These returning blacks would work to restore the lifeline in these communities. But Hamill was quick to add: "Obviously, I don't mean that you should move your family back to the ghetto. Or that your friends should do the same. That simply isn't going to happen in the immediate future. But in important ways, such a drastic commitment isn't necessary."[44] Hamill is wrong—such a drastic commitment is necessary. The plight of disadvantaged blacks requires that some middle-class blacks stay in poor communities as role models, even if they can afford to leave. Some middle-class blacks will need to return to these communities, especially if the goal is to keep the cultural flames lit and to impart middle-class values to poor blacks.

Black neoconservatives Thomas Sowell and Walter Williams think that members of poor urban communities lack those values that make them productive citizens. Williams, nonetheless, does not put much stock in the role model idea. He claims, "The point is that the role model theory has not delivered on its promised to provide the kind of incentives envisioned by its advocates. Those who advocate the role model theory of socioeconomic progress have never bothered to explain how they made their own achievements without role models."[45] Wilson, on the other hand, thinks that less-fortunate blacks need positive role models in the community. Let us assume that the behavior of poor blacks can be changed by "positive" black role models. It then seems clear that the type of role models needed for many black children must be close at hand. You cannot be an effective role model if you do not live in close proximity to the person who needs a model. Middle-class blacks often view those black individuals who have been very financially successful in America as role models. One prime example of a person who is often cited as a successful role model is former basketball player Dr. J. (Julius Erving). Playing a sport such as basketball offers an interesting example because many young blacks know what you need to do to play in the NBA—you have to be a great basketball player. Yet these same youths may not understand what it means to be in college, which is the major route to the NBA. Other examples of successful role models are Oprah Winfrey and rap artist Kool Moe Dee.

Children and the poor do need to see people who have "made it." But they also need to see people who go to work every day and men who stay with their families and pay bills and persons who are trying to make their community better. They need to see that you do not have to be rich and famous to live a productive life and strive for excellence in your endeavors.

But what happens when these individuals who care for their families and hold steady jobs finally change their economic status? They move out of the community. Even those persons who claim to speak for the urban poor are not immune to moving out.[46] When these blacks move, the economic and political drain on the community continues and the slide into social, political, and economic decay quickens.

It is also claimed that this drain on the black community has an adverse effect on intragroup black relations. A social schism is developing between more-affluent blacks and the black underclass. The black middle class is being blamed for the condition of poor urban blacks. Those who have more are being considered traitors to the race.[47]

It is suggested that there is a crisis of leadership, trust, and identity.[48] Many poor blacks, it is claimed, do not feel that they have the same political or economic interests as more-affluent blacks.[49] As a matter of fact, William Julius Wilson has also claimed that many social and political issues are decided now more by class position than by race.[50] And it must be admitted that class position does play a significant role in many of the social and economic decisions of the black middle class. While some blacks give lip service to race solidarity and generally vote and act on class grounds, these blacks still often want a strong black community.[51] But it should be noted that many blacks who return to the black community do so for economic reasons. Many inner cities have structurally sound housing at low cost, which serves as financial inducement. Some blacks see the black community as a source of potential customers for black-owned and -operated businesses. They want to be big fish in the black pond. Du Bois realized that some blacks were narrowly race loyal.[52] It would appear that one way to allay the fears of poor blacks that those blacks who have made some gains have forgotten them would be for well-off blacks to stay with them. Some well-off blacks must remain in the communities and fulfill their obligation of racial uplift.[53] After all, we do want the members of our family to do well.

The black community, it is argued, needs positive role models, and it is the duty of middle-class blacks to be such models. Survival of the black community as a spatial community seems to demand that some affluent blacks remain in poor areas in sufficient numbers to make a difference. This position, of course, assumes that their presence will have a stabilizing and socially uplifting effect and that the model notion really works. Tommy Lott, however, argues that if middle-class blacks are role models, the role model they represent, in fact, does nothing to change the basic structure of American society, and that this is needed if poor blacks are really to be helped.[54]

The End of Obligations?

Well-off blacks are pushed to see their help of less-fortunate blacks in the form of a social obligation; that is, it is the social responsibility of every well-off black to work to uplift the race. Yet there is another aspect to the racial uplift theory: uplifting the race is in fact to help eliminate societal racism. Whites would realize that blacks are no different culturally or that they have a culture that everyone receives value from and thus should be respected as social equals.

Some persons, both black and white, may have reasoned that, with the passage of the civil rights acts and various affirmative action programs, one day soon blacks would be integrated totally in the fabric of American society. The struggle for social uplift would be won. The burden of the historical moral imperative would be lifted.

The 1954 *Brown v. Board of Education* Supreme Court decision seemed to validate this reasoning. Blacks had pushed for political and social equality, and in the 1950s the Supreme Court broke down the barrier of discrimination in education, which caused many other social barriers to fall. The 1960s saw political and many residential barriers fall. American society seemed to be opening up, and true social integration seemed a reality. Jobs and political opportunities that never existed before became available for a segment of the black community. Like good Americans, those blacks who could rushed to take advantage of these new opportunities. In the forefront of almost everyone's mind was the idea that at some point America would truly be an integrated society. In the past twenty-five years, it has become clear that the majority of blacks are unable to take advantage of the social progress. There is still a great deal to be done to make the goal of complete racial uplift a reality.

On the one hand, blacks now generally believe that the percentage of blacks who have made significant progress is alarmingly small. What is more, the failure of many blacks to make significant progress is not entirely their own fault. It is not as if these blacks have cultivated warped preferences that systematically get in the way of their making social progress. There are, it is true, many poor whites. But many persons, both black and white, tend to think—rightly or wrongly—that poor whites bear the brunt of the blame for their poverty.

On the other hand, most blacks believe that there is still considerable racism in American society, and that it is because of racism that many blacks are not making the progress one would like to see them make. Very few successful blacks deny the existence of racism in American society. In fact, very few deny having had to contend with racism—and still having to contend with it.[55] Thus many successful blacks are morally torn because they realize that their good fortune is due more to fortuitous circumstances than to the absence of racism in society. Well-off blacks often resent the implication on the part of whites that their own good fortune shows just how little racism there is in society, since they think that it shows no such thing.

Racism and Racial Obligations

One may think that the obligation of blacks solely to help blacks would not exist with the elimination of racism. And, of course, this is the rub. There appears to be a concerted opinion among many blacks that America will never be free of societal racism. First, they feel that the government is out to get black people in general and black leaders in particular.[56] The government, it is argued, singles out black politicians and makes sure that drugs are easily available in poor black neighborhoods. Some persons have suggested that the AIDS virus was created in order to infect black people. Moreover, the police, it is claimed, work to keep blacks contained, rather than to protect the lives and property of blacks.[57]

Second, the history of blacks in America has produced much debate over the correct strategy to deal with societal racism. Racial integration and separatism are generally the focus of this discussion. Philosopher Howard McGary has examined the integrationist and separatist positions with the aim of clarifying the conceptual issues involved in the dispute. What he has to say about the separatist position is important for our discussion. He notes that there is no one separatist position and, of course, not all blacks are separatist. Nonetheless, separatist ideology is prominent in the black urban community. While different groups believe that blacks must separate from whites to achieve their aims, these groups also differ on what the end results should be.

McGary thinks, however, that a common line of reasoning underlies the separatist position, and that the arguments by the extreme or moderate separatists are persuasive, if we accept the following claims:

(1) that white racism is endemic in white American society, that it is central to the culture and economic interest of the white majority,
(2) that racial identification is functional from the standpoint of economic, psychological, and social development,
(3) that racial separatism can be a democratic solution to the race problem, and
(4) that a supported bond can/does exist between blacks.[58]

McGary notes that the empirical evidence needed to support these claims is sparse. But, as we have seen, lack of supporting evidence does not often undermine beliefs.

Let us assume that these claims are false: There is no government conspiracy to eliminate blacks, and whites do not always act with racist intent. If, however, the majority of blacks believe that the claims are true, then they must also believe that any black person may be a victim of racism, and that other blacks must help that person overcome societal racism. This would not be a problem if blacks thought that whites could be trusted. But why should blacks trust white Americans to do the right thing?

In his insightful work *Living Morally* philosopher Laurence Thomas discusses at length the notion of trust. Thomas think that real trust only comes about when persons or groups give other persons or groups evidence that they can be trusted. In many cases, it takes years to develop a relationship of trust.[59]

Thomas thinks that "these observations about trust reflect the reality that we do not trust a person whom we regard as not being trustworthy." Trust is something that develops over time. One may start out not trusting someone, but may find after a period of time that one can trust that person. This means that if blacks are to trust whites to look out for the well-being of blacks, whites must have communicated to blacks that whites respect the situation that blacks are in and are prepared to do the right thing. None of this means that there are not some individual whites that blacks can trust, but it does reflect a reluctance to trust whites as a group. Why should blacks believe that they can trust whites as a group?[60]

A review of black American history does not provide much hope for blacks putting trust in whites to do the right thing. Because of this history many blacks are reluctant to trust whites. They feel that most whites cannot be trusted not to act with racist motivation, or to act without racist intent. If blacks cannot for the foreseeable future think that they can trust whites, how can they believe that racism will end in America?

The implication of this belief is clear: If America will never be free of racism to the point that blacks will be elevated to full and complete social equality, middle-class blacks have no obligation to work for racial uplift. "Ought" implies "can." One cannot have an obligation to do something that cannot be done. Will whites in America ever see blacks as their social equals? If, indeed, the answer is no, the goal of racial uplift is impossible. Still, it does not follow that middle-class blacks no longer have any reason to be concerned with the plight of poor blacks. There may still be a moral justification given to help less-advantaged blacks, and there may be pragmatic reasons to be concerned about the fate of less-advantaged blacks. Either of these reasons may still require some middle-class blacks to remain in the black community.

Many blacks will be uneasy with any assertion that they should stay in a less well-off black community. Some blacks will not like my analysis. They will claim that any betterment of their own position is really helping blacks. They have what can be called a Reverend Ike (Frederick Eikerenkoetter) view of poverty: The best way to help the poor is not to be one of them.

Black Americans admittedly are influenced by the ideology of liberal individualism. In the theory of liberal individualism, the individual is the center of the social and political world. One should not be held back in one's life goals because of one's affiliation with a religious, ethnic, or racial group. This view plays out in the material world in the attitude that one ought to improve one's lot in life.[61] This will include moving up in one's profession, moving to a better neighborhood, and achieving higher social status.[62] Poussaint notes that some blacks claim "to feel no obligation to less fortunate Blacks and become angry and resentful when it is suggested that they owe something to others." Poussaint thinks that this is the American spirit of "rugged individualism" at its worst. "These people see their achievement as personal accomplishments, only vaguely and indirectly related to the overall Black struggle for civil rights and economic rights."[63]

Poussaint believes affluent blacks fall into three categories: those who take a "rugged individual" approach; those who "live a Spartan lifestyle," rejecting or hiding their prosperity because they feel that it may be an act of hostility toward poor blacks to display any affluence and are determined to prove that they remain part of the black masses; and those affluent blacks who are enjoying the fruits of their own success and still accepting some responsibility for their less well off brothers and sisters.[64] Poussaint thinks that most affluent blacks fall into this last category. Poussaint also seems to think that there is a moral obligation to help less-fortunate blacks.

But even if Poussaint is correct and most affluent blacks fall into his third category, blacks in this group can feel torn about the extent of their obligations to other blacks. One often has to choose between pursuing one's own interests and doing what one feels obligated to do. Sometimes the decision is agonizing. For example, the decision of where to live often raises this problem for middle-class blacks living in areas without a large black middle class. This is particularly problematic if one wants to enjoy the fruits of one's labor. Should one move one's family into a less-prestigious black neighborhood or to a "better" (often white) one? Individual blacks are pushed to achieve as individuals, but are always reminded never to forget the group.

Middle-class blacks also feel obligated to help immediate family members who have not been able to take advantage of the societal changes in the past twenty-five years. But all of this help is not without a cost to those who strive for middle-class status. In dozens of interviews cited in a *New York Times* article, middle-class blacks said that they were proud to be able to help their families, but were frustrated by their inability to get ahead.[65] That one is helping a family member is supposed to make the sacrifice easier to bear.

The question often arises, What do these well-off blacks get from less-advantaged blacks? This question has been raised by some upwardly mobile blacks who feel no obligation beyond self-interest and charity to aid those less well off. For example, it is often thought that there is a general duty of charity owed to those who, through no fault of their own, are less fortunate than we are. Yet blacks are not permitted to see their concern for other blacks as charity. One does not give charity to family members.

Since there is no immediate payback for helping the disadvantaged, it is generally thought that middle-class blacks are repaying other blacks who worked to make their middle-class existence possible. It is an obligation of reciprocity. Philosopher Bernard R. Boxill agrees and thinks that such an obligation means that each person who receives a benefit from the contributions of others "has a duty to contribute to it as well. It is wrong, and a dereliction of duty, to be a parasite." Everyone has a duty to "pull his own weight."[66]

What does it mean for each person to pull his own weight? It at least means that individuals should not be a burden to the race or society. But in the black community the notion of reciprocity often means working to pay back those who made one's present condition or situation possible. For example, black college students are told that they owe a debt to those blacks who struggled for the right of blacks to attend predominantly white universities. These students are obligated to keep up the struggle to ensure that other blacks will have the same opportunity. It would seem that if one were to do well in college and press for fair treatment of other blacks, one would have repaid one's debt to those blacks who struggled before one. This, however, turns out not to be the case. One is constantly reminded, like members of some families, not to forget that one's brothers and sisters have not been able to make it. It does not matter what one's past contributions have been to the family.

One other reason for supporting the race-as-family model has to be given. Those who push the racial uplift notion claim that if less-fortunate blacks are not respected and treated with dignity, the social situation of more-affluent blacks is always in danger. Respect for one black depends on the entire group's being respected. Helping less-fortunate blacks has the effect of securing the social position of more-fortunate blacks. This may seem like an appeal to self-interest; however, black leaders have resisted the appeal to self-interest. Like Du Bois, they realize that if allowed to act in what they perceive to be their own best interest, many blacks might not choose to help less-advantaged blacks. Middle-class blacks get the good feeling of helping family members. Even if racism will not be eliminated, middle-class blacks have to be concerned with the overall behavior of poor blacks. Whites, it is thought, do not generally make distinctions between the behavior of poor blacks and that of middle-class blacks. So middle-class blacks still need to be concerned with the social behavior of poor blacks. One way middle-class blacks can influence this "negative" behavior is to live with them and show them how to behave.

Race as Family, Again

Even if we think that races are families, can my obligation to the race be overridden by my concern for my more immediate family, my wife and child? If we do have absolute obligations to our racial families, should I put my immediate family in danger? If the question is whether one should move one's family into a disadvantaged neighborhood in hopes of helping disadvantaged members of one's race, many blacks are going to say "no."

If one has an obligation to provide one's own family with the comfort, security, education, social opportunities, and whatever else is associated with a "nice" neighborhood, that would override one's obligation to move into disadvantaged neighborhoods for at least three reasons. First, at least prima facie, one owes more to one's immediate family than to the distant cousin one has never met or to the stranger with the same skin color. Second, the benefits of my own family's remaining in a "nice" neighborhood are relatively certain compared to the merely possible and rather nebulous future benefit that my presence in the disadvantaged neighborhood may produce. Third, if it is true that all middle-class blacks do not have to move into the neighborhood, one might agree that somebody ought to do it, without feeling that one must do it.[67]

One more challenge to the concept of race as family as a justification for moral action is that it is self-defeating. That is, it is not a moral position that black Americans want to universalize. Blacks do not want whites to be totally committed to an intrinsic racist position of looking out for one's racial family first. Most blacks want to be treated as moral and social equals. The appeal to race-as-family morality would undermine the basic political and moral principles that have been used to get blacks what civil liberties they have. It does not matter whether the appeal to race as family is based on biology or lineage. Blacks lack sufficient political and economic power in America to push such a moral position as a universal moral principle. Races can still be considered families, but we do not want that concept to be the basis of moral obligation.

Finally, political scientist Adolph Reed, Jr., has argued that the discourse about blacks being responsible for uplifting other blacks ties in very nicely with the current negative ideology that surrounds poor blacks and urban black culture:

> Whites like it because it implies that blacks should pull themselves up by their bootstraps and not make demands on the government. Middle-class blacks like it because it legitimizes a "special role" for the black petite bourgeoisie over the benighted remainder of the race. In both views, "self-help" with respect to the ordinary black citizens replaces a standard expectation of democratic citizenship—a direct, unmediated relation to the institutions and processes of public authority.[68]

Conclusion

The goal of much of the political and social struggle in America by both blacks and whites has been and continues to be for blacks to have the opportunity to live where they want and associate with whom they please as full citizens. The partial fulfillment of these opportunities is one of the most cherished accomplishments of the civil rights struggle.[69] It must be constantly remembered what life was like in America before those blacks who could afford to move were allowed to do so. It has been more than twenty years since the death of Martin Luther King, Jr., and there have been, we must admit, many advances in line with King's vision of racial uplift and social integration. Few blacks want to return to the socially and politically segregated days of the 1870s to the mid-1960s—that is, to a time when the decision to buy homes in certain neighborhoods or to work or to apply for employment in certain professions was virtually closed to most blacks, regardless of qualifications. We must keep clear in our mind the memory of what society would be like if those blacks who could afford to move were not able to.

Neither well-off whites nor well-off blacks seem to feel obligated to live in poor white neighborhoods. As I have said, this is because there is a perception that poor whites are themselves at fault for being poor. It would seem to follow that when most blacks believe that less-fortunate blacks are responsible for their own economic and social situation, and not societal racism, the obligation to other blacks because of societal racism will be ended. However, if middle-class blacks believe that racism will never be eliminated or lessened to the point where the failings of blacks can be attributed seriously to some other factor, they will be obligated to continue to work to make life tolerable for less-advantaged blacks for a number of moral and pragmatic reasons.

We now have some hint to the answer to the often-asked question, How long must there be governmental programs to eliminate the effects of past and present racism? The answer, in part, seems to be: When blacks think that race is not a negative factor in the life of any black who wants to achieve in America. This does not mean that America must be free of racially discriminatory acts; there may always be cases of individuals acts of racial discrimination. What it means is that all or nearly all blacks must believe that if a black American fails to achieve in America, it is because of lack of individual effort and not societal racism.

Nothing I have said here is meant to imply, nor should it be taken to imply, that middle-class blacks are responsible for the creation or continuation of urban poverty.[70] Nor does it follow that the black middle class has no obligation to the urban poor. What it means, at best, is that some alternate theory of obligation other than the family model must be given.

Wilson can, of course, claim that he is only describing what events have led to the rise of the urban underclass and that he is not suggesting that middle-class blacks move back, as "family members" or for any reason. He also argues that there should be governmental programs to help eliminate many of the adverse conditions of the urban poor. But his remarks about the relationship of middle-class blacks to the condition of urban blight raises questions about the moral obligation of not causing suffering. If the movement of middle-class blacks out of these neighborhoods causes social harm, do middle-class blacks have obligations to the larger black community that can override their personal interest? If there is a general moral obligation not to cause unnecessary harm, then, if Wilson is correct, middle-class blacks must think long and hard about moving out of black communities. However, this does not mean that the government has no responsibility for alleviating urban poverty and making members of the underclass full citizens.

The knowledge that a segment of the black community, or any community, will never enjoy the benefits of full American citizenship shows that there are some systemic problems in America. While it may be a truism that the poor will always be with us, those persons who aspire to change their economic and social position should at least have some faith that the system is not closed to them. Many black Americans believe, with good reason, that the system is closed to people of color. These blacks do not think that they can trust whites to do the right thing. The fact that many African Americans do not trust white Americans as a group is a problem for all Americans.[71] Even more depressing is the knowledge that many black Americans have no faith that this nation will do what is necessary to make their citizenship real. This lack of basic trust, coupled with the seeming reluctance of America to make the citizenship of blacks real, is what makes many of the urban poor the "truly disadvantaged."[72] Establishing trust in America has to be part of any government public policy to eliminate urban poverty.

NOTES

1. William Julius Wilson, *The Truly Disadvantaged* (Chicago: University of Chicago Press, 1987), p. 54.

2. Nicholas Lemann, "The Origins of the Underclass," *Atlantic Monthly*, July 1986, p. 54; idem, *The Promised Land* (New York: Alfred A. Knopf, 1991).

3. Pete Hamill, "Breaking the Silence," *Esquire*, March 1988, p. 99.

4. Kenneth L. Karst, *Belonging to America* (New Haven: Yale University Press, 1989), p. 133.

5. Alvin F. Poussaint, "The Price of Success: Remembering Their Roots Burdens Many Blacks in Mainstream with Feelings of Either Guilt or Denial," *Ebony*, August 1987, p. 76.

6. Signithia Fordham, "Racelessness as a Factor in Black Students' School Success: Pragmatic Strategy or Pyrrhic Victory," *Harvard Educational Review* 58, no. 1 (February 1988): 232.

7. See Chapter 2 of this volume for a discussion of the race school of thought on black progress.

8. This position has been denied by Thomas Sowell, Walter Williams, and Glenn Loury.

9. Thomas Jo Durant and Joyce Louden, "The Black Middle Class in America: Historical and Contemporary Perspectives," *Phylon* 47, no. 4. (Winter 1986): 253–63.

10. See, for example, Lawrence Becker, "Reciprocity and Social Obligations," *Pacific Philosophic Quarterly* 61 (1980): 411–21.

11. W.E.B. Du Bois, "Three Centuries of Discrimination," *The Crisis*, December 1947, p. 363.

12. Wilson, *The Truly Disadvantaged*, p. 60.

13. W.E.B. Du Bois, "The Talented Tenth," in *Negro Social and Political*

Thought 1850–1920, ed. Howard Brotz (New York: Basic Books, 1966), pp. 518–32.

14. BeBe Moore Campbell, "Staying in the Community," *Essence*, December 1989, pp. 96–112.

15. Laurence Becker, *Reciprocity* (New York: Routledge and Kegan Paul, 1986), pp. 177–226.

16. Kwame Anthony Appiah, "Racisms," in *Anatomy of Racism*, ed. David Theo Goldberg (Minneapolis: University of Minnesota Press, 1990), pp. 3–17.

17. Ibid, p. 4.

18. Ibid, p. 5.

19. Kwame Anthony Appiah, "The Uncompleted Argument: Du Bois and the Illusion of Race," *Critical Inquiry* 12 (Autumn 1985); reprinted in *"Race," Writing, and Difference*, ed. Henry Louis Gates (Chicago: University of Chicago Press, 1986), pp. 21–37.

20. Appiah, "Racisms," p. 5.

21. Ibid.

22. Ibid., p. 6.

23. Ibid.

24. Ibid., p. 11.

25. Ibid.

26. Ibid.

27. Ibid.

28. Ibid.

29. Ibid.

30. Ibid., p. 12.

31. Ibid.

32. Ibid.

33. Ibid.

34. Ibid., p. 14.

35. Ibid.

36. Ibid., p. 15.

37. For discussion of the role of the concept of race in social and political theory see Appiah, "The Uncompleted Argument"; idem, "The Conservation of 'Race,'" *Black American Literature Forum* 23, no. 1 (Spring 1989): 37–60; Houston A. Baker, Jr., "Caliban's Triple Play," *Critical Inquiry* 13 (Autumn 1986): 182–96; and Bill Lawson, "Individuals and Groups in the American Democracy: Group Interest and Civil Rights," *Logos* 6 (1985): 105–16.

38. Wilson, *The Truly Disadvantaged*, p. 136.

39. Poussaint, "The Price of Success," p. 76.

40. "Harlem: Its Promise Is the Draw," *New York Times*, April 25, 1988, p. B1.

41. See Chapter 5 of this volume.

42. "Harlem: Its Promise Is the Draw," B1.

43. See, for example, Glenn Burkins, "Choosing North Philadelphia," *Philadelphia Inquirer Magazine*, November 25, 1990, pp. 18–26.

44. Hamill, "Breaking the Silence," p. 100.

45. Walter Williams, "Myth Making and Reality Testing," *Society* 27 (May–June 1990): 4–7.

46. Rapper Ice-T, whose album *The Iceberg/Freedom of Speech . . . Just Watch What You Say* was ruled obscene in 1990 by a Florida grand jury, recently bought a $700,000 house off Hollywood's Sunset Strip. The 2,500-square-foot gated home, complete with a city-to-ocean view from almost every room, has two bedrooms, three baths, a hot tub, a large garden, and a private drive. *Jet*, February 18, 1991, p. 52.

47. Many black college students complain that when they return to their old neighborhoods they are accused of abandoning the black community and of no longer being black.

48. E. Franklin Frazier claimed that members of the black middle class really had contempt for poor blacks (*The Black Bourgeoisie* [New York: Free Press, 1957], p. 236).

49. Kenneth Maurice Jones, "The Buppies," *The Crisis* 93 no. 4 (April 1986): 17–64.

50. William J. Wilson, *The Declining Significance of Race* (Chicago: University of Chicago Press, 1978).

51. I take their position to be the belief that the historical and cultural importance of the black community remains constant.

52. Du Bois, "Three Centuries of Discrimination," p. 363.

53. Bernard Boxill, *Blacks and Social Justice* (Totowa, N.J.: Rowman and Allanheld, 1984), p. 183.

54. See Chapter 5 of this volume.

55. George Davis and Glegg Watson, *Black Life in Corporate America* (New York: Anchor Books, 1982).

56. Jason Deparle, "Talk Grows of Government Being Out to Get Blacks, *New York Times*, October 29, 1990, p. B6.

57. See my article, "Crime, Minorities and the Social Contract," *Criminal Justice Ethics* 9, no. 2 (Summer/Fall 1990): 16–24.

58. Howard McGary, "Racial Integration and Racial Separation: Some Conceptual Clarification," in *Philosophy Born of Struggle*, ed. Leonard Harris (Dubuque, Iowa: Kendall/Hunt, 1983), p. 205.

59. Laurence Thomas, *Living Morally* (Philadelphia: Temple University Press, 1989), p. 177.

60. Claire Safran, "What It's Really Like to Be Black," *Women's Day*, May 28, 1991, pp. 60–68.

61. Shelby Steele, *The Content of Our Character* (New York: St. Martin's Press, 1990), p. 109.

62. Poussaint, "The Price of Success," p. 76.

63. Ibid.

64. Ibid., p. 77.

65. Isabel Wilkerson, "Middle-Class Blacks Try to Grip the Ladder While Lending a Hand," *New York Times*, November 26, 1990, p. B7.

66. Boxill thinks that the dilemma can be resolved if blacks give up the position of cultural pluralism. See "Separation and Assimilation," in Boxill, *Blacks and Social Justice.*

67. This section draws on discussions with my colleague Kate Rogers.

68. Adolph Reed, Jr., "The Rise of Louis Farrakhan: All for One and None for All," Parts 1 and 2, *The Nation*, January, 28, 1991, p. 91.

69. See my article, "Politically Oppressed Citizens," *Journal of Value Inquiry* 25, no. 4 (October 1991): 335–38.

70. Douglas Massey and others have challenged Wilson's thesis that the migration of middle-class blacks has given rise to the underclass. See, for example, Douglas S. Massey, "American Apartheid: Segregation and the Making of the Underclass," *American Journal of Sociology* 96, no. 2 (September 1990): 329–57; Douglas Massey and Mitchell L. Eggers, "The Ecology of Inequality: Minorities and the Concentration of Poverty, 1970–1980," *American Journal of Sociology* 95, no. 5 (March 1990): 1153–88; Nancy A. Denton and Douglas S. Massey, "Residential Segregation of Blacks, Hispanics, and Asians by Socioeconomic Status and Generation," *Social Science Quarterly* 69, no. 4 (December 1988): 797–817; and Karl E. Taeuber, "Racial Segregation: The Persisting Dilemma," *Annals of the American Academy of Social Sciences* 422 (November 1975): 87–96. For Wilson's response, see "Public Policy Research and *The Truly Disadvantaged*," in *The Urban Underclass*, ed. Christopher Jencks and Paul Peterson (Washington: Brookings Institution, 1991), pp. 460–81.

71. See, for example, "The New Politics of Race," *Newsweek*, May 6, 1991, pp. 22–31.

72. For a discussion of the disadvantaged, see Mario D. Fantini and Gerald Weinstein, *The Disadvantaged: Challenge to Education* (New York: Harper and Row, 1968).

PART *Three*

Social Policy

7   LEGAL RIGHTS FOR POOR BLACKS

Anita L. Allen

ANGLO-AMERICAN legal philosophers from Jeremy Bentham and John Austin to H.L.A. Hart and Ronald Dworkin have traditionally included complementary analyses of the concept of a *legal right* in their general theories of law. Social and political philosophers without general theories of law have sometimes offered stand-alone analyses of legal rights. For example, Joel Feinberg once defined legal rights, without first specifying a theory of law, as valid claims arising out of a system of official rules.[1]

In complementary and stand-alone analyses of legal rights, philosophers have addressed basic questions about the nature or, as it is sometimes put, the conceptual or theoretical properties of rights.[2] Their questions have included whether legal rights entail correlative legal obligations and whether legal rights exist apart from positive rules, principles, judicial pronouncements, or law enforcement practices. Philosophers have also queried whether legal rights may be waived, forfeited, or overridden by considerations of utility. They have inquired whether children, the unborn, future generations, and nonhumans may have legal rights.

This chapter discusses the theoretical conceptions of legal rights, embraced by philosophers and others, that guide legal practice relating to American blacks. Academic philosophers do not live in a social vacuum. They bring to their work beliefs and intuitions about legal rights formed through varied social experiences outside of academe. To an extent, what they say about legal rights in the abstract and about specific rights claims echoes pervasive public opinion. Indeed, some rights theorists may consciously view their task as the defense and elaboration of common sense.

Philosophers' conceptions of legal rights have influence, as well as origins, beyond the ivory tower. Through writing and teaching, they routinely impart philosophic conceptions of legal rights to new generations of voters, legislators, lawyers, and judges. Much of what they convey is learned from others. But they also disseminate subtle new perspectives and powerfully original expressions of old ideas. Thus, how rights theorists understand legal rights is significant, not only for its own sake or as a mirror of culture, but also for its potential to guide, inspire, and retard legal practice.

Our society's dominant conception of legal rights and its unwillingness to remedy one of its most severe social problems are connected. I argue that conceptions of legal rights embraced in good faith have worked along with racism, politics, and economic factors to further black inequality. Prevailing conceptions of who may have legal rights, what it means to have a legal right, and what kinds of legal rights it is possible to have, have contributed to the creation and persistence of black poverty.

The dispassionate philosopher must admit that good theories can have bad consequences. However, it does not follow that the most defensible theories of legal rights must—or even can—have disastrous consequences for poor blacks. Be that as it may, by calling attention to the adverse material consequences of mainstream theories for impoverished blacks, I hope to encourage committed rights theorists to be more circumspect in their ascriptions and formulations of legal rights. I also hope to prompt reconsideration of certain hard-and-fast notions about the conceptual properties of legal rights.

My brief remarks are not primarily intended to defend a particular conception of legal rights or to fuel critical doubts about the existence and efficacy of legal rights. A more or less liberal egalitarian by instinct and education, I maintain the hope that there is an important sense in which legal rights exist and can be marshaled to promote important interests. However, I share some of the skepticism of theorists who have raised grave doubts in recent years about the existence of rights in American jurisprudence and about the utility of legal rights discourse as a means to achieving racial justice.[3]

Law and the "Black Underclass"

In 1962, in *Challenge to Affluence*, Gunnar Myrdal used the expression "underclass" to refer to the desperately poor whose poverty was a traceable consequence of the postindustrial economy. The expression "black underclass" was used a decade ago by Douglas G. Glasgow in a study of unemployment among young urban blacks. He used the now-controversial term to designate a permanently entrapped population of impoverished and underutilized victims of racism and the free enter-prise economy.[4] The population that Glasgow intended to denote by "black underclass," and that I will denote by the same term, substan-tially overlaps with the group William Julius Wilson recently termed the black "ghetto poor."[5] Many of the social and economic problems of the black ghetto poor, the "truly disadvantaged" segment of the black community, are problems characteristic of inner-city poor of all races.[6] Yet the predicament of the black underclass is shared, to a degree, by middle- and upper-income blacks throughout the United States. American blacks as a group persistently fare badly when compared to whites as a group.[7] Blacks as a group are more likely than whites to be poor, jobless, and homeless.[8] Blacks are more likely to die in infancy, to be reared by a single parent, and to be poorly educated.[9] Blacks as a group are more likely to be victims of violent crimes, to wind up in prison, to receive inadequate health care, and to die in middle age.[10]

Blacks join other racial and ethnic minorities in being underrepre-sented in government, business, the professions, and the media. Several major cities—Los Angeles, Atlanta, Seattle, Detroit, Baltimore, Phila-delphia, Memphis, and Washington, D.C.—have elected black mayors. L. Douglas Wilder took office in 1990 as Virginia's first elected black governor. But in most parts of the country, blacks do not hold high elected office or enjoy collective political power. William Gray, Jesse Jackson, and Ron Brown are the exceptions that prove the rule,[11] for blacks lack political clout on the national level, too. Only a handful of blacks are in Congress, advise the president, and preside over the federal courts.[12] Blacks are barely visible in the higher echelons of our universities and of most professions.[13] The number of black-owned businesses is small. Blacks boast proprietary or managerial control over only a smattering of the major print and electronic media.[14]

African Americans regardless of class are burdened by racism and race consciousness. Ours is a deeply race-conscious and, indeed, racist society.[15] Discrimination, prejudice, and mistreatment are the common experiences of individuals, families, and groups identified as black. Blacks from all income groups report that they are still excluded on account of race. Blacks are unwelcome in many social, religious, civic, fraternal, and business organizations. Even today blacks are denied entry to some commercial establishments.[16]

American law is not a natural ally of the black underclass.[17] As the Supreme Court would acknowledge in *Dred Scott v. Sandford,* the Con-stitution of 1787 condoned slavery "distinctly and expressly." [18] Few legislative impediments to the enslavement of blacks were on the books prior to the Civil War. Yet legal change has made it possible in recent decades for blacks to be citizens rather than slaves, voters rather than bystanders.

The Thirteenth, Fourteenth, and Fifteenth Amendments[19] and the nineteenth-century civil rights acts[20] were major steps toward racial equality. The Supreme Court attempted further steps in that direction in the 1950s, when it supplanted the principle of *Plessy v. Ferguson*[21] that "separate is equal" with the mandate of *Brown v. Board of Education* to desegregate public schools "with all deliberate speed."[22] In the 1960s, Congress enacted the Civil Rights Act of 1964 and other sweeping legislation calling for voting rights, equal employment opportunities, and equal access to public accommodations.[23] In the same decade, equal housing legislation was passed and courts ordered the busing of public school children to impose racial integration on communities resistant to change.[24] In the 1970s, the Supreme Court upheld affirmative action principles in education and employment,[25] with only partial retrenchment in the 1980s.[26] In the 1980s, cutbacks were made in legislated welfare entitlement programs,[27] but Aid for Dependent Children, food stamps, Medicaid, Medicare, and Social Security survived as entitlements for some of the seriously needy.[28]

In light of all this judicial and legislative intervention aimed at achieving equal justice and social welfare, what explains the persistence of a black underclass? The putative explanation racists favor is that blacks innately lack intelligence, moral conscience, and industry.[29] Even some blacks see the source of the problem as a social pathology within the black community, a pathology of indifference and dependence for which blacks must take primary causal and curative responsibility.

Social problems within the black community may have a role in blacks' underclass status. However, part of the explanation both for those social problems and for blacks' underclass status would appear to be that legal efforts have fallen short of ending racism and indifference, and that the massive redistributive overhaul needed to take the elimination of black inequality seriously has always been politically and, some would argue, constitutionally and morally unattainable.[30]

Few have the resources credibly to explain so complex a phenomenon as the persistence of the black underclass. I will highlight a single factor contributing to the phenomenon: how American courts—and those, such as rights theorists, with an ability directly or indirectly to influence them—think about legal rights. The law and the conceptions of legal rights persons of authority and influence interpret it to embody continue to be a barrier for blacks. As previously asserted, popular conceptions of who may have a legal right, what it means to have a legal right, and what kinds of legal rights it is possible to have contribute to the perpetuation of the black underclass.

Who May Have Legal Rights?

Two notable twentieth-century positivists commenced their analytic theories about the nature of law with theories of legal personhood. As John Chipman Gray and Hans Kelsen conceived it, a theory of legal personhood is a theory about, on the one hand, who or what may have legal duties and, on the other, who or what may have legal rights.[31] Theories about who or what may have legal rights can be referred to as theories of rights-ascription.[32] Positivist theories of rights-ascription assume that propositions of the form "X has a legal right to ———" are sometimes true, and proffers characterizations of the entities over whom the variable X may range.

Gray and Kelsen maintained that there are virtually no conceptual barriers to rights-ascription in the law. They argued that, in principle, legal rights can be ascribed to anything. Whether human or nonhuman, real or imagined, tangible or intangible, an entity may have legal rights so long as it has or can be imputed a choosing will and interests. They argued that the devices of legal representation, guardianship, and "next friends" take care of the problem that some entities do not in fact have wills or subjective interests.

The conclusion that, in principle, in a legal system virtually anything can have a right to anything should hold special interest for legal theorists in the United States. Our nominally egalitarian courts have often refused to ascribe important legal rights to human individuals and groups on account of their race, religion, alienage, gender, and age. For example, before the Civil War, American courts in slave states were reluctant to ascribe legal rights to blacks. Statutes and lower-court opinions frequently did ascribe legal rights to black slaves against third-party tort-feasors, contractual obligors, and kidnappers.[33] At the same time, courts treated black slaves as property with few basic common law rights against their owners. In the infamous *Dred Scott* case, the Supreme Court held that blacks are not citizens of the United States and hence have no standing to sue for wrongful enslavement in a federal court. This was a powerful, if somewhat oblique, way of announcing to blacks that they lacked the most important kind of legal rights of all—constitutional rights.

If the positivists were correct that the concept of a legal right is so flexible than even inanimate objects may be ascribed rights, and if the ascription of rights in our law is deemed to be something more than the brute or arbitrary exercise of power, it is imperative to understand how lawmakers purport to justify their exclusive rights-ascription practices. Two questions direct the jurisprudential inquiry mandated by such an understanding. First, what kinds of reasons count in law as good reasons for ascribing and refusing to ascribe rights to human claimants? Second, what kinds of reasons have courts actually given for refusing to ascribe to "new" classes of claimants rights readily ascribed to paradigm classes of rightholders?

In their best-known works, Kelsen and Gray did not reach these crucial questions. They took no position on the details of legal rights–ascription practices in the United States. In fact, the actual and ideal norms of legal rights–ascription practices have commanded the attention of few legal philosophers or lawyers. This is not to say that rights theorists primarily interested in legal rights or in moral rights have not contributed insights about the norms of rights-ascription.[34]

Foundational aspects of rights-ascription arguably have been addressed by Hart and Dworkin as special instances of deciding difficult or controversial lawsuits. Indeed, Hart's writings about the concept of law and jurisprudence offer a broad account of the norms and practices of rights-ascription. In *The Concept of Law*, Hart characterized law as the union of primary and secondary rules. Primary rules of duty or obligation require human beings "to do or abstain from certain actions whether they wish to or not."[35] Secondary rules of recognition, adjudication, and change "confer rule-related powers."[36] They are rules about rules. They permit public or private parties to "introduce new rules of the primary type, extinguish or modify old ones, or in various ways determine their incidence or control their operations."[37] For Hart, legal rights are the mirror images of legal duties or obligations established through primary and secondary rules. Rights claimants are entitled to the rights sought if, pursuant to rules of law, they are designated beneficiaries of correlative legal duties or obligations. In practical terms, contested legal rights are what judges ostensibly acting in accordance with secondary rules say they are.[38]

But Hart did not address just what combinations of primary and secondary rule-following or rule-making are called for by cases inviting novel or controversial rights-ascription. He hinted that utilitarian interest-balancing is called for when courts find they must fill gaps in the law. But he did not address the kinds of reasons by which courts have been and should be swayed to admit new classes of rightholders. At best, Hart provided a plausible, sophisticated positivist account of where courts' reasoned rights-ascriptions or refusals to ascribe rights are formally situated in law and judicial practice.

Dworkin's insights about the relationship between legal institutions and legal paradigms offer similarly formal clarification of rights-ascription practices.[39] In *Taking Rights Seriously* and *Law's Empire*, Dworkin drew attention to what he termed "hard cases" to illustrate his belief that "even when no settled rule disposes of the case, one party may nevertheless have a right to win."[40] Law as integrity "holds that people have as legal rights whatever rights are sponsored by the principles that provide the best justification of legal practice as a whole."[41] The process by which courts determine the existence of rights is deeply interpretative. Judges must interpret, not only particular rules of law and precedent, but the law as a whole.[42] Dworkin's familiar analysis of the jurisprudence of "hard cases" has broached certain questions raised by controversial rights-ascription, including whether racial minorities,[43] children,[44] and the unborn[45] have the legal rights white adults have. And Dworkin has made plain his belief that all persons are entitled to equal respect and concern. Yet Dworkin has not revealed how his ideal judge Hercules would handle cases that threaten to break a tradition of law precisely by bringing a category of claimant into a corner of the common law or constitutional rights framework for the first time or in a dramatically new way. In short, Dworkin has not focused on the details of the theory of rights-ascription presupposed by his theory of legal rights.[46] Except to argue that fetuses are not constitutional persons because they have not been treated uniformly as such in the law, Dworkin has not put forward an explicit conception of what kinds of persons or nonpersons count in American law and why. Like Hart's, Dworkin's theory provides mainly formal guidance.[47]

In a recent book, Christopher Stone attempted what Hart and Dworkin did not: He took a close, explicit look at the norms and actual judicial practice of legal rights–ascription in the United States. As a prelude to a moral argument that plants and animal life and their habitats deserve legal protection, Stone mounted a jurisprudential argument in the tradition of Kelsen and Gray that anything can have a legal right to anything. Stone concluded that there are few general reasons of law for courts to refuse to ascribe rights to nonpersons.[48] He argued that the only real legal barriers to legal rights–ascription are instrumental barriers of practicality and intelligibility. Any right can be ascribed to any person or thing so long as a guardian or lawyer can be designated, a court can fashion a remedy, and the right would have a coherent purpose.[49] Stone observed that just as people are ascribed legal rights appropriate for entities with personhood, other entities could easily be ascribed rights appropriate for their types. Thus trees could be ascribed legal rights of treehood protecting their integrity as trees, but properly be denied the personhood right of jury service.[50]

Stone short-circuited the jurisprudential branch of his inquiry by too quickly concluding that our law permits anything to have a legal right to anything, subject only to instrumental constraints. He failed to show that what is conceptually possible for a legal system—that anything can have a right to anything—is in fact the law of the United States. He failed to take seriously the possibility that, rightly or wrongly, American law opposes the ascription of rights to certain classes of people or things. Conceived as a complex set of rules, principles, or other norms limiting what courts legitimately may do, it is far from evident that existing American law permits the ascription of rights to, as Stone concluded, nonhumans.[51]

Anglo-American legal philosophy has not yet generated a general, detailed descriptive and prescriptive theory of the rights-ascription practices of American courts. Nonetheless, contemporary rights theorists such as Stone and Dworkin are quick to stipulate that all normal adult human beings are members of the class of paradigm moral and legal rightholders.[52] Though appropriate, the easy assertion by mainstream philosophers that all normal adult human beings are paradigm rightholders rings hollow against the background of American history, in which the opposite proposition has been quietly believed and loudly defended in the courts and legislatures to the detriment of nonwhites, women, and the unpropertied poor.

The philosophers' stipulation of legal peerage is welcome, but not necessarily comforting to blacks. Debates have raged over whether Native Americans, blacks, aliens, women, and children[53] should be accorded important rights. Denial to these groups of constitutional personhood, citizenship, voting rights, and access to public accommodations and schools has called into question criteria employed in the ascription of legal rights.[54] Until and unless rational and compelling criteria for inclusion in the law are articulated, blacks and other excluded groups understandably wonder: Whence comes the sudden intuition of equal rights and how stable is it?

It could be argued that theoretical concern and personal insecurity about legal rights–ascription practices are unwarranted in the post–civil rights era.[55] American law now ascribes equal rights to blacks. Indeed, critics of affirmative action have argued that black equality is black superiority, to the extent that courts uphold "preferential treatment" policies in employment and education. This portrait of blacks' legal status as one of equality or advantage rather than exclusion is contested. For example, Derrick Bell has argued in his constitutional scholarship and fictional chronicles that blacks' nominal legal rights have always been merely the unstable byproduct of political compromises reached among competing factions of white majority interest groups. Whites in pursuit of their interests subject blacks to "involuntary sacrifice."[56]

In the 1990s there is still cause for concern about the ascribability of legal rights to some blacks. While outright judicial denials of all legal rights for blacks is not the crisis it once was, the long-term effects of such denials remain and grow as a public crisis. Refusing legal rights to blacks in the past has contributed to creating and perpetuating a black underclass for the present. The black underclass exists in large part because of eighteenth- and nineteenth-century judicial and legislative refusals to ascribe rights readily ascribed to paradigm rightholders (propertied white males) to "new" classes of claimants. Denied legal rights, blacks were unable to develop the material and social basis for well-being or effectively combatting prejudice and racism.

The official understanding of who may have a legal right has been broadened to include blacks. However, the full practical benefits of having rights is still beyond the reach of the black underclass. Henry Shue has argued that "being socially guaranteed is probably the single most important aspect of a standard right."[57] Lower levels of compliance with the law and ineffective law enforcement in underclass communities may signal the absence of meaningful rights, partially undercutting the sense in which legal rights or equal legal rights can be meaningfully ascribed.

City dwellers know from experience that black homes and neighborhoods in the inner city are insufficiently policed to reduce the incidence of crime to tolerable levels. Crime in the inner cities gives lie to the idea of property rights and a state that is a "nightwatchman" to all groups equally. The high incidence of black-on-black crime gives lie to the existence of rights to bodily integrity. Solitude, secrecy, and autonomy are forcibly yielded as a condition of obtaining public welfare benefits, giving lie to the idea of privacy rights.

Feinberg and many other philosophers have written with eloquence about the importance to human dignity of being able to conceive of oneself as a rightholder with legitimate claims against others. Feinberg argued that having rights enables persons to stand up like men and women, to look others in the eyes, and to feel the equals of anyone.[58] Although officially endowed with a panoply of rights, many in the black underclass, because some of their important rights are nominal only, may not have the self-concept of bearers of a full compliment of basic legal rights. They dwell in the ugly version of "Nowheresville," the world of Feinberg's thought experiment where "no one, or hardly anyone . . . has rights."[59]

Justice would seem to require that blacks be brought de facto—as well as de nomine—within the realm of those who possess legal rights. The public's unwillingness to devote resources to making legal rights for the black underclass a practical reality can be viewed as evidence that the concept of blacks as rightholders has not been fully accepted. The ascription of legal rights to the poorest blacks is perhaps better viewed as in progress, rather than as fully realized.

What Does It Mean to Have a Legal Right?

The law helped to create the black underclass by denying legal rights to blacks wholesale. To this it must be added that the law serves to perpetuate the black underclass when certain philosophical conceptions of what it means to have a right are cemented into the edifice of constitutional jurisprudence.

A good example is the Supreme Court's interpretation of abortion rights after *Roe v. Wade*.[60] Unwanted children are especially burdensome to the poor. *Roe* purportedly secured reproductive autonomy, enabling poor women safely to avoid giving birth to children for whom they cannot be responsible. Studies show that when abortion is unavailable, black women are disproportionately represented among the fatal victims of self-induced and back-alley abortions.[61]

In theory, *Roe v. Wade* and subsequent cases through *Thornburgh v. American College of Obstetricians and Gynecologists*[62] firmly established a legal right under the liberty clause of the Fourteenth Amendment for all women to obtain medically safe abortions. But a few years after *Roe*, the Supreme Court in *Maher v. Roe*,[63] *Poelker v. Doe*,[64] and *Harris v. McCrae*[65] held that state and federal governments may refuse to pay for the elective abortions of poor women. The court upheld denial of Medicaid funding for abortions other than those elected by victims of rape or incest or women whose lives were at risk, even though the federal government routinely paid for poor women's prenatal care.

In *Webster v. Reproductive Health Service*,[66] a majority of the Supreme Court relied on the earlier three abortion funding cases to uphold the constitutionality of Missouri legislation prohibiting performance of abortions by state employees and at state facilities. The court appealed to the federalist argument that states are free under the Constitution to implement policy preferences against abortion. The court concluded that the Constitution does not require government to endorse, finance, or provide abortion services. Because most second- and third-trimester abortions in Missouri had been performed in a state-supported facility, the Court in *Webster* effectively ruled out two categories of abortion permitted under *Roe v. Wade* for women unable to travel to private or out-of-state facilities.

Teenage pregnancy has been cited as a major problem among the urban poor.[67] Limited access to birth control and abortion contributes to the high incidence of children giving birth to children. Nonetheless, in 1990, the Supreme Court held that states may require parental notification and judicial approval for minors' abortions.[68] Dissenting Justices Thurgood Marshall, Harry A. Blackmun, and William J. Brennan lamented the decision, arguing that the court had upheld laws premised on the false belief that minors seeking abortion come from two-parent, intact, nuclear families. Most minors voluntarily notify parents or other responsible adults of pregnancy and abortion. Minors who shun notification often come from homes where parents are ineffective, or where there is a history of violence or sexual abuse that parental notice could aggravate. Legal barriers to minors' abortions generally only delay the inevitable, and are thus a causal factor in a higher number of second- and third-trimester abortions.[69]

One way to characterize the result of the Supreme Court's abortion funding decisions is this: Poor women are denied the legal right of meaningful reproductive choice that other women enjoy. Despite the enormous interest philosophers have shown in the abortion debate, few have reacted in print to the crucial funding issue. However, relying on the distinction between negative and positive rights, George Sher devoted an article to defending the court's early abortion funding decisions. He argued that the court's holdings are consistent with the philosophically most-defensible theory of rights.[70] Debunking the idea of reproductive privacy, Sher argued that the right to abortion is better viewed as a negative right to be at liberty to obtain an abortion if one has the means, rather than as an affirmative entitlement to the means of obtaining an abortion. He also argued that no right to abortion funding exists because contraception is available and because abortion is lower on the scale of basic needs than transportation, education, and money.

The "only poison" poor women and children need is "the classic 'liberal's' main prescription for the good life—do not interfere with thy neighbor."[71] One response to Sher's "poison" is that rights as fundamental to women's autonomy as abortion rights should not be characterized as "negative" rights against unwanted interference rather than as "positive" welfare rights. According to government figures, 30 percent of all blacks and nearly 50 percent of all black children live in poverty. Given the notorious respects in which unwanted children increase the basic needs of poor households, it seems shortsighted to argue against abortion funding on the grounds that abortion is lower on the scale of basic needs.

Moreover, the Supreme Court does not take abortion rights seriously even as negative rights when it permits state legislatures to restrict reproductive autonomy severely. The clear point of all of the abortion funding statutes upheld to date by the court has been to impede poor women's access to disfavored abortions. If a substantial number of those who seek abortion may be thwarted at will by political majorities or elites, it strains the concept to refer to abortion as a *right*. Sher wrongly assumed that safe, effective contraception is available to all women. First, availability implies affordability. At an estimated cost of $300 a year and requiring a medical prescription, oral contraceptives are not universally affordable. Second, the most effective forms of contraception are oral contraceptives and subdermal implants—but neither is 100 percent effective. Moreover, neither is recommended for all women. For some women, the use of hormonal contraceptives carries significant health risks. Many physicians now recommend hormonal contraception for no more than ten of a woman's thirty fertile years. Little research is being conducted on new contraceptive alternatives, especially on male contraception. "Pro-life" politics has thus far kept RU 486, the contragestational drug one French official called the "moral property" of women, out of the American market.

In sum, the distinction between negative and positive rights does not mask the sense in which abortion funding constraints are affirmative constraints. Teenage pregnancy, medically safe abortion, and contraception are major concerns for poor black women. Some philosophers and philosophically sophisticated judges prefer to view the Constitution as "a charter of negative liberties" that "does not require the federal government or the state to provide services, even so elementary a service as maintaining law and order."[72] A philosopher concerned about the implications of law for the black underclass would have good reason to reexamine carefully arguments such as Sher's about the most defensible understanding of legal rights.

What Kinds of Legal Rights Is It Possible to Have?

Possibly, "discrimination [is] less of a factor affecting incomes now than in the past."[73] Nevertheless, inescapable poverty linked to unemployment, low wages, and limited opportunity is a central feature of the black underclass. That the "deserving poor" are fit subjects for charity is a tautology no one would bother to dispute. That the poor have a right to a national full-employment policy, better wages, or a subsistence income is controversial. The proposition is particularly controversial among those who believe adult poverty in the inner-city is largely self-inflicted. Yet, "if subsistence rights seem strange, this is more than likely because Western liberalism has had a blind spot for severe economic need."[74]

Against the strenuous objections of economic conservatives who fear waste and inefficiency, it is sometimes argued that a guaranteed subsistence income would alleviate the "cycle of poverty" that sustains the black underclass.[75] I would surmise that only a tiny percentage of legal experts in this country would argue that such an income is a constitutional right. Most lawyers would agree that while Congress could legislate or the Constitution could be amended to create a subsistence income right, no such right currently exists in the positive law.[76] Peter Edelman is the rare lawyer who has gone on record defending both a moral rights claim and a constitutional claim to a survival income for the poor.[77] Edelman argued, first, that constitutional guarantees, including the Fourteenth-Amendment guarantee of "life, liberty and due process," imply an affirmative governmental duty to provide the fundaments of well-being as a matter of substantive due process; and second, that as a matter of constitutional equal protection, our nation must make amends to the poor for its very real contributions to poverty.

Numerous discussions of the philosophical bases, if any, of welfare rights can be found in the literature.[78] Shue has defended the existence of basic subsistence rights to "unpolluted air, unpolluted water, adequate food, adequate clothing, adequate shelter, and minimum preventative public health care."[79] While some philosophers are willing to admit welfare rights, many still view them as doubtful. Some presume that because welfare rights are positive rights to goods and services they merit automatic controversy.[80] Libertarians have argued that welfare rights are inherently inconsistent with property rights, the ideal of the limited state, and economic efficiency. With the problem of the black underclass squarely before them, philosophers have good reason seriously to examine the arguments of moral philosophy and constitutional jurisprudence respecting economic welfare rights. Indeed, the failure of lawyers and judges to be convinced by arguments such as Edelman's and Shue's may go a distance to explaining why there is persistent poverty and a black underclass. Philosophers will also want to consider whether some special characteristic (e.g., deserving reparations for slavery) makes the argument for a subsistence income especially strong in the case of the African-American underclass.

As an economic rights issue, affirmative action bears more directly

on opportunities for college-bound and employed blacks than on the
fate of the black underclass.[81] For underclass blacks, education, families, health care, crime, drug abuse, and homelessness are more pressing
concerns. Nevertheless, it is worth adding here that the affirmative
action question can be viewed as another relating to the legal rights
of blacks that falls under the rubric of "what kinds of legal rights it is
possible to have."

The primary issue in the philosophical literature has been whether
distributive or compensatory principles apply to create rights and
duties of preferential treatment.[82] Against compensatory theories it has
sometimes been argued that contemporary whites cannot be attributed
duties based on the wrongs of earlier generations of whites. In a different vein, some have argued that affirmative action is justified, if at all,
only as an individual remedy and not as a group remedy, because racial
groups as such cannot have moral or constitutional rights.[83]

Closely related to the affirmative action question is the question of
government reparations to blacks for slavery. Reparations are seldom
proposed as solutions to the problems of the underclass, although cash
grants could conceivably aid isolated families or individuals in their
efforts to escape poverty. The major nonutilitarian argument of principle against black reparations is that the only deserving victims of
reparations for slavery are the deceased men and women who were actually enslaved. Cross-generational rights are rejected in connection with
reparations, much as cross-generational rights and duties are sometimes rejected in connection with affirmative action.

Conclusion

Barriers to the elimination of the black underclass include conceptual
barriers relating to how society thinks about legal rights. Rights discourse conveys that public and private actors have serious, if not compelling, obligations to others. Once denied virtually all the legal rights
whites enjoyed, blacks are now nominally whites' legal peers. Yet legal
rights continue to be interpreted by mainstream courts, theorists, and
the general public in ways that deny validity to blacks' claims and deny
urgency to alleviating the problems of the black underclass.

The paramount task for sympathetic rights theorists is to grapple
with the substance of exclusive rights-ascription theories and practices.
Assumptions about legal rights that I have identified—namely, that
"official" ascription is meaningful possession; that fundamental constitutional rights are "negative" liberties; and that there can be no eco-

nomic welfare rights, group compensatory rights, or cross-generational group rights to reparations—are useful starting points for philosophical reconsideration of the nature and extent of the legal rights of the black underclass. No guarantee can be given that active reconsideration by numerous theorists would yield reconceptualization, or that academic reconceptualization would in turn soon yield material improvement. Nevertheless, effort on behalf of the black underclass to show that current conceptions of rights are not the straightforward product of irrefragable logic, maximally astute interpretation, and moral vision is effort well spent.

NOTES

1. Joel Feinberg, "The Nature and Value of Rights," *Journal of Value Inquiry* 4 (Winter 1970): 243.

2. See, for example, Alan R. White, *Rights* (Oxford: Clarendon Press, 1984); Jeremy Waldron, ed., *Theories of Rights* (New York: Oxford University Press, 1984); A. I. Melden, *Rights and Persons* (Berkeley: University of California Press, 1980); Joel Feinberg, ed., *Rights, Justice and the Bounds of Liberty* (Princeton: Princeton University Press, 1980); and David Lyons, ed., *Rights* (Belmont, Calif.: Wadsworth Publishing, 1979).

3. Black legal scholars who have raised doubts about rights include Kimberlie Crenshaw, "Race, Reform and Retrenchment: Transformation and Legitimation in Antidiscrimination Law," *Harvard Law Review* 101 (1988): 1331; Christopher Edley, "Affirmative Action and the Rights Rhetoric Trap," in *The Moral Foundations of Civil Rights*, ed. Robert K. Fullinwider and Claudia Mills (Totowa, N.J.: Rowman and Littlefield, 1986), pp. 56–76; and Girardeaux Spann, "Secret Rights," *Minnesota Law Review* 71 (1987): 669.

4. Douglas G. Glasgow, *The Black Underclass* (San Francisco: Jossey-Bass Publishers, 1980), pp. 3–11.

5. William Julius Wilson, "Studying Inner-City Social Dislocation: The Challenge of Public Agenda Research," *American Sociological Review* 56 (February 1991): 1–14. In this chapter I use the familiar term "black underclass" as a rough synonym for "persistently poor blacks such as live in major urban centers of the Northeast and Midwest." As Wilson notes, some have urged abandoning the term as imprecise and stigmatizing. However, my present effort does not require the precision of quantitative social science, and I do not intend by use of the term "underclass" to imply that poor blacks are undeserving.

6. William Julius Wilson, *The Truly Disadvantaged* (Chicago: University of Chicago Press, 1987).

7. See National Urban League, *The State of Black America 1989* (New York: National Urban League, 1989). See also National Urban League, *The*

State of Black America 1991 (New York: National Urban League, 1991). Hereafter, unless otherwise noted, I will rely upon U.S. Bureau of Labor Statistics, U.S. Bureau of the Census, and other federal government figures cited in *The State of Black America 1989*; *The State of Black America 1991*; *Runta* 2 and 3 (1989–90), a monthly newsletter published by the National Urban League Research Department; and the National Urban League Research Department's *Quarterly Report on the African American Worker*, Reports 25 and 26 (1990).

8. In 1989, 30.7 percent of blacks lived in households with incomes below the poverty level, compared to 10 percent of whites; black children had a poverty rate of 43.2 percent, compared to 14 percent for white children; and 46.5 percent of black female-headed families had poverty level incomes, compared to 25.4 percent for white. Black per capita income has averaged three-fifths of white per capita income since 1989. In 1990, an estimated 11 percent of the black population was unemployed, compared to 4.5 percent of the white population.

9. In 1985, 18.2 black infants died per thousand live births, compared to 9.3 deaths for white infants. In 1990, more than half of all black children lived with their mothers only, compared to less than a quarter of all white children. A 1986 report showed that the high school completion rate for black students was 76.4 percent, compared to 83.1 percent for white. By 1990, the high school drop-out rate for black boys and girls was 16 percent, compared to 10 percent to 12 percent for whites. In 1985, only 26 percent of black high school graduates went on to college. In 1990, black women accounted for only 5.2 percent of all college and university students, 3 percent of all baccalaureate degree graduates, and 1.8 percent of all doctoral degree recipients.

10. Homicide is the leading cause of death for black males aged 15–24 years. Although blacks make up about 5.9 percent of the U.S. population, nearly 50 percent of prison inmates in 1990 were black. Nearly one-fourth of black males are either in jail, in prison, or on probation on any given day. In 1986, 33.4 per thousand of the black population over the age of twelve were victims of violent crimes, compared to 27.5 per thousand of the white population. In 1986, there were 634 deaths per one hundred thousand of the black population between the ages of 45 and 54, compared to 319 per one hundred thousand for the white population.

11. The Reverend Jesse Jackson campaigned for the Democratic national presidential nomination in 1984 and 1988. Ron Brown, who directed Jackson's 1988 presidential campaign, became head of the Democratic National Party in early 1989. In the same year, Congressman William H. Gray from Pennsylvania was chosen as House majority whip.

12. In 1989, approximately 24 of 535 members of Congress and 50 federal judges were black. President George Bush appointed a black, Dr. Louis Sullivan, as secretary of the U.S. Department of Health and Human Services. Bush appointed black four-star general Colin L. Powell as chairman of the Joint Chiefs of Staff.

13. For example, in 1985, it was estimated that 90 percent of the full-time faculty in higher education were white and 4.1 percent were black.

14. A 1982 survey of minority-owned businesses revealed that 301,000 businesses were owned by blacks, compared to 14,315,000 businesses owned by whites. A 1984 study reported that 97 percent of all newspaper news executives were white, and 60 percent of the nation's daily newspapers employed no minority journalists. Additionally, blacks owned less than 2 percent of the licensed and operating radio and television stations. A 1985 study showed that blacks owned less than 0.9 percent of the nation's 1,138 commercial television stations, only 0.3 percent of the 15,647 cable television stations, and only 1.5 percent of the nation's 8,996 commercial radio stations.

15. A national survey showed that 31 percent of a random sample of Americans polled agree that "Blacks come from a less able race and this explains why blacks are not as well off as whites in America" (Paul A. Sniderman and Michael Gray Hagen, *Race and Inequality: A Study in American Values* [Chatham, N.J.: Chatham House Publishers, 1985], p. 30).

16. University of Wisconsin law professor Patricia Williams has described being refused admittance to a popular retail boutique in Manhattan, New York because of her race (black). See her "Spirit-Murdering the Messenger: The Discourse of Fingerpointing as the Law's Response to Racism," *University of Miami Law Review* 42 (1987): 127–28.

17. See Kenneth L. Karst, "Citizenship, Race, and Marginality," *William and Mary Law Review* 30 (Fall 1988): 1, for a discussion of the constitutional dimensions of "the conditions of human life among the marginalized poor in our urban ghettos."

18. Dred Scott v. Sanford, 60 U.S. (19 How.) 393 (1857).

19. U.S. Constitution, Amendment XIII, Article 1 provides that "neither slavery nor involuntary servitude, except as a punishment for crime whereof the party shall have been duly convicted, shall exist within the United States, or any place subject to their jurisdiction." See also U.S. Constitution, Amendment XIV, Article 1, providing that "all persons born or naturalized in the United States, and subject to the jurisdiction thereof, are citizens of the United States and of the State wherein they reside. No State shall make or enforce any law which shall abridge the privileges or immunities of citizens of the United States; nor shall any State deprive any person of life, liberty, or property, without due process of law; nor deny to any person within its jurisdiction the equal protection of the laws." Far from successful in establishing the black franchise when first ratified, U.S. Constitution, Amendment XV, provides that "the right of citizens of the United States to vote shall not be denied or abridged by the United States or by any state on account of race, color, or previous condition of servitude."

20. The Civil Rights Act of 1866 stated that as citizens of the United States blacks "shall have the same right . . . as is enjoyed by white citizens," including the right to contract and to own property. The 1870 act added criminal penalties to the 1866 act and was designed principally to protect the right

to vote as set forth in the Fifteenth Amendment. The 1871 so-called Ku Klux Klan act established civil liabilities for the deprivation of rights "under color of" state law. The 1875 act, later invalidated in the Civil Rights Cases, 109 U.S. 3 (1883), addressed racial discrimination in public accommodations.

21. 163 U.S. 537 (1896).

22. Brown v. Board of Education of Topeka, 347 U.S. 483 (1954), 349 U.S. 294 (1955).

23. The Civil Rights Act of 1964 contained new voting rights provisions and dealt with desegregation of schools and places of public accommodation. The Voting Rights Act was adopted in 1965. The Civil Rights Act of 1968 declared that it is national policy "to provide, within constitutional limits, for fair housing throughout the United States."

24. See, for example, Swann v. Charlotte–Mecklenberg Board of Education, 402 U.S. 1 (1971).

25. Regents of the University of California v. Bakke, 438 U.S. 265 (1978), upheld an affirmative action plan in medical school admissions; United Steel Workers v. Weber, 443 U.S. 193 (1979), upheld a private employer's affirmative action plan.

26. The Supreme Court upheld civil rights and affirmative action principles in cases including Wygant v. Jackson Board of Education, 476 U.S. 267 (1986); Sheet Metal Workers International Association v. EEOC, 478 U.S. 421 (1986); Johnson v. Transportation Agency, 480 U.S. 616 (1987); and United States v. Paradise, 480 U.S. 149 (1987).

However, as Justice Blackmun observed in his dissenting opinion in Wards Cove Packing Co. v. Antonio in 1989, 490 U.S. 642 (1989), the court has taken "major strides backwards in the battle against race discrimination." Recent cases some commentators view as setbacks to civil rights and affirmative action principles include Martin v. Wilks, 110 S. Ct. 11 (1989); Richmond v. Croson, 488 U.S. 469 (1989); Lorance v. AT&T Technologies, Inc., 490 U.S. 900 (1989); Jett v. Dallas Independent School District, 491 U.S. 701 (1989); and Patterson v. McLean Credit Union, 491 U.S. 164 (1989).

27. The Aid for Dependent Children (AFDC) budget cuts enacted in 1981 removed 400,000 working poor families from the rolls and reduced AFDC benefits for another 300,000 families. Federal spending for food stamps was cut by 15 percent between fiscal years 1981 and 1987. Blacks comprised 40 percent of the recipients of these programs.

In 1989, the State of New York announced plans to cut Medicaid spending available to its 2.3 million poorest residents by $50 million. The state expended $11 billion on Medicaid in 1988 ("To Control Costs, New York Is Planning to Limit Medicaid," *New York Times*, August 17, 1989, p. 1, col. 5).

28. See 42 U.S.C. 1395 (1982) (Medicare); 42 U.S.C. 601 (1982) (AFDC); 42 U.S.C. 1396(a) (1982) (Medicaid); 7 U.S.C.S. Sec. 2013 et. seq. (1990) (Title 7, food stamps). The Census Bureau reported in 1985 that 19 percent of all households in the United States received benefits from need-based programs such as food stamps, subsidized housing, and Medicaid.

29. See Sniderman and Hagen, *Race and Inequality*, p. 30. Fifty-five percent of the group polled agreed that "God made the races different"; 69 percent agreed that "if blacks would only try harder, they could be just as well off as whites"; 52 percent agreed that blacks "teach their children values and skills different from those required to be successful in American Society"; and 31 percent agreed that "blacks come from a less able race."

30. Law professor Kenneth L. Karst attributes the persistence of urban poverty to the inadequacy of existing law and to the ease of excluding the poor from our understanding of who counts ("Citizenship, Race and Marginality," *William and Mary Law Review* 30 [1988]: 1).

31. Hans Kelsen, *Pure Theory of Law* (Berkeley: University of California Press, 1967); idem, *General Theory of Law and State* (Cambridge, Mass.: Harvard University Press, 1945); and John Chipman Gray, *The Nature and Sources of Law*, ed. Bernard D. Reams, Jr. (1921; reprint, Buffalo: W. S. Hein, 1983–84).

32. Theories of both moral and legal rights presuppose theories of rights-ascription. The problem of responding to questions about why we ascribe or refuse to ascribe moral rights presents a fundamental challenge to any rights theory. The inability of a theory to respond to questions of ascription may be evidence that rights are phantoms or theorizing about them pointless. Until theorists get a grip on puzzling cases of questions of ascription involving the rights of the dead, fetuses, animals, species, the mentally incompetent, plants, and future generations, they cannot be said to grasp any coherent concept of a right at all. See Joel Feinberg, "The Rights of Animals and Unborn Generations," in *Responsibilities to Future Generations: Environmental Ethics*, ed. Ernest Partridge (Buffalo, N.Y.: Prometheus Books, 1981), pp. 139, 140.

It is sometimes assumed that moral and legal rights share theoretical properties; that is, both can be waived, alienated, claimed, forfeited, and so on. Moral rights are also sometimes depicted as the basis of the law, meaning that we can appeal to them to characterize, justify, criticize, or invalidate positive law. If moral rights are in some sense the basis of law, the conclusions philosophers reach about the proper ascription of moral rights will be relevant to jurisprudence. In venturing such conclusions one must be mindful that the practice of moral rights–ascription and the practice of legal rights–ascription have important differences. We are all equally able to assert that someone has a moral right or lacks it; we are also able to assert that someone has a legal right or lacks it. But only certain courts, politicians and bureaucrats have the special powers to imbue having a legal right with practical meaning.

33. See Mark Tushnet, *The American Law of Slavery, 1810–1860: Considerations of Humanity and Interest* (Princeton: Princeton University Press, 1981).

34. See, for example, Michael Tooley, *Abortion and Infanticide* (Oxford: Clarendon Press, 1983); Tom Regan and Peter Singer, eds., *Animal Rights and Human Obligations* (Englewood Cliffs, N.J.: Prentice-Hall, 1976).

35. H.L.A. Hart, *The Concept of Law* (Oxford: Clarendon Press, 1961), pp. 78–79.

36. Ibid., p. 92.

37. Ibid., p. 92.

38. Ibid., p. 139.

39. Hart wrote: "The connection between the institution and the paradigms of the day will be . . . intimate. . . . Someone who rejects a paradigm will seem to be making an extraordinary kind of mistake. . . . Paradigms anchor interpretations, but no paradigm is secure from challenge by a new interpretation that accounts for other paradigms better and leaves that one isolated as a mistake" (ibid., p. 72).

40. Ronald Dworkin, *Taking Rights Seriously* (Cambridge, Mass.: Harvard University Press, 1977), pp. 81–130.

41. Ronald Dworkin, *Law's Empire* (Cambridge, Mass.: Belknap Press, 1986), p. 152.

42. According to Dworkin: "Each judge's interpretative theories are grounded in his own convictions about the "point"—the justifying purpose or goal or principle—of legal practice as a whole. . . . Law as integrity asks judges to assume, so far as this possible, that the law is structured by a coherent set of principles about justice and fairness and procedural due process, and asks them to enforce these in the fresh cases that come before them, so that each person's situation is fair and just according to the same standards" (ibid., pp. 88, 243).

43. Ibid., pp. 387–97.

44. Ibid., p. 402. Dworkin hints that Hercules might sacrifice the consistency of ascribing adult rights to children to political fairness.

45. Dworkin, *Taking Rights Seriously*, p. 125.

46. Even Dworkin's extensive discussion in *Law's Empire* of the snail darter case did not bring out some of the most interesting issues of rights-ascription the case brings to mind. In TVA v. Hill, 437 U.S. 153 (1977), the court had to decide whether the fact that a multimillion-dollar federally funded dam project was substantially complete and subsequently refunded at and beyond the time endangered species legislation went into effect entailed that the project should continue notwithstanding the loss of the snail darter's presumably unique habitat. The case raised a question of rights-ascription that forces direct comparisons of the relative values of costly human projects and animal survival. If having a serious right is having a trump against arguments of social utility, there is a sense in which the little perch known as the snail darter has been effectively ascribed rights, albeit indirectly, by the Supreme Court.

47. His critics commonly suggest that the formal guidance Dworkin gives is useless, since no judge and no court could be expected to view decisions as an interpretative reconciliation of principles embodied in the legal system as a whole.

48. Stone maintained that few distinctly legal barriers obstruct the ascription of legal rights beyond paradigm rightholders. The more daunting barriers, he argued, are extralegal, moral barriers, chiefly in the form of pervasive "monistic" moral theories that preclude the complex reasoning needed for plausible inclusion of nonhumans into the moral realm. Whatever one may

think of Stone's idiosyncratic moral pluralism as an alternative to monistic utilitarian or rights-based theories, it would seem that he dismissed too quickly the possibility that reasons of legal value and precedent internal to law can limit the ascription of legal rights in principle.

49. Environmental philosopher Brian G. Norton influenced my characterization of Stone's arguments as "instrumental."

50. Christopher D. Stone, "Should Trees Have Standing? Toward Legal Rights for Natural Objects," *Southern California Law Review* 45 (1972): 450; idem, *Earth and Other Ethics: The Case for Moral Pluralism* (New York: Harper and Row, 1987). According to Stone: "Issues regarding the legal status of 'things' other than individual normal persons crop up all the time. . . . Can a defective newborn have 'rights' assertable against its parents? Can a fetus have rights? A robot? . . . [Can] the unborn? . . . [Can] a *people* or a *nation*[?] . . . [Can] a corporation?" (ibid., p. 12).

51. Stone may have been implicitly assuming the prescriptive perspective of the legal realist or what Dworkin in *Law's Empire* terms the "pragmatist." Realism and pragmatism assert that courts should not approach adjudication as though their hands were tied by preestablished formal rules or past political acts that do not coincide with norms of independent validity.

52. See, for example, Feinberg, "The Rights of Animals," p. 140. Feinberg asserted that "normal adult human beings, then, are obviously the sort of beings of whom rights can meaningfully be predicated." Compare Stone, *Earth and Other Ethics*, pp. 12, 20, who presumes that individual normal persons are unproblematic rightholders.

Where normal adult human beings are treated as "paradigm" rightholders, by implication, the rights status of children, the unborn, and the disabled is deemed a legitimate subject of controversy, along with the rights status of animal and plant life, the environment, and future generations.

53. See Neil MacCormick, "Children's Rights: A Test-Case for Theories of Rights," in his collected works, *Legal Right and Social Democracy* (Oxford: Clarendon Press, 1982), p. 154.

54. See, for example, Spann, "Secret Rights"; and Mark Tushnet, "An Essay on Rights," *Texas Law Review* 62 (1984)· 1363.

55. Philosophical questions bearing on how to explain, justify, or remedy the political, economic, and social problems of underclass blacks are carefully examined in Ellen Frankel Paul et al., *Equal Opportunity* (New York: Basil Blackwell, 1987).

56. Derrick A. Bell, *Race, Racism and American Law*, 2d ed. (Boston: Little, Brown and Co., 1980), pp. 7–8, 29–30; and idem, *And We Are Not Saved: The Elusive Search for Racial Justice* (New York: Basic Books, 1987).

57. Henry Shue, *Basic Rights: Subsistence, Affluence, and U.S. Foreign Policy* (Princeton: Princeton University Press, 1980), p. 16.

58. Feinberg, "The Nature and Value of Rights," 243.

59. Ibid.

60. 410 U.S. 113 (1973).

61. The implications of limited access to abortion for poor and minority

women were detailed in the brief *amici curiae* filed with the U.S. Supreme
Court in Webster v. Reproductive Health Services, 88–605 (October Term
1988) by the Center for Constitutional Rights on behalf of more than a
hundred minority organizations.

62. 476 U.S. 747 (1986).
63. 432 U.S. 464 (1977).
64. 432 U.S. 519 (1977).
65. 448 U.S. 297 (1980).
66. 5492 U.S. 490 (1989).
67. However, the highest fertility rate for black females occurs, not among
teenagers, but among adults age twenty to twenty-four. Still, the fertility rate
for black females between ten and nineteen years of age is triple that of whites.
National Urban League, *Runta* 2, no. 2 (1989): 2.
68. See Hodgson v. Minnesota, 110 S. Ct. 2926 (1990); and Ohio v.
Akron Center for Reproductive Health, 110 S. Ct. 2972 (1990).
69. Anita L. Allen, "Court Disables Disputed Legacy of Privacy Right,"
National Law Journal 12 (August 13, 1990): S8.
70. George Sher, "Subsidized Abortion: Moral Rights and Moral Compromise," *Philosophy and Public Affairs* 10 (Fall 1981): 361.
71. Shue, *Basic Rights*, p. 19.
72. Bowers v. DeVito, 689 F.2d 616, 618 (7th Cir. 1982) (R. Posner, J.).
73. June Ellenoff O'Neill, "Discrimination and Income Inequality," in
Ellen Frankel Paul et al., *Equal Opportunity*, pp. 169–87.
74. Shue, *Basic Rights*, p. 27.
75. But see Richard Allen Epstein, *Takings: Private Property and the Power
of Eminent Domain* (Cambridge, Mass.: Harvard University Press, 1985).
76. Frank Michelman, "In Pursuit of Constitutional Welfare Rights: One
View of Rawls' Theory of Justice," *University of Pennsylvania Law Review* 121
(1973): 962; and idem, "Welfare Rights in a Constitutional Democracy,"
Washington University Law Quarterly 1979, no. 3 (1979): 659.
77. Peter B. Edelman, "The Next Century of Our Constitution: Rethink-
ing Our Duty to the Poor," *Hastings Law Journal* 39 (1987): 1.
78. A systematic discussion of the law and philosophy of welfare rights is
presented in Carl Wellman, *Welfare Rights* (Totowa, N.J.: Rowman and Little-
field, 1982). See also Rea Bruno, "John Locke: Between Charity and Welfare
Rights," *Journal of Social Philosophy* 18 (Fall 1987): 13; and Rodney Peffer, "A
Defense of Rights of Well-being," *Philosophy and Public Affairs* 6 (1976): 58.
Useful discussions of welfare rights to health and income include Loren E.
Lomasky, "Medical Progress and National Health Care," *Philosophy and Public
Affairs* 10 (Winter 1981): 65 nn. 1–2, 66 n. 3, 76; Allen E. Buchanan, "The
Right to a Decent Minimum of Health Care," *Philosophy and Public Affairs* 13
(Winter 1984): 55; and Norman Daniels, "Fair Equality of Opportunity and
Decent Minimums: A Reply to Buchanan," *Philosophy and Public Affairs* 14
(Winter 1985): 106.
79. Shue, *Basic Rights*, p. 23.
80. "Of course, since welfare rights are positive rights—are rights not

merely to be left alone but rather to be provided with goods and services, their very existence is a matter of controversy" (Sher, "Subsidized Abortion," 363).

81. Mainstream philosophers have focused on the justice of affirmative action much more than on the justice of, for example, a subsistence income. This is no doubt because controversial affirmative action policies have actually been implemented and litigated, whereas subsistence income policies have the character of wistful or "radical" thinking. In addition, academic philosophers often have personal or institutional experiences with affirmative action policies, but no similarly direct contact with efforts to address the problems of the black underclass.

82. For example, see Marshall Cohen, Thomas Nagel, and Thomas Scanlon, eds., *Equality and Preferential Treatment* (Princeton: Princeton University Press, 1977); Robert K. Fullinwider, *The Reverse Discrimination Controversy: A Moral and Legal Analysis* (Totowa, N.J.: Rowman and Littlefield, 1980); and Kent Greenawalt, *Discrimination and Reverse Discrimination* (New York: Alfred A. Knopf, 1983). Compare Bernard Boxhill, *Blacks and Social Justice* (Totowa, N.J.: Rowman and Allanheld, 1984).

83. See Owen Fiss, "Groups and the Equal Protection Clause," *Philosophy and Public Affairs* 5 (1976): 107; and Richard Delgado, "The Imperial Scholar: A Review of Civil Rights Literature," *University of Pennsylvania Law Review* 132 (1984): 561, citing Casteneda v. Partida, 430 U.S. 482, 494, 496, which holds that Mexican Americans are a group for purposes of class-based legal relief. See also Patricia Williams, "Alchemical Notes: Reconstructing Ideals for Deconstructed Rights," *Harvard Civil Rights and Civil Liberties Law Review* 22 (1987): 401, 412–13.

8   Affirmative Action and the Urban Underclass

Albert G. Mosley

IN THIS CHAPTER I review some recent attacks made against affirmative action by prominent African-American scholars. These scholars approach the problem of the urban black underclass from both conservative and liberal perspectives and advocate commensurately different solutions. Notwithstanding, each has argued that race-specific policies are inappropriate and ineffective in alleviating the plight of the urban black underclass. Focusing on the works of Thomas Sowell, Glenn Loury, and William Julius Wilson, I attempt to show that, despite their differences, they share a misguided view of the proper role of affirmative action policies in eliminating the effects of slavery and segregation.

Thomas Sowell and Affirmative Action

In his book *Civil Rights: Rhetoric or Reality*[1] Sowell makes a sharp distinction between activities meant to bring about "equal opportunity" and activities meant to bring about "affirmative action." Equal opportunity activities, instituted with the *Brown v. Board of Education* Supreme Court decision, are meant to abolish legal and social barriers to educational, employment, and political opportunities and to guarantee that individuals be able to maximize their benefits without being penalized for race, sex, religion, or ethnic background. Affirmative action activities are predicated on the view that the accumulated disadvantages of institutional racism make it more difficult for African Americans to compete on the basis of merit alone; therefore, affirmative action activities are designed to offset such disadvantages. For Sowell, the move from equal opportunity to affirmative action is equivalent to the difference between proscribing discrimination and insuring equal representation.

140

He expresses sympathy for the plight of African Americans and the uniqueness of the injuries they have sustained under slavery, segregation, and racism. He objects, however, to the tendency to generalize from the African-American situation to any group that finds itself underrepresented in a particular field. He illustrates the fallacy in such generalizations as follows: "Even if A is known to cause Z, we still cannot infer A whenever we find Z, if B, C, etc. also cause Z."[2] This means that many statistical disparities involving Asian, Italian, Irish, German, and other ethnic groups in America cannot be ascribed to discriminatory practices, but may instead derive from cultural patterns that preceded that group's presence in America.

Sowell's point is well taken. But by focusing on the truth of his general thesis, he shifts our attention away from the particular case of African Americans and the fact that discriminatory practices have been an important factor in their overrepresentation among the least well off.

Sowell argues that differences in ability or skill between two groups need not derive from discriminatory policies favoring one group over the other, but rather may derive from cultural patterns that have been passed from generation to generation. He cites black West Indians living in the United States, whose attainments tend to exceed those of American-born blacks, as evidence that racial discrimination is not the sole or even primary determinant of achievement—since black West Indians are presumably subject to the same discriminatory practices as American-born blacks.

Of course, Sowell is aware of the "selective migration" explanation of why certain immigrant groups achieve far above the norm for native-born groups,[3] and it is not clear why he does not elaborate on it. Selective migration is the phenomenon in which the most highly motivated, skilled, and intelligent members of a population migrate to another location and are better able to exploit opportunities there than groups already present. Initially, southern blacks who migrated to the north often did much better than blacks already residing there, and West Indian immigrants to the United States often have done better than African Americans born here because the educational and/or motivational levels of such 'immigrant' groups were generally much higher than those of the residents they encountered.

Sowell acknowledges the special case of African Americans and suggests that his approach is meant to dissuade spurious claims based only on the existence of statistical disparities. But his treatment of African Americans does not focus on the debilitating effects of slavery, segregation, and unequal treatment justified by racism. Instead he argues that, just as cultural differences may account for many disparities in wealth between well-off and disadvantaged blacks, so cultural differences may account for many of the disparities in wealth that exist between black and white communities. By so arguing, he effectively nullifies his acceptance of African Americans as a "special case."

Glenn Loury and Affirmative Action

In his essay "Why Should We Care about Group Inequality?"[4] Loury continues Sowell's attempt to assimilate differences between African-American and European-American communities to class differences between African Americans. "Why should the mere existence of group disparities evidence the oppressive treatment of individuals?" Loury asks. "There is little support in the historical record for the notion that, in the absence of oppression based upon group membership, all socially relevant aggregates of persons would achieve roughly the same distribution of economic rewards."[5]

Loury and Sowell proceed by cleverly constructing a pseudo-issue, which they then discredit. That pseudo-issue is the false generalization that all group disparities are the result of discriminatory practices. By disproving that generalization, Sowell and Loury are able to cast doubt upon the legitimacy of citing discrimination as the principle cause of Afro-American overrepresentation among the least well off. But clearly the claim that the striking economic, educational, and political disparities between Euro- and Afro-American achievements are the result of historical oppression is not the claim that all disparities between any two groups result from the oppression of one group by the other.

By means of this sleight of hand, Loury proposes "to shift our focus from disparities among groups per se to disparities in the rewards to the different types of activities toward which various groups' members incline."[6] His claim, as I understand it, is that members of the underclass reap certain kinds of rewards for the kinds of activities they are inclined towards, though those rewards might provide no monetary benefits and indeed might involve economic penalties.

But instead of explicating this claim, Loury proceeds to a scathing ad hominem: "Why is inequality among individuals of the same group acceptable when inequality between the groups is not?"[7] Again Loury does not spell out the implications of his rhetorical question. He appears to be asking why inequality between wealthy and poor African Americans should be acceptable when inequality between European and African Americans is not. And if wealthy blacks are not willing to redistribute their incomes to poor blacks, why should whites be willing to redistribute their advantages to blacks? Loury offers no answer to this question, but this does not mean there is no satisfactory response. Intragroup differences in wealth derive from different causes than intergroup differences. The historical fact is that the wealth transferred from blacks to whites is of substantially different kind and quantity than the wealth transferred from poor blacks to well-off blacks. Americans of African descent had their wealth appropriated by their masters under slavery, and after slavery they were legally excluded from educational and employment benefits available to Euro-American ethnic groups. Thus, slavery and segregation are causes of intergroup differences that have no parallels in intragroup differences between African Americans.

There will always be some group on the bottom, Loury proposes, but the fact that they are on the bottom is not necessarily a result of their having been oppressed: "there is 'group inequality' whenever there is inequality—one need only take those at the bottom to constitute a 'group.'"[8] And if the underrepresentation of whites in college and professional basketball is not a moral problem, then why is the underrepresentation of blacks in professions requiring sophisticated mathematics a moral problem?

Again, Loury does not pursue the questions he raises. Yet it is clear that such questions need discussion. To illustrate, I would argue that the underrepresentation of whites in professional basketball relative to blacks is not a moral problem because such underrepresentation has negligible effects on the well-being of whites as a group. On the other hand, the underrepresentation of blacks in professions requiring sophisticated verbal, mathematical, and manual skills places serious limits on their ability to take advantage of the employment opportunities typical of the current workplace. This, in turn, has very serious effects on the well-being of blacks as a group.

Loury acknowledges that a capitalist economy would perpetuate the results of past racial discrimination, even if discrimination were totally eliminated in the present. "We cannot expect *laissez faire* to produce equality of results between equally endowed social groups if these groups have experienced differential treatment in the past," he writes. Thus, "state action . . . is *legitimated* by the claim that, in its absence, the consequences of historical wrongs could be with us for the ages. It is necessitated by the fact that individuals, in the course of their private social intercourse, engage in racial distinctions which have material consequences."[9]

But given this admission, Loury merely proceeds to reiterate that not all acts of racial discrimination should be rectified by state action:

> A black woman . . . does not have an opportunity equal to that of a white woman to become the wife of a given white man. . . . Since white men are on the whole better-off financially than blacks, one could imagine calculating the monetary damages to black women of this kind of racial discrimination. . . . That such a notion strikes most people as absurd is mere testimony for the fact that we all basically accept the legitimacy of the practice of racial discrimination in the intimate, personal sphere.[10]

This example, however, is not as transparent as Loury makes it out to be. Even if it is granted that the notion "of calculating the monetary damages to black women" of their inability to become the wives of white men appears absurd, that is no proof that it is absurd. Black women have not benefited from the access white men have had to them in the way that white women have benefited from similar access. Black women and their mulatto children have not received inheritances from the estates of white men in any degree comparable to that which white women and their children have. Just because many might deny compensation for this at first glance does not mean that the claim is morally absurd. And even if compensation were refused, dissimilar rewards for similar service would still be morally wrong.

That I might prefer straight-haired to curly-haired people is a personal preference that I am entitled to. But my preference cannot allow me to exclude curly-haired people from equal educational, employment, and inheritance opportunities. As Ronald Dworkin emphasizes (in distinguishing internal and external preferences), such intrusions of the private into the public sphere, even if they cannot be eliminated altogether, are what civil rights laws are meant to prohibit.[11]

Loury rejects the view that affirmative action is a form of restitution for the wrongs committed against African Americans through slavery and segregation. He asks: "Why do the wrongs of this particular group and not those of others deserve recompense? . . . No amount of recounting the unique sufferings attendant to the slave experience makes plain why a middle-class black should be offered an educational opportunity which is being denied to a lower-class white."[12]

Here again, Loury shifts the focus from why African Americans deserve restitution to the question of why a middle-class African American should get preferential access to some valued opportunity over a lower-class Euro-American. Clearly, these questions are not equivalent. One can certainly believe that African Americans deserve restitution, yet not believe that a middle-class person deserves an advantage over a lower-class person merely because the former is black and the latter is white. The kind and amount of restitution necessarily varies with the kind and degree of harm suffered. To cite an extreme example, some African Americans may have profited from racial discrimination and passed that profit on to their progeny. Why should such persons, having inherited wealth through the restrictions imposed upon other blacks, be provided with entitlements as restitution? Clearly, race should not be a sufficient condition for the receipt of employment and educational opportunities as restitution for harm from slavery and segregation. At best, race could be considered only a necessary condition for restitution, in so far as Africans were the principle victims of slavery and segregation.

Loury stacks the deck by posing his question as one between a middle-class black and a lower-class white. One wonders why it is not posed in the more likely case of a middle-class black being given preference over a middle-class white, or a lower-class black being given preference over a lower-class white. Other things being equal, race might determine a preference in such cases. But this would in no way "devalue the injustices endured by others."[13] It would, however, recognize that Americans of African descent have historically had their interests sacrificed to the interests of European-American ethnic groups, and that some redress of this situation is necessary.[14] The advantages accruing to whites at the expense of blacks have produced a sizable deficit in the black community, and that is a debt that should be acknowledged. African Americans are owed restitution in order to correct for the historical transfer of wealth from the African-American community to the Euro-American community.[15]

While insisting that affirmative action is just, it is also possible to acknowledge that "affirmative action is . . . doomed to be controversial . . . should it . . . continue to favor blacks of comfortable social backgrounds over whites of more modest circumstances."[16] Indeed, I argue above that affirmative action used in this way shows neither political nor moral wisdom.

Loury categorically denies, however, that restitution is owed for the deprivations of slavery and segregation. He writes: "The evocation of slavery in our contemporary discourse has little to do with sociology, or with historical causation. Its main effect is moral. It uses the slave experience in order to establish culpability."[17] But if Loury considers slavery historically irrelevant, then even more irrelevant must be the Jim Crow and legal segregation that replaced slavery. This suggests that African Americans have suffered no greater hardships than that of any other ethnic group that has come to the United States.

Of course, there are advantages to ignoring the distinctiveness of the African-American experience. By so doing, it is possible to deny that European Americans have benefited from the subjugation of African Americans, and that they continue to benefit from the advantages accruing from that subjugation. The belief that every group has suffered hardships and that every group should be able, through its unassisted efforts, to achieve equity requires a studied ignorance of the peculiar exploitation suffered by African Americans. Slavery and segregation transferred labor value and professional opportunities from African-American to European-American groups, and the effect of this transfer continues to manifest itself.

Loury worries that "preferential selection will undermine the ability of those preferred to garner for themselves the honorary, as distinct from pecuniary, benefits associated with the employment."[18] But we can expect this only if the presumption already exists that the person preferentially selected is incompetent for the job. To illustrate, the boss's son does not feel that the advantages his hereditary status confers on him suggest his incompetence. On the contrary, being the boss's son is taken as conferring a right to expect preferential treatment. Likewise, the preference shown for European Americans over African Americans under slavery and segregation was not interpreted as indicating less competence on the part of the former. Europeans did not believe they needed some kind of unfair advantage to compete with Africans. Rather, being a European was taken as indicative of a right to preferential treatment over Africans. These examples are meant to show that how one takes preferential treatment depends on the perspective from which one approaches it. Clearly, Loury approaches preferential treatment from a perspective that gives benefit to the prevailing doubt as to African-American competence. He thus reinforces the view that African Americans have only themselves to blame for their fate.[19]

Loury ignores the fact that lack of opportunity is likely if past racial discrimination has created a situation in which it is rational to discriminate. As a result of policies designed to limit black educational and employment opportunities, blacks are generally less qualified than whites. Thus, on the basis of race alone, an employer would come out better hiring whites rather than blacks. To illustrate, on a scale of one to ten, if whites score above five 70 percent of the time while blacks score above five only 50 percent of the time, then in every ten blacks hired, we can expect five of them to score below five, while of every ten whites hired, we can expect only three to score below five. A 20 percent difference is generally something any firm would want to exploit. And if ten percent of the blacks and, say, 15 percent of the whites score above a nine, it is even more profitable for the employer to discriminate. Civil rights legislation is designed to make it costly rather than prudent for employers to discriminate openly, and affirmative action is one means of offsetting covert discrimination that continues to manifest itself. Loury, I conclude, affirms the very conditions that affirmative action is meant to challenge.

William Julius Wilson and Affirmative Action

The civil rights movement focused on gaining equality of opportunity for individuals. However, once laws were passed making it illegal to discriminate, it became obvious that past discrimination made it impossible for many individuals to take advantage of opportunities they were now legally entitled to. During the very period when institutionalized racism came under attack by the judiciary and the federal government, the U.S. economy exhibited structural changes that essentially trapped the urban poor into a deteriorating position. Removing artificial racial barriers was not enough to

> enable poor blacks to compete equally with other groups in society for valued resources because of an accumulation of disadvantages flowing from previous periods of prejudice and discrimination, disadvantages that have been passed on from generation to generation. Basic structural changes in our modern industrial economy have compounded the problems of poor blacks because education and training have become more important for entry into the more desirable and higher paying jobs and because increased reliance on labor-saving devices has contributed to a surplus of untrained black workers.[20]

In his book *The Truly Disadvantaged*, Wilson chronicles the growth in the number of children born out of wedlock, female-headed families, poverty, crime, and joblessness that has become identified with the urban black underclass. But he is careful to distinguish himself from the view (which I have associated with Sowell and Loury) "that poverty is a product of 'deeply ingrained habits' that are unlikely to change following improvements in external conditions."[21] Instead, Wilson argues that efforts to alleviate the conditions of the urban poor should be directed to changing their joblessness and social isolation rather than to changing their "cultural traits."[22]

Unlike Loury, Wilson does not suggest that race-specific policies are somehow morally suspect. Rather, he sees no prospect of their receiving sustained support from the American population as a whole.

"In order to draw sustained public support . . . it is necessary that training or retraining, transitional employment benefits, and relocation assistance be available to all members of society who choose to use them, not just to poor minorities."[23] For Wilson, the hidden agenda for liberal policy makers is to pursue policies that would be available to all without regard to race, but which would disproportionately benefit the black urban underclass.

To achieve this, Wilson advocates a policy of full employment and programs that are "positive sum" in the sense that everyone benefits from them. He rejects race-specific programs because of the perception that such programs benefit one group at the expense of other groups. Yet it is not at all clear why a program of full employment in itself should lead to the elimination of the black urban underclass. Even if there were jobs available, it is not clear why these jobs would go disproportionately to poor blacks.

Wilson takes it as an act of faith that full employment would create a demand for labor that would penetrate even the most recalcitrant structural impediments. But even if labor became scarce and more expensive, it is not obvious that a stage would be reached where it would be profitable for businesses to hire and train otherwise undesirable workers. The introduction of labor-saving devices, immigrant labor, and relocation to areas with cheaper labor sources are viable alternatives that businesses actively explore in times of labor shortage. Thus, it is not at all clear that full employment without affirmative action would provide a solution to the problems of the urban black underclass.

Conclusion

Both conservatives and liberals have as their goal full employment. But in the absence of race-specific programs, it is not clear that the black urban underclass would be capable of taking advantage of the opportunities that either political agenda might make available. John Kenneth Galbraith, Lester C. Thurow, and others have argued that pockets of poverty persist, irrespective of the extent of a tight labor market, simply because people within those pockets lack the skills for or access to the available jobs. Even under a socialist regime, a particular racial or ethnic group might remain caught in a position that precluded its members from taking advantage of opportunities made available by antidiscrimination legislation. Without affirmative action, then, neither conservative nor liberal schemes might alleviate the problems of the urban black underclass.

A persistent criticism is that affirmative action and preferential treatment have helped those who are better prepared for employment and educational opportunities more than they have helped the "truly disadvantaged." But this is not an anomaly to be eliminated. Slavery and segregation penalized those who were better prepared for educational and employment opportunities more than it did those who were least prepared: The more education and training a black person got, the smaller the proportion of the white income for similar employment he or she would be paid.[24] In other words, jobs that required low skills were more likely to pay black workers the same wage as white workers than were jobs that required extensive skills. The result was a disincentive for African Americans to invest in extended skill preparation. Affirmative action is a means of counteracting this historical phenomenon, by taking steps to insure that the qualifications of African Americans are not discounted.

Because the truly disadvantaged, by definition, lack the skills necessary to take advantage of available opportunities, Sowell, Loury, and Wilson argue that the black urban underclass has been relatively unaffected by affirmative action programs because these programs benefit only those who at least have minimal qualifications for existing opportunities. Unfortunately, recognition of the limitations of affirmative action is taken to imply that such policies are somehow redundant and unnecessary. Race-specific policies are considered discredited because they do not solve the problem of the urban black underclass. But affirmative action is not meant to solve all problems deriving from racism and monopoly capitalism. In particular, affirmative action is not meant to solve the problem of the existence of an underclass. Rather, it is meant to contribute to ending the disproportionate representation of African Americans among the underclass. Thus, any African American achieving minimal qualifications is given an extra push away from the underclass by the existence of affirmative action policies.

Both Sowell and Loury suggest that the situation of the black urban underclass results from habits its members have acquired that are dysfunctional. They are therefore in direct opposition to "radicals" who suggest that an underclass is an inevitable outcome of monopoly capitalism, and that the current underclass in the United States simply happens to be black. As they differ in their account of the source of the underclass, radicals and conservatives also differ in their solutions to the problem of the black underclass. Radicals believe that the workings of capitalism must be exposed so that the existence of an underclass is seen as a necessary outcome of the development of monopoly capitalism. The solution to the problem of the black underclass is the elimination of the mechanism that produces an underclass. Conservatives, on the other hand, believe that the underclass results from the fettering of the individual's ability to exhibit rational preferences between alternative courses of action. Racial discrimination makes it impossible for employers to hire the most competent employees, independent of racial, gender, religious, and ethnic differences. The cost of labor is artificially raised and economic activity is ultimately dampened. Economic stagnation, in turn, leads to unemployment.

In their discussion of the relevance of affirmative action policies, Sowell and Loury tend to shift from the specific case of African-American overrepresentation among the least well off to the more problematic generalization regarding the source of all ethnic disparities. Wilson prefers to focus on eliminating joblessness rather than on eliminating the disproportionate representation of blacks among the jobless. In both cases, the legacy of racial discrimination is not addressed directly, but only indirectly, by focusing on a different problem considered to be more germane, more central. The fact that African Americans tend to be overrepresented among the members of the underclass is treated as a contingent, historical fact that should not blind us to a supposedly more important problem. This attitude, this "view from nowhere," is akin to ignoring the patient in favor of fighting the disease. It is an attitude I find common between Sowell, Loury, and Wilson.

NOTES

1. Thomas Sowell, *Civil Rights: Rehtoric or Reality* (New York: William Morrow, 1984).
2. Ibid., p. 17.
3. Ibid., p. 79.
4. Glenn Loury, "Why Should We Care about Group Inequality?" in *Social Philosophy and Policy* 5, no. 1 (1988): 249–71.
5. Ibid., p. 249.
6. Ibid., p. 250.
7. Ibid.
8. Ibid.
9. Ibid., p. 256.
10. Ibid., p. 259.
11. Ronald Dworkin, *Taking Rights Seriously* (Cambridge, Mass.: Harvard University Press, 1978).
12. Loury, "Why Should We Care?" p. 260.

13. Ibid.

14. Stanley Lieberson, *A Piece of the Pie: Blacks and White Immigrants Since 1880* (Berkeley, University of California Press, 1980).

15. Albert Mosley, "Preferential Treatment and Social Justice," in *Terrorism, Justice, and Social Values*, ed. Creighton Peden (Lewistown, N.Y.: Edwin Mellen Press, 1990).

16. Loury, "Why Should We Care?" p. 262.

17. Ibid., p. 263.

18. Ibid., p. 264.

19. Alan Chase, *The Legacy of Malthus* (Urbana: University of Illinois Press, 1980).

20. William Julius Wilson, *The Truly Disadvantaged* (Chicago: University of Chicago Press, 1987), p. 126.

21. Ibid., p. 137.

22. Ibid., p. 138.

23. Ibid., pp. 151–52.

24. Charles Sacrey, *The Political Economy of Urban Poverty* (New York: W. W. Norton, 1973), p. 72.

9 Social Policy, Ethical Life, and the Urban Underclass

Frank M. Kirkland

SCHOLARS CONCERNED with urban poverty, social welfare, and public policy have bestowed much critical acclaim upon William Julius Wilson's *The Truly Disadvantaged*. Wilson's text provides a formidable and comprehensive analysis of the problems of the urban underclass, while simultaneously laying the groundwork for the kind of social policy necessary to meet the ever-worsening socioeconomic conditions of that group. Wilson's thesis basically asserts that the long-term poverty and protracted welfare dependency of the urban underclass is due primarily to persistent bouts of unemployment and underemployment spawned by a complex set of structural problems endemic to American society's macrosocioeconomic arrangement.

Recently, however, Wilson has expressly complemented his thesis with a "cultural argument," claiming that the poverty and welfare dependency of those comprising the underclass are reinforced by the behavior of other members of the underclass in the same social environment.[1] Although Wilson discusses this matter in *The Truly Disadvantaged* in terms of the "concentration effects" of the social isolation of members of the underclass from institutional resources enabling social mobility, he implicitly or minimally refers to it as part of the cultural argument of his thesis in that book. He makes the reference minimal primarily because he wants to annul the binding force of the "culture of poverty" argument for explaining the plight of the urban underclass and, in so doing, to insulate the cultural components ("concentration effects," "social isolation") of his thesis from any of the trappings of that argument. This tack gives the impression that Wilson is linking the plight of the underclass exclusively to structural problems in extant economic arrangements without any strong consideration of the cultural aspects of the underclass's life in poverty.

What truly distinguishes Wilson's thesis with its own "cultural argument" from the "culture of poverty" thesis is the following: Whereas the latter claims that the underclass's life in poverty is due to the self-induced pathological behaviors of its own culture, that its plight is culturally rooted, the former claims that the underclass's life in poverty is reinforced by pathological cultural traits, which are themselves the result of structurally adverse economic arrangements in society. Unlike the "culture of poverty" thesis, this makes Wilson's thesis both bilateral and serially ordered. His thesis is bilateral because it brings together arguments affirming the negative impact of the economy *and* culture on the underclass. But, more importantly, it is serially ordered, because cultural arguments explaining the plight of the underclass cannot be justified, as they are in the "culture of poverty" thesis, independently of arguments explaining that plight by structural problems in the economy. Cultural arguments are indeed necessary for Wilson's thesis, but they can neither precede nor exclude the socioeconomic ones.

On the level of analysis, the bilateral and serially ordered framework of Wilson's thesis undoes the impression that he connects the dire circumstance of the underclass solely to socioeconomic problems and not even partially to culture. But, on the level of remedy, as we shall see, this impression is revitalized despite the thesis's framework.

To remedy the position of the urban underclass, Wilson proposes a social policy of universal economic reform whose social welfare program is informed by the moral principle of equality of life chances. The policy promotes the establishment of full employment and of balanced economic growth and is designed to do two things. First, it addresses the plight of the urban underclass in terms of that group's inextricable connection with the structure and functioning of the national economy, not in terms of the currency of racism, the culture of poverty, or the work motivation of the poor. Second, it calls for socioeconomic reforms beneficial to both advantaged and disadvantaged groups in the United States regardless of racial or ethnic background. This second point carries what Wilson calls the social policy's "hidden agenda," an agenda whose purpose is "to improve the life chances of truly disadvantaged groups such as the ghetto underclass by emphasizing programs to which the more advantaged groups of all races and class backgrounds can positively relate."[2] In short, programs targeted specifically for the urban underclass would have to be incorporated in a comprehensive economic reform package beneficial to all social groups in order to gain and sustain widespread political acceptance for such programs. Consequently, social policy on the urban underclass, Wilson asserts, requires "rational government involvement in the economy"[3] as well as ongoing deracialization of the targeted groups of domestic social programs.

Obviously the need for "cultural arguments" on the level of analysis has been rendered superfluous by the remedy, since social policy, aimed at resolving the structural problems of the nation's macrosocioeconomic arrangement, can engender changes for the better in the socioeconomic circumstance of the underclass that, according to Wilson, "will lead to changes in [its] cultural norms and behavior."[4] This signifies that improving economic conditions alone are sufficient for changing for the better the cultural values and behavior of the underclass. But if that is the case, there is no call for Wilson to integrate socioeconomic *and* cultural arguments in his theoretical framework, because cultural aspects pertinent to understanding the plight of the underclass would be simply epiphenomenal features of that group's real, materially based deprivation. Social policy of economic reform, as described by Wilson, would then be enough to resolve that group's persistent bouts with poverty *and* problems in behavior. Since Wilson's theoretical framework for comprehending the problems of the underclass provides a bilateral and serially ordered analysis with policy-generating intentions, a bilateral and serially ordered remedy dealing with the group's economic and behavioral problems, respectively, would be anticipated. Unfortunately Wilson's proposal of a social policy of universal economic reform is essentially *unilateral* and reduces the remedy for cultural problems to the remedy for economic ones. It thereby moots the necessity for cultural arguments in both the analysis of and the remedy for the plight of the urban underclass, a necessity which, as we saw, Wilson explicitly endorsed at least on the level of analysis.

The main thrust of the remainder of this chapter will be to delineate what I take to be critically assailable facets of Wilson's remedy for the plight of the urban underclass. Yet I trace them not for the sake of rejecting wholesale Wilson's remedy or even, for that matter, his analysis. Rather, I carry out this enterprise for the sake of demonstrating that these facets belie the importance of and need for "cultural arguments" in the remedy for the plight of the urban underclass. I show that even a social policy of universal economic reform, as proposed by Wilson, must frame limits, once cultural questions, or what I shall hereafter call questions of "ethical life,"[5] come to the fore.

A social policy of universal economic reform is geared to resolve systemic problems in the economy, which negatively affect the advantaged and, more severely, the truly disadvantaged. It neither resolves nor mitigates the underclass's problems in behavior. Repairing structural and functional problems in the economic system does not coincide with restoring the meaningfulness of institutions and practices that culturally and psychologically prepare members of the underclass for entrance into the economy. Social policy, therefore, must be bilateral and serially ordered, on the one hand strategically executing universal economic reform of the economic system and on the other hand, politically enabling social institutions to be culturally integral and motivationally plausible to lives of those of the underclass.

Joblessness and Social Policy

Wilson rightly goes to the heart of the material deprivation of the urban underclass when he claims that a significant reduction of joblessness, particularly among young black men, must be a top priority issue in social policy agendas in order to restore and enhance the material base of economically impoverished black families.[6] The material impoverishment of the underclass is due to structural transformations in the economy that have placed this segment of the general population outside of the sphere of gainful employment. Automation, the burgeoning segmentation in the labor market, and the relocation of industry from urban centers contribute enormously to that group's lack of economic opportunity and marginalized status. Capital disinvestment and the "red-lining" policies of banks are among major factors in the material erosion of its social environment.

Given this scenario, Wilson proposes for the urban underclass a socioeconomic policy designed to "promote both economic growth and a tight labor market [in which] the latter affects the supply-and-demand ratio [with] wages tending to rise. It would be necessary, however, to combine this policy with fiscal and monetary policies to stimulate non-inflationary growth and thereby move away from the policy of controlling inflation by allowing unemployment to rise."[7] In this claim we find Wilson affirming the basic function of welfare state social policy, namely, to effect the ongoing transformation of the unemployed into the employed. But he also wants to expand the function of that policy to effect the ongoing transformation of the *jobless* into the employed. This entails that the formulation and execution of policies, aimed to neutralize or mitigate the liabilities of the labor market, must cover a wider segment of the population, namely, the jobless rather than simply the unemployed. Before proceeding with an examination of Wilson's position, I will discuss briefly labor market liabilities.[8]

As we are well aware, capitalist economies societally generate labor market liabilities such as unemployment and underemployment in a widely extensive and repetitive fashion. In the context of this discussion, the urban underclass is that group, comparatively speaking, upon whom labor market liabilities exact the greatest toll. These liabilities take the form of above-average unemployment, inordinate frequency of above-average length of unemployment, insuperable difficulties gaining access into employment relations, and overexposure to exceptional risks that render qualifications to work superfluous. The degree of exemption from these liabilities depends on a group's relative control of the means of production of goods, of the means of consumption for the satisfaction of needs, and of the means of acquisition for skills. In short, it depends on class position. The lesser the control, the lesser the group's exemptions from these burdens. Therefore, class position as well as a specific orientation toward achievement and market success more than likely determine the level of economic wherewithal, which relatively insulates members of a class from societally generated labor market liabilities.

Returning to Wilson's claim, we see that he proposes a social policy engendering a "tight labor market," that is, a labor market in which the demand for labor would be greater than the supply. Given the severe and heavy impact of labor market liabilities on the urban underclass, Wilson argues that a tight labor market provides a significant remedy because, in such a market, job openings would increase, wages would rise, and bouts of unemployment would decrease and shorten, factors which would sharply counteract labor markets liabilities on the urban underclass.

However, Wilson eventually makes a conceptual error, I believe, on the level of remedy when he speaks of the benefits of a tight labor market to the urban underclass. A tight labor market would be beneficial to those *already participating* in the labor market, and Wilson does not demonstrate that members of the underclass participate in it. Bear in mind that, on the level of remedy, Wilson advances a social policy effecting the ongoing transformation of the jobless into the employed. Yet on the level of analysis, he employs the concept of joblessness generically to include the unemployed as well as nonparticipants in a labor market.[9] This means that unemployment and nonparticipation in a labor market are forms of joblessness. With that in mind, Wilson can then claim that the benefits of a tight labor market extend to both the unemployed and nonparticipants in a labor market since both are jobless. The problem with Wilson's claim is that the unemployed are participants in a labor market and, hence, would be the only segment of the jobless to benefit from a tight labor market. Clearly this is not the intent of Wilson's remedy, especially since the underclass would be a segment of the jobless that does not participate in a labor market.

Rather than exclusively employing the concept of joblessness generically, it is important also, I believe, to employ it *analogically*. In so doing, unemployment and nonparticipation in a labor market are not forms of joblessness; they are rather as forms of joblessness different. Allow me to explain with the following classification scheme.[10] The unemployed are those who are not involved in a contractual employment relationship yet ardently seek such a relationship by making themselves available for work. In contrast, the employed are involved in such a relationship and, hence, depend on contractual income or wages. Both groups, however, are participants in a labor market. Nonparticipants in a labor market involve those who are self-employed, that is, those whose income is not dependent on a contractual employment relationship but rather on the difference between profits and expenses, since they also control the means of production. In contrast, there are nonparticipants who have been rendered inactive, that is, who have been withdrawn from the labor market.

From this scheme, it would be fair to claim that the unemployed and the inactive are jobless but in different fashions. And when we explore more closely this inactive group, we find that the underclass constitutes a peculiarly distinct segment of that inactive population—a segment whose joblessness stems from conscious withdrawal from the labor market because its material condition renders it incapable to withstand labor market liabilities. Indeed, there are other segments of the inactive population (the elderly, children, and the chronically ill) whose style of life either cannot entail "labor" as its central, primary activity or, if "labor" is entailed, cannot secure its means of subsistence in terms of compensation for that work (e.g., housework). The underclass also shares this characteristic. Nonetheless, the joblessness of these other inactive segments, their withdrawal from the labor market, results from political regulation, mandating the conditions according to which nonparticipation in a labor market is possible. The joblessness of the underclass, its withdrawal from the labor market, is established by the burdens of labor market liabilities and "social dislocation" (to use Wilson's term).

Construing joblessness analogically enables us to show the rationale for a bilateral and serially ordered social policy executing universal economic reform and encouraging sociocultural reintegration. Although Wilson advocates a social policy effecting the ongoing transformation of the jobless into the employed, his conception of joblessness at the levels of analysis and remedy is exclusively generic. As a consequence, it fails to capture the difference in joblessness between the inactive and unemployed populations and between the underclass and the other segments of the inactive population. Since a plan for tightening the labor market can bear fruit only for those already participating in a labor market, such a plan apparently would have no effect on those who have consciously withdrawn from it. This criticism, however, is neither asserting nor suggesting that a tight labor market as a significant part of the package of universal economic reform ought to be jettisoned. Rather, it addresses the boundaries or limits of the unilateral social policy of economic reform that Wilson endorses.

I make this claim because a jobless segment like the urban underclass can benefit from a tight labor market only if members of it are prepared to enter or reenter the labor market—prepared not simply in the sense of gaining skills of some kind, but prepared in the sense of being both socioculturally and sociopsychologically equipped to entertain and undergo as cognitively adequate and motivationally plausible the risks associated with participation in a labor market. In short, they have to muster the culturally shaped motivation of entering a labor market. Such a position appeals to the significance of coupling cultural arguments with economic arguments at the level of remedy, with one side of a social policy clearing away economic obstacles to employment, and the other prompting the reintegration of the urban underclass into institutionally viable sociocultural arrangements.

As we know, familial and educational institutions have usually provided the normative obligations and motivations to individuals through socialization for entrance into the labor market. They have also been the spheres where the inactive population in general has, so to speak, taken residence for material and ethical support and for exemption from labor market liabilities. Yet when we turn our attention to that distinctive inactive segment, the urban underclass, we find that these same institutions have undergone steady and constant deterioration over the past thirty years, a deterioration that in families can be traced back, Wilson claims, to joblessness.

The debilitation of these areas of sociocultural life for the underclass reflects (1) that this group's basis for reproducing its life materially or economically has been destroyed and (2) that this destruction has compelled those of the underclass to call into question their belief in the norms and values of the society and to withdraw their recognition of key institutional arrangements and social practices. Although tight labor markets in conjunction with fiscal and monetary policies controlling matters such as inflation are necessary for addressing (1), they are inadequate for settling (2), because they are formulated to respond to malfunctions in the economic system and not to disturbances or problems in cultural forms of life. The impact of both (1) and (2) on the underclass leads totally to what Wilson calls the "social isolation" of the underclass[11] and partially to what I call the desiccation of ethical life within the underclass, both notions addressing the social problems of behavior pertinent to that group.

The two notions, I believe, bear similarities, the primary one being that the social problems of behavior pertinent to the underclass are not culturally induced alone, but are the result of the adverse consequences wrought by unchecked structural problems in economic modernization. The major difference, I believe, between Wilson's notion and mine is the extent to which I argue that social policy, unilaterally and exclusively tied to a universal program of economic reform, must have a disintegrative effect on areas of cultural and personal existence responsible for shaping, developing, and reproducing norms and motivations necessary for the integrity of ethical life and must contribute to the desiccation of ethical life within the urban underclass, because it must be bureaucratically and administratively implemented in an acute fashion. For Wilson, however, so long as social policy is unilaterally and exclusively tied to a universal program of economic reform and is bureaucratically formulated and implemented to approximate conditions of full employment and to provide compensatory relief from economic problems in those above-mentioned areas of social life, there appears no way that such a policy could contribute to the "social isolation" of the underclass. He pays no attention to the bureaucratic effects. In the following sections I focus on these issues.

Ethical Life and the Urban Underclass

Before proceeding with my analysis, a few words must be offered concerning the meaning of ethical life. Ethical life is the interdependence and reproduction of the practices, norms, patterns of meaning, and motives embedded in a given community. It functions as the context-forming cultural background of that community and sustains for it what does and does not count as reasonableness in knowledge, what is involved in failure to understand or appreciate cultural fidelities, conceptions of various moral norms and aesthetic ties that bind, and a stock of exemplary individuals for members to extrapolate proper conduct and behavior. Patterns of meaning, norms, and motives are reproduced in a threefold process for maintaining the integrity of ethical life, and this process involves reproducing (1) interpretive schemes through language and tradition for a group's "parochial knowledge," (2) group solidarity through norms and values, and (3) competent and responsible social actors through motive formation. This threefold process entails, respectively, cultural transmission, social integration, and socialization.[12] Individuals and groups, therefore, establish their social identity in the light of the norms, motives, needs, and patterns of meaning available to them in ethical life. Indeed, the socioeconomic and sociopolitical realms, particularly their occupational and administrative sectors, respectively, are heavily dependent on the achievements of this threefold process maintaining the integrity of ethical life, namely, individuals with moral and technical competences and with a good sense of motivation and collective allegiance.

If this characterization of ethical life is plausible and acceptable, then we need to be wary of those who too easily claim that culture alone induces the social problems of behavior of the urban underclass.[13] Ethical life, left to its own design, neither animates nor incurs systematically distorted interpretive schemes, normatively deficient patterns of behavior, and morally incompetent role models without external incursions. These deficiencies never originate endemically in ethical life, are never the "enemies within," so to speak. Rather, they are deficiencies of ethical life only as the by-product of other societal factors. For the urban underclass, these external incursions are the unchecked systemic problems in macrosocioeconomic modernization, especially joblessness (as discussed in the previous section), *and* the legacy of racial discrimination, since the bulk of the urban underclass is as a consequence racially black and culturally African American. Yet despite the impact of racism's legacy, or even for that matter its currency, it is not sufficient to set in motion the desiccation of ethical life within the urban underclass. To comprehend the structure and extent of this desiccation requires the consideration of the other external incursion discussed in the previous section. However, with this claim, I do not want to be entangled either gratuitously or trivially in the debate concerning race and class. So before proceeding with my examination of what sets the desiccation of ethical life in motion, allow me to digress very briefly on the premises of my claim.

As stated previously, class position and specific orientation toward achievement and market success determine the level of economic wherewithal that relatively insulates members of a class from societally generated labor market liabilities. At first sight these liabilities appear to be connected *only* with a group's control or lack of control of the means of production for goods and of means of acquisition for skills, thus giving the impression that the impact of these burdens is homogeneous with respect to class position. But these liabilities are also connected, and not in any ancillary manner, with a group's socially ascriptive features, that is, race, gender, and age, insofar as these liabilities are societally allocated in a highly uneven manner. This point is important, because social scientists are proximately and for the most part committed to a kind of analysis in which socially ascriptive qualities can at best be of only ancillary significance for theories on social stratification in which the concepts of class and status predominate.[14] Furthermore, the state's social policies dealing with the labor market are no longer formulated only in terms of employment, qualifications, and mobility. Increasingly, they are formulated in terms of enhancing, in accordance with race, gender, and age, the market position of specific segments of the labor market. All told there would be a certain amount of heterogeneity within classes due to both socially ascriptive characteristics and social policies on the labor market. In the context of our discussions, the societal allocation pattern of labor market liabilities would correspond to race and, in spite of or because of this correspondence, the state would enact social policy to influence selectively the labor market racially. So the degree of exemption to labor market liabilities would not be strictly uniform within class position, but would characteristically vary within class position due to race.[15]

Returning to the topic of this section, what is sufficient to set in motion the desiccation of ethical life are the unchecked systemic problems and transformations in macrosocioeconomic modernization. The main problem is joblessness, which renders the underclass as a sector of the population outside of the sphere of gainful employment. Other problems are inflation, interruptions in the realization and circulation of capital, and constraint on the rate of profit due to the improved negotiating position of organized labor. These problems serve only to explicate the self-paralyzing tendencies of the economic system to economic growth; therefore, the plight of the urban underclass cannot be interpreted in the context of the economic system. It is only when these economic problems have an existentially critical impact on individuals and groups that they aid in interpreting the underclass's plight. They have such an impact when they destroy the basis of a group to reproduce its life materially and compel members of a group to call into question their supportive belief in the norms, practices, and patterns of meaning of the society. The urban underclass meets these two conditions.

Moreover, unchecked structural transformations in the macrosocioeconomic arrangement significantly contribute to those two conditions in the following ways. First, automation, the burgeoning segmentation of the labor market, and the relocation of industry from urban centers, all completely rational from the standpoint of economic strategy, simply contribute to the underclass's lack of economic opportunity. Second, those who subscribe to the flourishing of these transformations on the basis of economic rationality alone have a tendency to stigmatize those who lack economic opportunity as those who lack the will or the drive to work. They are usually neoconservative theorists or supporters of the "culture of poverty" thesis. By claiming that there is no connection between the unchecked structural transformations and the lack of will or drive to work among the urban underclass, they remoralize work and treat it as a pivotal point for a morally and materially good life and as a remedy to the moral and material impoverishment of the urban underclass.[16] Such a proposal presupposes a restoration of full employment on the basis of the flourishing of the above-mentioned transformations and a conviction that the urban underclass would benefit therefrom once it assumes the proper moral orientation toward work. Although both presuppositions are quite dubitable, the attempts to remoralize work plainly fail to consider that the conception of work as a moral duty requires conditions that enable people to be recognized as moral persons through their work. Since economic rationality dictates the necessity of making the production process ever more efficient through the above-mentioned transformations in the macrosocioeconomic arrangement, large areas of social labor are subject either to technological innovation or to deskilling and depreciation, and in doing one or the other, the production process is made as separate and autonomous as possible from the human element. But if that is the case, there is then absolutely no reason either to presume or to prescribe that people, especially those of the urban underclass, bear moral orientations toward work where the structures for fulfilling those orientations have been rationally eliminated or neutralized in favor of the production efficiency of the macrosocioeconomic arrangement. Hence the appeal to remedy the plight of the urban underclass through structural transformations in the economy and remoralizing work is hollow, because those transformations increasingly do away with the need for moral orientations toward work while increasingly depreciating and eliminating job opportunities.[17]

Certain consequences follow from the foregoing analysis. First, systemic problems in the macrosocioeconomic arrangement render the urban underclass more vulnerable than most to the adverse side effects of structural transformations in that arrangement. Second, this group's conscious withdrawal from the labor market and its problems in social behavior do not reflect its subscription to endemic "pathological cultural traits" as much as they reflect the effects of the depth of its material impoverishment and of the intensity of its sociopsychological recant of socially current norms and patterns of meaning, both of which threaten its socially integrative capacity or the integrity of its

ethical life, and both of which are due to structural problems and transformations in the macrosocioeconomic arrangement. Third, outside of
these effects, the ethical life of the urban underclass would be proximately and for the most part nothing other than the ethical life of the
African-American mainstream, given the de facto racial and cultural
identity of both. Indeed, this mainstream would be better insulated,
although not exempt, from labor market liabilities, and the basis for
reproducing its life materially would be relatively intact, such that it
would be less compelled to recant its support of socially current norms
and practices. Hence the ethical life of the African-American mainstream would be viable enough to enable its members to assume as
cognitively adequate and motivationally plausible the risks and burdens
associated with participation in a labor market.[18]

It is not difficult to comprehend that if structural problems
and transformations in the macrosocioeconomic arrangement go unchecked for a protracted period of time, then their existentially critical
impact on the urban underclass is exacerbated over that period. This
state of affairs has devastating consequences for the integrity of ethical
life, because long-term material impoverishment and protracted sociopsychological recants of socially current norms and patterns of meaning
can severely disrupt the reproduction of ethical life, in which cultural
transmission, social integration, and socialization occur. It can deplete
or desiccate the "resources" necessary for reproducing and replenishing the norms, patterns of meaning, motivations, and exemplars that
comprise the integrity of ethical life.

As stated previously, Wilson calls for "rational government involvement in the economy" to check its systemic problems and transformations through social policies of economic reform that are beneficial
to and serviceable for *all* members of society and not just the urban
underclass. First, Wilson makes this appeal for government involvement because he subscribes to the view that the state must and can
manage economic problems and fiscal crises by stepping into the functional gaps, so to speak, of the market economy. Here the state is
construed as either rationally mitigating or eliminating the existentially
critical impact of the liabilities of economic problems and transformations on the general public for the purpose of preventing salient loss in
social productivity and weightier losses in the quality of life of future
generations.[19] Second, he makes the appeal for social policies that are
de jure universally beneficial to and serviceable for all members of society rather than group-specifically beneficial to and serviceable for the
underclass, because the former are capable of greater and wider political support. In Wilson's eyes, this does not mean that group-specific

programs targeted for the urban underclass are eliminated. Rather, they are formulated as a component of the universal programs whose broad political support would *surreptitiously* carry and protect those targeted for the underclass. This then becomes the universal social policy's "hidden agenda."

There are, however, a number of difficulties with Wilson's proposals on social policy. First, he does not consider the possibility that state involvement in the economy may not produce the *universal* economic reform necessary to mitigate, if not eliminate, the negative impact of economic problems on the public in general and the urban underclass in particular and that, indeed, its involvement in the economy may itself reflect deficits in rationality. Second, he does not account for the possibility that state involvement in the economy coupled with a bureaucratically intense implementation of social welfare programs may contribute to the desiccation of ethical life within the urban underclass. Third, he does not explicate the possibility that the ancillary character of the group- and race-specific social program may undo the significance of cultural arguments pertinent to the formulations of a bilateral and serially ordered social remedy for the plight of the urban underclass. I shall deal with these issues in the following section.

Social Policy Problems and the Desiccation of Ethical Life

RATIONALITY DEFICITS IN GOVERNMENT INVOLVEMENT IN THE ECONOMY

Given Wilson's call for "rational government involvement in the economy," it is clear that he does not regard the social welfare state as an ad hoc random invention impinging on and interfering with the market economy. He regards the state as an irreversible social institution having a structural rationale, namely, to manage economic dysfunctions through administrative measures and reforms. What he fails to see, however, is that with the state's structural rationale comes poignant structural dilemmas.

I have already discussed one set of tasks entailed in the state's rational involvement in the economy, namely, to stabilize and supplant the market economy through policies that (1) handle the self-paralyzing tendencies or problems of the economy such as labor market liabilities and inflation and (2) substitute for the economy in providing primary economic goods to those areas of social life (such as family, health services, environmental protection, and education) where economic problems have yielded devastating consequences. However, the other set of tasks the state performs is that of safeguarding and subsidizing the market economy through policies that (3) protect private appropriation of wealth within the economy and (4) cultivate elements most conducive to capital investment and the business cycle as well as to investment in economically significant scientific and technological research. In short, the social welfare state manages structural problems in the macrosocioeconomic arrangement, yet its political and administrative steering of the economy occurs only with the proviso that private enterprise in matters of capital investment be basically safeguarded. As a result, the state performs dissonant sets of tasks of shaping for the public domain, on the one hand, policies for mitigating the negative side effects of the economy or for effecting the ongoing transformation of the jobless into the employed, which are the exclusive focal point of Wilson's analysis, and, on the other hand, shaping for private enterprises policies serviceable for capital investment.

Since Wilson fails to account for the latter set of tasks, he is unable to consider that the state's performance of these two dissonant sets of tasks reflects the state's structural dilemmas. Policies formulated to do (1) and (2) *cannot* be implemented in a manner that mitigates the effectiveness of policies formulated to do (3) and (4) because of the indispensability of capital investment to the macrosocioeconomic arrangement. And for this reason, policies formulated to do (3) and (4) *can* be implemented in a manner that mitigates the effectiveness of policies formulated to do (1) and (2).[20] The universal economic reform Wilson seeks seems undermined, not because of the political advantages that come to the state by giving priority to policies stimulating the accumulative performance of capital investment, but because of the political disadvantages that accrue to it by not giving priority to them.

So, for example, Wilson's proposal of tightening the labor market for the purpose of politically securing and generating opportunities of employment, a proposal representative of (1) and (2), could be accepted only on the condition that in the economic arena capital investment could still flourish optimally, if not maximally, despite such a proposal or because of it. If that condition is not met, then such a proposal could be viewed only as an impediment to capital investment and, hence, as a rationale for the curbing, if not the withdrawal, of such investment in that arena. If that should occur, it would either render moot the proposal of a tight labor market leading to full employment or give rise to proposals for increasing jobless economic growth.

The "rational" character of government involvement in the economy, then, cannot signify simply the proposals of a tight labor market and balanced economic growth as Wilson suggests. It signifies rather the ability of the state to give politically satisfying reasons for preferring the implementation of (1) and (2) over (3) and (4) or for preferring the implementation of the converse to solve economic problems or to effect sweeping economic reform. In the light of Wilson's concerns, doing the former can threaten capital investment, which in that event poses risks for and sets constraints on employment opportunities, especially for the urban underclass; doing the converse can exacerbate the conditions of joblessness, again especially as they pertain to the urban underclass. The dissonance of and the lack of equiponderance between (1) and (2) on the one hand and (3) and (4) on the other make the possibility of the state generating a "rational" involvement in the economy or providing politically satisfying reasons for implementing one set over the other an inordinately difficult affair.

Wilson's failure to come to terms with the dissonance and lack of equiponderance of social policies oriented toward universal economic reform is due to his belief that the state could assume a political form capable of yielding broad consensus on full employment, economic growth, and social welfare issues. This political form is called "corporatist democracy" or "corporatism." Citing the work of Harold Wilensky, Wilson defines "corporatism" as

> the interaction of solidly organized, generally centralized, interest groups —particularly professional, labor, and employer associations with a centralized or quasi-centralized government either compelled by law or obliged by informal agreement to take the recommendations of the interest group into account or to rely on their counsel. This arrangement produces a consensus-making organization working generally within a public framework to bargain and produce policies on present-day political economy issues such as full employment, economic growth, unemployment, wages, prices, taxes, balance of payments, and social policy (including various forms of welfare, education, health, and housing policies).[21]

The corporatist political arrangement "produces a situation whereby, in periods of rising aspirations and slow economic growth, labor—concerned with wages, working conditions, and social security—is compelled to be attentive to the rate of productivity, the level of inflation, and the requirements of investments, and employers—concerned with profits, productivity, and investments—are compelled to be attentive to issues of social policy."[22]

Wilson believes that a corporatist political arrangement would undo the dissonance and lack of equiponderance between the two above-mentioned sets of social policy, because it supposedly establishes strong political coalitions and parity among organized interest groups such as business associations and labor unions, as well as allegedly enforcing a discipline and constraint on the kinds of demands such groups bring to the political discussions with the government in the concerted effort of resolving economic problems and producing equitably binding political decisions on social policy. But the state's corporatist form carries difficulties, which undermine the facility toward consensus Wilson emphasizes.

The parity between business associations and labor unions is established by generically referring to them as "interest groups." They are thus regarded as sharing formal properties in common such as "voluntary membership, a more or less bureaucratic structure of decision-making, dependence upon material and motivational resources, efforts to change the respective environments into more favorable ones."[23] Yet the generic reference as well as the utilitarian paradigm of collective action *conceal* their respective structural differences as interest groups, differences constituted by the indispensability of capital investment. That requirement is uncircumventible and, hence, establishes the boundaries of political discussion among the three corporate members, namely, business associations, labor unions, and the government. Negotiating and deciding social policy and economic reform are heavily shaped by that requirement, which designates and delineates what can and cannot be subject to political discussion. Because of the indispensability of capital investment, corporatism produces a political situation whereby labor is *more* compelled to be attentive to the requirements of investments than employers are compelled to be attentive to issues of social policy. This is why that requirement is almost always challenged by organized "interest groups" other than business associations. Their challenges would thus convey a corporate political arrangement fraught with political antagonism and disparity rather than with political consensus and parity.

Even if we counterfactually assume that capital investment is a dispensable item in corporatist political discussions, Wilson cannot proffer the grounds on which the state assigns or authorizes political or public status to business associations and labor unions (or any organized interest group) such that in the corporatist arrangement these groups are able to make politically binding decisions affecting the rest of the citizenry.[24] Indeed, corporatism is constructed to shape politics pragmatically in accordance with the conditions of an advanced industrial-technological society and in accordance with ways that by-pass the political conflicts manifest in the competition for power among the numerous segments of the citizenry. As we just saw above, corporatist arrangements do not themselves escape political conflicts per se. Furthermore, these reasons do not nullify the requirement of the state to maintain legitimate recognition from its citizens. And such recognition or legitimacy seems threatened when citizens are bound to the decisions of a corporatist arrangement in which they have had no say regarding its composition or agenda. In short, deficiencies in rationality and threats to legitimacy still plague the government in its involvement in the economy and social policy, even as a member of a corporatist arrangement. Given these problems surrounding corporatism, and in the light of Wilson's explicit concerns, there is no reason to believe that a political agenda favorable to the urban underclass would be best raised in a corporatist arrangement.

BUREAUCRATIC EFFECTS ON ETHICAL LIFE
WITHIN THE UNDERCLASS

We move now to the next difficulty that Wilson's proposal on social policy raises, namely, that state involvement in the economy coupled with a strong bureaucratically implemented social welfare program may contribute to the desiccation of ethical life in the urban underclass. For the sake of argument, I shall not be raising here the problems of rationality and corporatism.

Wilson is in agreement with the longitudinal empirical research of David Ellwood and Mary Jo Bane, which purports that "welfare simply does not appear to be the underlying cause of the dramatic changes in family structure of the past few decades." [25] He employs their results to counter, if not refute, claims endorsing the view that the receipt of welfare subsidizes idleness and rewards failed (i.e., fatherless) families, [26] as well as to support ex negativo his view that joblessness is the cause of failed families. Although I agree with Wilson that joblessness (as I characterized it above) is the predominant factor in this matter, I want to argue further, in contrast to Wilson, that the long-term receipt of welfare revamps the family in particular and ethical life in general according to administratively defined criteria. This produces a situation in which norms and roles of the family and its members, for example, usually supplied and shaped by ethical life for the sake of guiding action in family matters, are brought into line with and ultimately supplanted by bureaucratic regulations that establish the condition for welfare receipt.

As stated earlier, the state assumes responsibility for managing economic problems as they arise and for rectifying the debilitating consequences thereof. One of these consequences would be the material impoverishment of a group such as the urban underclass. The state responds with social welfare policies whose administrative regulations are to define eligibility and to insure that a certain modicum of economic and social goods and services reaches those eligible. Indeed, such policies are meant to compensate for the inadequacies of economic modernization and their existential critical impact on the urban underclass. They are also meant to sustain credibility in the eyes of the underclass for both the market economy and the state by reforming in a positive manner the conditions of life for that group. Paradoxically, however, as these policies are bureaucratically administered, the informal and personal areas that comprise the ethical life of the urban underclass become increasingly subject to a kind of legalistic regulation, which does not formally overlay the norms and patterns of meaning that demarcate these areas, but which formally strips these norms and patterns of any significance for these areas. The reason for this circumstance lies in the fact that the bureaucratic and legalistic channels through which social welfare programs are implemented are not inert, but are rather mediums for managing, regulating, normalizing, monitoring, and regimenting those areas.

The bureaucratic implementation of social welfare policies incessantly and unavoidably spawns pressures toward revamping the underclass's everyday situations, usually concretely structured by ethical life, as genuine instances of legalistically defined abstract states of affairs, according to which the needs of the underclass are interpreted and the conditions of its welfare receipt are established. It compels those of the underclass who receive welfare to assume vis-à-vis the state the position of dependent clients or objects of administrative care rather than of independent citizens. As a consequence, it preempts the influence of ethical life on areas of daily concern (such as family relations) and exerts a stultifying paternalism on those of the underclass, which prevents them from dealing with and interpreting their situation in an autonomous fashion and heightens individual helplessness and social weightlessness.

If the existential critical impact of macrosocioeconomic problems has seriously challenged the credibility of motives for participating in the labor market, and if the state's regulatory welfare measures to mitigate this impact have overridden the norms and patterns of meaning that previously organized the everyday situations of those of the urban underclass, then it is virtually impossible to conceive of what remains that is of motive-orienting force in their actions and of morally binding force in their lives. This state of affairs is made especially more evident when we keep in mind that neither the macrosocioeconomic arrange-

ment nor the state can monetarily or administratively produce or re-
plenish normative and motivational patterns of behavior. Under these
societal circumstances the desiccation of ethical life within the urban
underclass can make fuller sense and can best explain the problems of
social behavior connected with its members.

The desiccation of ethical life within the urban underclass, as stated
above, is the depletion of the cultural resources necessary for reproducing and replenishing norms, patterns of meaning, and motives. It
occurs when the problems and transformations of the macrosocioeconomic arrangement and the paradoxically adverse effects of social welfare policy have (1) destroyed the long-term basis of a group to reproduce its life materially, (2) compelled the group's members to disavow
socially current norms and patterns of meaning, and (3) bureaucratically eviscerated the moral conceptions, traditions, and motive formation culturally organizing everyday life. Since the integrity of ethical
life is maintained by a threefold process of reproducing patterns of
meaning, norms, and motives, the desiccation of ethical life appears in
three distinct ways.

When the process of reproducing patterns of meaning is desiccated,
the result is *loss of meaning*. For the urban underclass, this signifies that
there is no obvious connection between the norms and motives required by the economy and political decision-making processes, on the
one hand, and its experiences, needs, and possibilities for action on the
other. This scenario is exemplified by the diminishing opportunities
for those of the urban underclass to sustain a quality of life without
protracted deprivation and by their demoralizing belief that nothing
really matters.

When the process of reproducing norms and values is subject to
desiccation, the result is *anomie*. For those of the urban underclass, this
signifies that the stabilization of group solidarity and the coordination
of action among them through conventional norms and values cannot be sustained. This scenario is exemplified by the ever-burgeoning
intraracial criminal activity of blacks.

When the process of reproducing competent social actors is subject to desiccation, the result is *disorientation in the individual*. For
those of the urban underclass, this signifies that there are no socially
recognized role models and patterns of social identity at their disposal.
They only have role models and patterns of identity that already embody structural identity conflicts, already reflect a deprivation of social
recognition, and are already marked with disturbances to a positive
self-image.[27] Social actors interpret rationally their needs and wants,
which constitute the motives of their action, in terms of values, norms,

and patterns of meaning available to them in ethical life. Moral and motivational patterns can be generated and renewed only through social actors convinced of the binding force these patterns have on their experience. This is why ethical life, if desiccated and lost, cannot be restored by a discretionary exercise of the will (as neoconservative theorists would have us believe). In short, the desiccation of ethical life explains why problems of social behavior among the urban underclass have an ongoing character.

THE RACE-SPECIFICITY OF
SOCIAL PROGRAMS

I have shown that the state's administrative regulation of social programs can be a significant factor contributing to the "social isolation" or, more appropriately, the desiccation of ethical life within the urban underclass. We now turn to the final difficulty of Wilson's proposal on social policy, namely, that the auxiliary character of race-specific social programs may undo the importance of cultural arguments pertinent to the formulation of a bilateral and serially ordered social remedy for the plight of the urban underclass.

As we are aware, Wilson wants to treat the social programs for the urban underclass as an ancillary and hidden component of the overall social policy of universal economic reform because of the political antagonism such programs would generate given their race-specific cast and the tendency to present them independently of any kind of economic reform. He treats these programs in this fashion, not simply because he contends that their success is dependent on a tight labor market and economic growth but, more importantly, because he contends that their success is not to be construed as the result of politically establishing benefits for a specific racial group. If their success were perceived to be so hinged, political conflict over the legitimacy of these programs, bearing strong racial overtones, would be a certainty. So long as the success of these programs is perceived as the result of influencing the labor market and stimulating economic growth beneficially for any group, regardless of race, political support for them, Wilson believes, would not be difficult to secure. "The important goal is to construct an economic-social reform program in such a way that the universal programs are seen as the dominant and most visible aspects by the general public. As the universal programs draw support from a wider population, the targeted programs included in the comprehensive reform package would be indirectly supported and protected."[28]

It does appear strange, however, that Wilson's concern focuses on the political antagonism that could ensue from the acceptance of race-specific social programs disconnected from a nonracial package of universal economic reform. As stated above, political antagonisms also ensue from the formulation of the social policy of universal economic reform, because even such reform must affirm both the indispensability of capital investment *and* the dispensability of employment security as a civil right in political discussions and decisions about social and economic policy. Contrary to Wilson's view, even in the preferred corporatist political arrangement, political conflict would still flourish. But it would not flourish as visibly as that over race-specific social programs for two reasons. First, the state tends to pacify the conflict over universal economic reform through compromise and, hence, to render it dormant, although such compromise neither surmounts it nor surmounts the structural inequality favoring the indispensability of capital investment in political decisions concerning economic reform. Furthermore, such compromise neither enhances nor necessarily guarantees rationality in the government's involvement in the economy. Second, the state tends to quicken racialized political conflict over race-specific social programs through advocacy or opposition and, hence, to invigorate it. The state's advocacy of or opposition to these programs is usually based on its subscription to either the principle of equal opportunity affirming individual rights and enabling socially affirmative action on the basis of individual merit or the principle of equal condition affirming group rights and enabling socially affirmative action on the basis of being a member of a group subject to past discrimination.[29] Subscription to the former yields de jure opposition to race-specific social programs; subscription to the latter yields de jure advocacy for them. Since different principles of equality and social justice can be applied in the political decision to implement or not to implement these programs, political conflict over the implementation of them is simultaneously over questions of justice and equality, and such conflict is quite patent and quite unamenable to compromise.

This potential for political conflict is a major reason why Wilson holds that race-specific social programs cannot be separated from measures of universal economic reform. He subscribes to neither of the two principles to govern the implementation of race-specific social programs for the same reason. Other significant grounds for Wilson's rejection of the two principles are the following: (1) the principle of equal opportunity cannot adequately address the complexity of structural problems comprising group or racial inequality in America; and (2) the application of either principle, especially the principle of equal condition, is more advantageous to the black mainstream than to the truly disadvantaged, specifically the black urban underclass.

Wilson thus endorses the principle of equal life chances, formulated by James Fishkin,[30] to govern the implementation of race-specific social programs. This principle affirms the rights of those deprived of an equal life chance comparable to others not so deprived, and it enables socially affirmative action on the basis of being a member of a group subject to the lack of resources associated with current class background. Nonetheless, Wilson's endorsement comes only with the understanding that this principle is informing the implementation of race-specific social programs already connected to measures of universal economic reform promoting full employment and balanced economic growth. If such programs are disconnected from these measures, Wilson would not find the principle of equal life chances any more compelling than the other two.[31]

Seen in this light, Wilson believes he now has a principle of equality and social justice that can justifiably govern the implementation of race-specific social programs without engendering racialized political antagonism and without benefiting the materially advantaged segment of a racial group. He holds this belief for the following reasons: (1) the justification for blacks to be de facto targeted or specified for the programs' benefits is not based on membership to a racial group subject to past discrimination but on current deprivation of economic resources; (2) given (1), materially advantaged blacks cannot be targeted; and (3) given (1) and (2), racialized political conflict over these programs cannot arise since the justificatory basis for them does not prohibit members of any racial group from being targeted so long as they are economically disadvantaged.

Wilson's proposal on social policy addressing the plight of the urban underclass would offer a nonracial solution of universal economic reform whose social program would de facto target blacks but would justify such a targeting, not racially, but economically. The race-specificity of the program would thereby be rendered politically benign or innocuous, and the program itself would become compatible with Wilson's totally unilateral economic solution to the plight of the underclass and would be serviceable as a component of it.

But herein lies the rub. There is only one explanation for a program informed by the principle of equal life chances to de facto target blacks, namely, the significant overrepresentation of blacks within the urban underclass. Such a program would target blacks, because their overrepresentation would be construed as dependent upon current deprivation of economic resources, as the principle asserts. This claim, however, is fallacious, because the *explanatory basis* for targeting blacks is being employed confusedly with the *justificatory basis* for targeting them. The fallacy of the claim can be made clearer by posing the claim's contrary. Assuming that whites are significantly underrepresented within the urban underclass, such a program would not target whites, because their underrepresentation would not be construed as dependent upon current deprivation of economic resources, as the principle asserts. Clearly the principle of equal life chances does not justify the prohibition of white members of the underclass from being targeted on the basis of their underrepresentation. The principle renders the issue of the underrepresentation of a racial group immaterial. It does likewise to the issue of a racial group's overrepresentation, because the group at issue under a program informed by the principle of equal life chances is simply that which is materially impoverished by virtue of current deprivation of economic resources. The racial composition of that group is irrelevant. This signifies, then, that programs informed by that principle cannot be race-specific—they are class-specific.

Wilson's error arises from confusing what he rightly finds as compelling in the racial composition of the truly disadvantaged, namely, the overrepresentation of blacks in the urban underclass, with what is compelling in targeting the truly disadvantaged itself, namely, current deprivation of economic resources. Only under the auspices of this error or fallacy could Wilson assert that social programs informed by the principle of equal life chances could be race-specific.[32] Only their class-specificity, not their fallaciously construed race-specificity, can make them politically benign in the context of successful universal economic reform, in which case the state could dispense with the need to hide them.[33]

However, since Wilson rightly finds the overrepresentation of blacks in the urban underclass a compelling reason for social programs to target them, the principle informing those programs would be that of equal condition, as described above. Although this principle provides the justificatory basis needed to target blacks—namely, being a member of a racial group subject to past invidious discrimination— it also renders these programs subject to the political antagonism that Wilson believes the state should avoid or minimize. In the context of seeking measures of universal economic reform, the adoption of race-specific social programs would compel the state to make them the "hidden agenda" of that reform for the following reason. Since the measures of universal economic reform (i.e., a tight labor market and balanced economic growth) are established with the intention, Wilson believes, to undo politically the racial competition over economic and employment opportunities, the adoption of race-specific programs would undermine the intention of the reform and could stimulate or exacerbate racialized political conflict over them. Despite the justificatory basis for race-specific programs,[34] the state is to remain consistent with its solution of universal economic reform and is to forge and conceal those programs in ways that do not substantially thwart that solution politically. This is in keeping with the unilateral social remedy Wilson advances. But it does become difficult to fathom how the ancillary and hidden character of those programs contributes to meeting adequately the overrepresentation of blacks in the urban underclass.

Concluding (and Very) Unscientific Postscripts

In my introductory remarks, I claimed that there were assailable aspects of Wilson's unilateral social remedy for the plight of the urban underclass that camouflaged the importance of "cultural arguments" in that remedy. The admission of these arguments into the remedy would transform Wilson's unilateral social remedy into a bilateral and serially ordered one. Allow me by way of synopsis to demonstrate those facets that, in belying the significance of cultural issues or issues of ethical life, indicate the points where those issues *can* enter into the social remedy for the plight of the urban underclass.

1. In the first section of this essay, "Joblessness and Social Policy," I showed that a tight labor market as a remedy for the jobless urban underclass is not sufficient, because the joblessness of that group derives not from its participation in the labor market as the unemployed, but from its conscious withdrawal from the labor market. Its withdrawal is due to long-term material impoverishment annulling its ability to bear that market's inherent liabilities. Reintegrating the urban underclass into institutionally viable sociocultural arrangements is necessary to equip that group's members with the motivation to assume the risks associated with participation in a labor market.

2. In the second section, "Ethical Life and the Urban Underclass," I claimed that institutionally viable sociocultural arrangements reflect the integrity of ethical life. Familial, communal, and cultural arrangements, responsible for providing patterns of meaning, normative obligations, and motivations to all as members of cultural groups, have steadily deteriorated for those of the urban underclass. Although Wilson readily discusses this phenomenon under the terms of "social isolation," "social dislocation," and "concentration effects," he offers no proposal specific to reversing the deterioration of ethical life within the underclass other than the economic one.

3. Wilson's proposal for universal economic reform, which entails that the state's involvement in the economy be ever rational, is to

do all the remedial work on the plight of the urban underclass. The issues of ethical life are ruled out in Wilson's proposal but, on the basis of my analysis of it in the section "Rationality Deficits in Government Involvement in the Economy," their importance emerges ex negativo once the structural weaknesses of Wilson's proposal reveal that it cannot do all the remedial work as Wilson holds. I argued that the state's involvement in the economy is not secured from deficits in rationality. Those deficits are inherent in the state's involvement in the economy, because it must perform dissonant sets of tasks and accept the set favoring capital investment as preponderant over the set favoring employment security (such as tight labor markets). Wilson does not even consider this point, which appears to threaten the proposal for universal economic reform.

Furthermore, the political sphere, in which this universal economic reform is to be initiated and hammered out, is a corporatist one. The political actors Wilson envisions in this sphere are interest groups and elites. Such political actors have detached themselves from the needs and orientations of their members or constituents, have focused their concerns toward maintaining and disciplining themselves, and have predetermined through their organizational power the limits within which political and economic matters are raised and settled. Wilson thinks that interest groups and political elites can form coalitions on universal economic reform that, in benefiting all, benefits the underclass. Yet Wilson fails to comprehend the connection between the potential for political friction among interest groups and elites on economic reform and the potential for the state's involvement in the economy to be secure from deficits in rationality. Since such deficits are structural, the ability of the state to bring about political coalition among those interest groups on economic reform is not as potent or as simple as Wilson would have us believe. Hence the strength of universal economic reform as a sufficient remedy for the plight of the urban underclass is severely mitigated by the state's own structural deficits in rationality when involved in the economy and its consequent inability to engender political coalitions on such reform. This leaves open the question of whether coordinating the political action around a social remedy for the plight of the urban underclass should occur in the sphere of ethical life.

4. Let us assume, however, that the state does not suffer from deficits in rationality when involved in the economy and, as a consequence, can forge the political coalition among interest groups on universal economic reform. Even under this circumstance, universal economic reform is still not sufficient, because of the excessive bureaucratic appa-

ratus necessary to implement it. Like other scholars and policy makers with strong liberal agendas, Wilson pays no intellectual attention to the bureaucratic effects on the daily lives of those, such as the urban underclass, in receipt of public assistance. Indeed, the goal of such assistance is to put those in receipt of them on the way toward independence, but the consequence has been putting those in receipt of them on the way toward dependence. However, this independence and dependence is not simply economic or material but, more importantly, sociopsychological. Therefore, an unintended consequence of welfare receipt is not just dependence on the dole, but dependence on the conditions for welfare receipt, that is, dependence on or obedience to bureaucratic regulations regarding one's daily existence. This bureaucratic effect eventually divests the binding force of ethical life on one's daily existence, especially if one, like members of the underclass, has been subject to persistent and protracted bouts of unemployment. Once bureaucratic effects on daily living are coupled with the destruction of a group's long-term basis for reproducing its life materially and the group's disavowal of socially current norms and patterns of meaning, the desiccation of ethical life is in motion. Since this desiccation cannot be prevented or reversed either monetarily or bureaucratically, then clearly we must look past economic reform alone to do all the remedial work on the plight of the urban underclass. Indeed, if "cultural arguments" are necessary for a social remedy of the underclass's plight, then such arguments must not simply address controlling the structural problems of the macrosocioeconomic arrangement (as liberals do) or controlling the strongly interventionist welfare state (as conservatives do). They must address controlling *both,* and must do so from the sphere of ethical life.

5. Social programs informed by the principle of equal life chances cannot be race-specific as Wilson maintains. They can be race-specific only if informed by the principle of equal condition. The justificatory basis needed to target blacks in the underclass for a program's benefits can be membership in a racial group subject to past invidious discrimination, not just membership in a group subject to current material impoverishment. This means that for the black urban underclass there are two sources of structural inequality pertinent to their plight. Wilson, however, subordinates the harm based on past discrimination to the harm based on current deprivation of economic resources, because he wants to make all race-specific social programs a subsidiary part of the overall package of universal economic reform. However, since neither source of structural inequality is derivable from the other, there is nothing logically compelling to subordinate one to the other,

although there may be political grounds to do so, as we have seen with Wilson. Nevertheless, it is still possible to consider the black urban underclass in terms of the harm of past discrimination without minimizing the importance of the harm of material impoverishment. This consideration can take the shape of establishing the significance of that harm for ethical life "in black" or, put another way, the significance of race in and for the African-American mainstream in order to see how it can contribute politically to reversing the desiccation of that life within the black urban underclass.

In showing where issues of ethical life can enter into the social remedy for the plight of the urban underclass, the question to be raised is: How is a bilateral and serially ordered remedy involving the issues of ethical life possible? Here my reflections become quite tentative, provisional, even nebulous, as they now advance to the "never-never land" of the normative. Nonetheless, let me set some material premises or constraints.

First, my critical discussion of Wilson's proposal for "rational government involvement in the economy" holds. That is to say, the state does operate with structural, not ad hoc, deficits in rationality when involved in the economy. Although, like Wilson, I too endorse a state oriented toward universal economic reform, I recognize that such an orientation is not guaranteed fulfillment due to the rationality deficits of the state. (Wilson gives the impression that this orientation is guaranteed fulfillment if the state only adopt a liberal agenda.)

Second, given its rationality deficits, the state is accepting the indispensability of capital investment while still oriented toward controlling structural problems of the economy due to the indispensability of capital. On the basis of these two constraints, it becomes clear that the social remedy for the urban underclass does not involve a socialist mode of societal transformation.[35] Rather it will involve some kind of civic incorporation which, I believe, is not inconsistent with Wilson's goals.

Third, the state cannot act upon the plight of the urban underclass in an excessively bureaucratic manner without further risk to the ethical life of that group.

These constraints do not serve as grounds to remove the state from involvement in the economy, from transforming the jobless to the employed, or from instituting social welfare programs. But they do serve as limits to the state's effectiveness and, when kept in view, clear the way for insight into how the state can reach an impasse if its policies brush against their grain, and how the state can be counterproductive even in its capacity to effect a high degree of social justice through universal economic reform. This is why the social remedy for the urban underclass cannot be unilaterally economic, as Wilson proposes. A bilateral and serially ordered social remedy for the plight of the urban underclass calls for the state to set and implement policy on universal economic reform for the sake of bringing social justice to the truly disadvantaged, but without moving against those limits. This means that a bilateral remedy at this level requires the state not only to check politically an unfettered economy, but also to check itself politically with regard to the negative impact of both on ethical life, since the urban underclass is a group whose ethical life has been devastated by the problems of an unfettered economy and excessive bureaucratic regulation.

The state's check on itself presupposes, however, a state administration politically reflective about the impact of its power on ethical life. If the state is reflective enough to pull back bureaucratically to some extent from ethical life while continuing to orchestrate as far as possible a tight labor market within universal economic reform, it enables ethical life to exert influence not only on daily existence, but also on how daily existence is politically shaped. Here is the level where ethical life plays its role, where the solidarity it generates among its members can make the state greatly sensitive to its influence. If a bilateral and serially ordered social remedy is to become a social policy in which issues of ethical life could emerge, it would have to be dependent upon the capacity of the state's administration to be sufficiently reflective to avoid bureaucratically encroaching on ethical life while protecting it from the problems of the macrosocioeconomic arrangement.[36] As a consequence, the state would be open to the claims arising out of ethical life. Indeed, these would be the ideal circumstances for a bilateral and serially ordered social remedy to emerge.

Such circumstances are, however, highly unusual, and that is why on matters of ethical life a state administration is usually itself subject to being checked politically by those "below" the political sphere, in which the corporatism that Wilson endorses flourishes. The political actors, who occupy the sphere "below" that of corporatism, are those determined by their solidarity with their constituencies' attempts at defining themselves and gaining some kind of popular "sovereignty" in terms of the integrity of their ethical life. Wilson does not give much credence to this political sphere, and his reluctance to embrace its politics seems to be due to the tendency of this politics to be at times nothing other than a cultural or racial group's unbridled symbolic self-assertion. Hence it would be possible to construe the politics arising out of ethical life as lacking in intelligent self-restraint and discipline just as the politics of corporatism is subject to the state's rationality deficits.

The major difference, however, between the two is that, whereas in the politics of corporatism the state's rationality deficits are inherent to it and pose structural obstacles to its involvement in the economy and to its forming corporate coalitions regarding economic and social policy, the lack of intelligent self-restraint in the politics of ethical life is *not* structural, leaving open the *real* possibility that the politics of ethical life can be coupled with intelligent self-restraint. This possibility is essential once the black urban underclass is brought into the picture. Since I have argued that the ethical life of this group has undergone desiccation, it appears that this group's plight would be best resolved by corporatist politics and not by the politics arising out of ethical life. But if this matter is thought with care, it is not difficult to see how the plight of the black urban underclass can be addressed successfully from the politics of ethical life once the African-American mainstream is introduced.

As stated earlier, outside of the desiccation process, the ethical life of the black urban underclass is nothing other than that of the African-American mainstream. Furthermore, the overrepresentation of blacks in the urban underclass is measured by the same significant harm that has been integrally factored in the ethical life of African Americans, namely, the legacy of racism. Although the desiccation of ethical life within the urban underclass is *not* set in motion by that legacy, the heavy concentration of blacks subject to that process is due to that legacy. That numerical concentration has given the false, if not racist, impression that the desiccation process is endemic to the ethical life of blacks. Since ethical life is the point where the African-American mainstream and the black urban underclass converge, the reversal of the desiccation process becomes the issue around which the African-American mainstream mobilizes the potential of its ethical life politically.[37]

Reversing the desiccation process within the black urban underclass means that the African-American mainstream is politically concerned, not just with policies associated with a tight labor market and employment opportunities, but also with restoring social institutions as culturally integral and motivationally tenable to those of the black urban underclass. Determined by their solidarity with the underclass, those of the African-American mainstream are the political actors concerned as much with mobilizing that solidarity against threats to employment opportunity and training as with checking the encroachment of the state and creating enough slack in social institutions for the ongoing autonomous development of ethical life "in black" both materially and symbolically. Such action would entail, however, the use of intelligent self-restraint, because the space opened for the development of institutions culturally integral to those of black underclass as well as the African-American mainstream would require at least to some degree the support of extant economic and political institutions. Nonetheless, the coordination of that support would not take place behind the backs of those with whom the political actors are in solidarity and would not occur without the state administration being swayed by the decentralizing political goals of the politics of ethical life.

There are a number of consequences that follow therefrom. First, the politics of African-American ethical life is carried out in the light of day and oriented around shifting to some degree the political and economic balance of power to decentralizing institutions of that group's own making. Here the bilateral and serially ordered social remedy would be at work as the *result* of the politics emerging from "below" in the ethical life of African Americans and reflecting intelligent self-restraint. Such a state of affairs would represent a 180-degree turn from the politics of corporatism.

Second, the politics of African-American ethical life spawns a bilateral and serially ordered social remedy that can hold open the possibility that it can "lead to a revitalization of neighborhoods in the inner city, reduce the social isolation," but not "recapture the degree of social organization that characterized these neighborhoods in earlier years." [38] This possibility is open to this remedy, because the remedy involves universal socioeconomic reform in some measure *and* restoration of the meaningfulness of institutions and practices that culturally and psychologically prepare members of the underclass for entrance into the economy. This restoration does not mean, however, recapturing the degree of social organization that characterized these neighborhoods in earlier years. It rather signifies reversing the desiccation process and reconstructing a place for the development of institutions culturally integral to the black underclass and the African-American mainstream conducive with the *current* political deliberations regarding the state and the economy. Wilson's unilaterally economic social remedy encourages economic and geographical mobility and, hence, cannot hold open the possibility of the remedy revitalizing inner city neighborhoods.

Third, the major political actors here are the African-American mainstream. Yet there is a position that criticizes the political role this group undertakes and asserts that the African-American mainstream is not culturally aligned with the black underclass and cannot be the political vanguard in the "racial" uplift of the underclass. It is prohibited from doing so because it sustains "middle-class" and petit-bourgeois sentiments of cultural integration. The culture of the underclass is, then, regarded as adequate politically to address its problems without mediation from others.[39] Some brief remarks to this position are in order. First, my analysis has already argued for the commonality of ethical life "in black" between the African-American mainstream and the black urban underclass. Second, in the light of the problems of material deprivation and social behavior within the urban underclass, one would be hard pressed to claim that such a group, comprised of *victims* of the problems of the economy and the bureaucratic encroachments of the state, can by itself be the *carrier* of its own social empowerment. Third, assuming counterfactually that this group could be such a carrier, the politics generated from its cultural expressiveness would indeed mobilize, but without the intelligent self-restraint necessary to engage existing institutions effectively.

Finally, the success of the African-American mainstream in challenging the state to be reflective enough to pull back bureaucratically from ethical life does not rule out contesting the subsidiary character of race-specific social programs in packages of universal economic reform. Since the politics of African-American ethical life culturally constructs its defense of these programs, one would suspect that it cannot justify its defense, because it cannot show how such programs do not disadvantage other groups not of the same ethical life. Indeed, this is Wilson's position. But the nature of the harm was such that African Americans were for centuries never regarded as persons with moral status and as citizens with rights. Since that harm is factored in the ethical life of African Americans, the cultural construction for the defense of race-specific social programs is motivated, not by correcting the material deprivation of African Americans, especially the black urban underclass, at the expense of other groups, but by addressing the wrong that systemically excluded members of that ethical life from full participation in the socioeconomic and sociopolitical institutions writ large, a wrong whose legacy is reflected in the overrepresentation of blacks in the underclass. On this note, harm by material deprivation of economic resources and by past invidious discrimination yield two different and independent motives for social programs, regardless of similarity in benefits, and cannot compel anyone to construe race-specific social programs as subsidiary to non–race-specific ones.

I hope that my remarks have offered some signposts for the importance of a bilateral and serially ordered social remedy for the plight of the urban underclass. The need to curtail urban poverty *and* to reverse the desiccation process, which in my opinion is the source of that group's problems in social behavior, is pressing. That this remedy deal with both in a serially ordered way and that it can be pushed by a politics of ethical life from "below" speak to the importance, not just of economic arguments, but also of cultural ones.[40]

I should emphasize that the last point is motivated by the conviction that, for the time being, political conflict over the legitimacy of race-specific social welfare programs is with us for better or worse. For the foreseeable future, political actors of the African-American mainstream will have to operate where defenses of these programs are contestable. But this circumstance is not unfortunate, because at least one can now argue that these programs address a matter of justice that cannot be reduced simply to the distribution of social goods for material improvement.

NOTES

Acknowledgments: Variations of this essay have been delivered at the National Conference of Black Political Scientists (NCOBPS) Meeting in Chicago (April 1986); at Hampton University's Ninth Annual Conference on the Black Family in Hampton, Virginia (March 1987); and at Hunter College in New York City (March 1987), as a response to Glenn Loury's essay "Race and Poverty: The Problems of Dependency in a Pluralistic Society." An abbreviated version of this essay was delivered at the conference Meditations on Integration held at the University of Delaware in Newark (June 1989).

1. See William Julius Wilson, "Studying Inner-City Social Dislocations: The Challenge of Public Agenda Research," *American Sociological Review* 56 (February 1991): 10.

2. William Julius Wilson, *The Truly Disadvantaged* (Chicago: University of Chicago Press, 1987), p. 155.

3. Ibid., p. 121.

4. Ibid., p. 159.

5. Although I borrow the term from Hegel, I shall make use of it in ways consistent with the spirit, if not the letter, of it. I employ this term because it carries a wider and stronger sense of sociocultural cohesion than Wilson's "neighborhood."

6. See Wilson, *The Truly Disadvantaged*, pp. 41–46.

7. Ibid., p. 151.

8. Here I am indebted to the analyses of Claus Offe, *Disorganized Capitalism: Contemporary Transformations of Work and Politics*, ed. John Keane (Cambridge, Mass.: MIT Press, 1985), pp. 10–51.

9. See Wilson, *The Truly Disadvantaged*, p. 41: "Furthermore, the jobless rate (unemployment and labor-force non-participation) among young black males (aged sixteen to twenty-four) has increased sharply since 1969 in the large central cities of the Northeast and Midwest."

10. See Offe, *Disorganized Capitalism*, pp. 26–28.

11. See Wilson, *The Truly Disadvantaged*, p. 60.

12. See Jürgen Habermas, *The Theory of Communicative Action*, 2 vols., trans. Thomas McCarthy (Boston: Beacon Press, 1984, 1987). My conception of ethical life takes on the same functions as Habermas's conception of "lifeworld." Indeed, much of my discussion is inspired by this significant work in social theory.

13. The most prominent neoconservative representative of this position is Glenn Loury. See his "The Moral Quandary of the Black Community," *Public Interest* 79 (Summer 1985): 9–22; and "A New American Dilemma," *New Republic*, December 31, 1984, pp. 14–18. See also Thomas Sowell, "Culture—Not Discrimination—Decides Who Gets Ahead," *U.S. News and World Report*, October 12, 1981, pp. 74–75.

14. This issue is exemplified by social theorists as divergent as Paul A. Baran and Paul M. Sweezy, and Talcott Parsons, all of whom concur in characterizing the situation of black Americans as one of a disadvantaged lower class and regard its resolution as essentially tied to a class-based social movement, either through civic incorporation (Parsons) or through societal transformation (Baran and Sweezy). Wilson's position bends toward Parsons or, more aptly and notably, toward Bayard Rustin, whose views gave strong emphasis to the need of interpreting the plight of poor blacks less in terms of race relations than in terms of economic ones. Cf. Bayard Rustin, "From Protest to Politics: The Future of the Civil Rights Movement," *Commentary* 39 (February 1965): 25–31; and "The Blacks and the Unions," *Harper Magazine*, May 1971, pp. 73–81.

15. See Offe, *Disorganized Capitalism*, pp. 11–13.

16. See Glenn Loury, "Race and Poverty: The Problem of Dependency in a Pluralistic Society" (unpublished manuscript prepared for the American Enterprise Institute).

17. See Offe, *Disorganized Capitalism*, pp. 129–50.

18. Bear in mind that the assumption of those risks also involves the recognition that labor market liabilities are societally allocated in a highly uneven fashion corresponding both to race and to social policies influencing the labor market racially. Moreover, despite its relatively better insulation from labor market liabilities when compared to the underclass, the African-American mainstream is itself not wholly released from the condition of socio-psychologically recanting socially current norms and practices. The legacy and currency of racial discrimination and the inability of the dominant American culture to view the ethical life of African Americans as itself in the forefront of that culture have set the conditions through which even the African-American mainstream come to distrust to some degree the predominant norms, practices, and institutions of American society. Although I cannot argue this point here, I would claim that the communicative competence of the African-American mainstream, in both black vernacular English and the vernacular English to which a semantic form or standard is tied, yields for that group a prophylactic skepticism about those predominant norms, practices, and institutions when they are up for discussion.

19. See Wilson, *The Truly Disadvantaged*, p. 157.

20. See Offe, *Disorganized Capitalism*, pp. 170–220.

21. See Wilson, *The Truly Disadvantaged*, p. 155.

22. Ibid., p. 156.

23. See Offe, *Disorganized Capitalism*, p. 175.

24. Ibid., pp. 221–58.

25. Cited in Wilson, *The Truly Disadvantaged*, p. 81.

26. The primary representative of this view is Charles Murray. See his *Losing Ground: American Social Policy, 1950–1980* (New York: Basic Books, 1984). However, for a novel and incisive interpretation of how social meanings are sedimented in welfare programs and significantly contribute to the "feminization of poverty," see Nancy Fraser's excellent work *Unruly Practices* (Minneapolis: University of Minnesota Press, 1988), especially chaps. 7 and 8.

27. See Habermas, *The Theory of Communicative Action*, vol. 2, pp. 311–96. For an abbreviated yet concise and fascinating discussion of the issues raised in this section, see idem, "The New Obscurity: The Crisis of the Welfare State and the Exhaustion of Utopian Energies," in *The New Conservatism: Cultural Criticism and the Historians' Debate*, trans. Shierry Weber Nicholsen (Cambridge, Mass.: MIT Press, 1989), pp. 48–70.

28. See Wilson, *The Truly Disadvantaged*, p. 154.

29. Ibid., pp. 112–16.

30. See James Fishkin, *Justice, Equal Opportunity and the Family* (New Haven: Yale University Press, 1983).

31. On this point, Wilson is extremely ambivalent, if not outright contradictory. On page 118 of *The Truly Disadvantaged*, he states, "Only programs based on the principle of equality of life chances are capable of substantially helping the truly disadvantaged." Yet, on page 154, he asserts, "As long as a racial division of labor exists and racial minorities are disproportionately concentrated in low-paying positions, antidiscrimination and affirmative action programs will be needed even though they tend to benefit the more advantaged minority members." Clearly the programs to which Wilson refers in the latter quotation would be based on the principle of equal condition. Bear in mind that his discussion of programs in both citations has not separated the programs from measures of universal economic reform. Consequently, this signifies that race-specific social welfare programs informed by either the principle of equal life chances or the principle of equal condition can be connected with measures of universal economic reform. However, the former principle would make the race-specificity of the program innocuous, moot, even absurd, and would provide no racially political grounds for Wilson to "hide" the program within a comprehensive economic reform package. The program supposedly would be compatible with the nonracial package. The latter principle, on the other hand, would make the race-specificity of the program relevant, substantial, even reasonable, yet would provide grounds for Wilson to "hide" the program within the above-mentioned package, since the tangibly racial program would be incompatible with the nonracial solution of the economic package. The dilemma that arises in the consideration of these two principles stems from Wilson's admission in the second quotation that the degree of exemption

from labor market liabilities is not strictly uniform within class position but varies within class position due to race (and gender, if we want to account for the "feminization of poverty").

32. See ibid., p. 154: "Both race-specific and targeted programs based on the principle of equality of life chances (often identified with a minority constituency) have difficulty sustaining widespread political support."

33. The politically benign character of class-specific social welfare programs would be dependent upon the degree of rationality the government exercised in its involvement in the economy. Indeed, the degree to which the state is successful in pacifying political conflict over universal economic reform is the degree to which the state could render class-specific social welfare programs politically innocuous. However, since Wilson discusses the political arrangement for the formulation of such reform in a manner in which broad consensus on the measures of such reform is possible, it is safe to assume that he would believe that decisions to implement class-specific social welfare programs would be equitably binding on the political actors in that arrangement. If universal economic reform is not successful, yet the state can effect some kind of compromise, the potential for political conflict over class-specific social welfare programs certainly looms and the compulsion to "hide" them becomes evident.

34. One of the best and strongest philosophical defenses of race-specific programs is Bernard Boxill's *Blacks and Social Justice* (Totowa, N.J.: Rowman and Allanheld, 1984), especially chaps. 4–7.

35. By the socialist mode of societal transformation, I mean here the statist conception of such transformation found in orthodox Marxist doctrine. Whether there can be a socialist mode of societal transformation that is not statist remains to be seen, although it cannot be ruled out. The statist conception of such transformation involves the dispensability of capital investment and the indispensability of employment security with the sweeping bureaucratization of the economy and society, but contrary to doctrine gives the state a political form that is recalcitrant to its supposedly eventual elimination.

36. My concern for protecting the integrity of ethical life from both the problems of the economy and the bureaucratic encroachments of the state should not be construed with a neoconservative rendition thereof. Although that rendition argues against the state's intervening tendencies into ethical life, the protection of ethical life is *irrelevant* to its account. Neoconservatives see the state's intervention simply as a response to political claims arising out of ethical life that place inordinate fiscal and political pressure on the state to resolve. They call for the state to pull back from protecting ethical life in order to reduce its fiscal and political burdens and to allow the economy alone to make good the claims arising out of ethical life. With respect to the urban underclass, all claims to the state for compensatory justice are fiscally and politically burdensome. Since the plight of the underclass, according to neoconservatives, is due to that group being ethically and culturally degenerate and subversive (see Loury's "enemies within"), there is absolutely no reason for state intervention to resolve that group's plight.

37. I take the political orientation of the African-American mainstream to be less of a cultural pessimism with the aims and goals of the welfare state than a historical recognition of the insufficiency of those aims to enable the development of African-American institutions while still affirming the state's egalitarian measures. This orientation would not permit the call for dismantling the welfare state from the African-American mainstream because of the high degree of social justice that group has acquired from it. But it would permit the call for securing space for the autonomous establishment of black cultural institutions to avoid cultural impoverishment in the context of African-American engagement with extant and current political arrangements.

38. See Wilson, *The Truly Disadvantaged*, p. 157.

39. This sentiment extends far back into the African-American intellectual tradition and is found represented in this volume by Tommy Lott's essay "Marooned in America: Black Urban Youth Culture and Social Pathology."

40. I believe that the cultural or ethical life component of the remedy is made clear in the face of empirical evidence that the composition of the urban underclass is predominantly children and youths. On the basis of this evidence, there have been numerous outcries for a national social policy for the family, which would make childhood and adolescence politically significant. Yet it would be a mistake to regard their political relevance in terms of being a social class, because childhood and adolescence do not possess any feature from which the relative control over the means of production for goods and the means of acquisition for skills could be derived. Childhood and adolescence are politically relevant because they are significant phases in the socialization process of ethical life, in which it is resolved whether youth or adolescence, a phase already fraught with sociopsychological risks, can have, in accordance with ethical life, a conventional outcome after long-term desiccation has penetrated it. Hence, the political significance of childhood and adolescence within the urban underclass is connected with their transition to the adult phase and with those features stabilizing and perpetuating unconventional cultural and social identities that are not in accord with ethical life, are incompatible with the requirements of the economic and political system, and, more importantly, incorporate novel potentials for antagonism and apathy.

Epilogue: Back on the Block

10 PHILOSOPHY AND THE URBAN UNDERCLASS
Cornel West

WHAT DOES it mean to talk about the black underclass from the vantage point of being a black philosopher? It means that we have to engage in a kind of critical self-inventory, a historical situating and positioning of ourselves as persons who reflect on the situation of those different from us, even though we may have relatives and friends in the black underclass. We have to reflect in part on our identity as black intellectuals, as black philosophers, and more broadly as academicians within the professional-managerial class in the advanced capitalist society of the United States. We also must be cognizant of the kind of impact postmodern culture, the culture of this society, is having upon our perceptions, discourses, and perspectives.

The Identity of the Black Philosopher

We have been struggling with the issue of the identity of black philosophers for many years. It is an issue that all of us have had to come to terms with. What does it mean to be a philosopher of African descent in the American empire? This raises the question of our relation to the discipline of philosophy. What is our relation to the dominant paradigms and perspectives in that discipline? Analytic philosophy? Continental modes of philosophizing? To what degree are we willing to transgress these paradigms? What kinds of consequences follow therefrom, given the fact that the reward structure of the discipline is such that to transgress means that we will be marginalized? I want to argue that in fact to talk about philosophy in relation to the black underclass means that we have a conception of philosophy that is inexplicably bound to cultural criticism and political engagement. We begin with a historicist sensibility, by which I mean that we do something our

191

colleagues often find very difficult to do: we read history seriously and voraciously.

We engage in an interdisciplinary or even dedisciplinizing mode of knowledge. We traverse and cut across the disciplinary division of knowledge inscribed within the universities and colleges, or we radically call into question the very existence of the disciplines themselves. To dedisciplinize means that you go to wherever you find sources that can help you in constituting your intellectual weaponry. It is going to be very difficult to obtain tenure in a philosophy department by doing this kind of thing. All of us have had to struggle with this. How do we remain engaged in our discipline while also radically calling various aspects of it, if not the whole thing, into question? How do we deal with our marginal status, as if we are not "philosophers," or "serious philosophers," "rigorous philosophers," "precise philosophers"? This is not in any way peculiar to black philosophers, but is true for a number of philosophers who call into question in serious ways the dominant paradigms. But black philosophers, I think, have been especially prone to this kind of perception and treatment.

If one begins with an interdisciplinary or dedisciplinizing orientation, it means also that one begins to talk about the *worldliness* of one's philosophical project. Here, I of course borrow a term from Edward Said's work, *The World, the Text and the Critic*. "Worldliness" means you acknowledge quite explicitly the partisan, partial, engaged character of your work. Now of course, the immediate charge is that you engage in politicized forms of knowledge. The more charitable reading is that you are simply explicit about your values. You are explicit about your political commitment and yet you believe in a balanced dialogue and hope that others will be as explicit and unequivocal as to where they stand in relation to their values and political perspectives.

But if we take seriously historicist sensibility with dedisciplinizing modes of knowledge and the worldliness of our work, then I think it no accident that we find ourselves reflecting on something like the black underclass and thereby using tools that have not been bequeathed to us by philosophy departments. Instead, we look to cultural criticism, to sophisticated historical work, and to social theory.

When we make the shift to reflection on the black underclass, we begin by reflecting on where we are and what authorizes the claims that we make about the black underclass. Why? Because we know that we are especially for the most part, and certainly socially, distant from the very object we are investigating, namely, brothers and sisters who are locked within the black underclass plight. Where are we socially? Where are we in regard to class? Where are we culturally? What has been the impact of the degree to which we have been acculturated and social-ized into the culture of critical discourse, or the academic subculture? What kinds of values and sensibilities have shaped our socialization, given where we come from? Many of us do indeed come from working-class origins, some underclass origins, some rural black working-class origins, and so forth. What kind of new identity has been constituted in this black philosopher, given these origins and this acculturation? I am not arguing that one has to be autobiographical in this regard. But it seems to me that before we even begin to talk about our identity or agency as black philosophers, we must ask: Who are we speaking to? Who are we writing to? Who holds us accountable? Is it the profession? In part it must be the profession if we are going to be a part of the profession. But is it solely the profession? And if it is more than the profession, then who else is it? Is it the black intellectual community that cuts across disciplines? To raise these kinds of questions means that we engage in a kind of critical self-inventory. Where does that take us? I want to put forth three basic claims about this.

First, we find ourselves in many ways marginalized, not solely by white or mainstream philosophers, but also because we are humanistic intellectuals. Humanistic intellectuals in general are being marginalized in our society by the *technical* intellectuals, such as physicists, computer scientists, and so on, because they receive most of the resources from the huge private enterprises, the state, and the military-industrial com-plex that flows from the nation-state. Why? Because the products that they provide, of course, are quite useful for society, as deemed by their supporters.

Second, as humanistic intellectuals we find ourselves marginalized because middle-brow journalists have much more visibility and saliency than we do in the academy. By middle-brow journalists I mean those who work for *Time, Newsweek, Atlantic Monthly, Harpers*, and others who have a large constituency or at least a large audience. The conse-quence in part is that we find ourselves talking more and more to one another, hoping that this will serve as a way of sustaining our sense of identity as academic humanists who often feel as if we are becoming antiquated and outdated.

In addition to marginalization, there is the issue of demoralization, by which I mean the crisis of purpose among black intellectuals in gen-eral and black philosophers in particular. I think the recent work of Allan Bloom on the right and Russell Jacoby's book, *The Last Intellec-tuals*, on the left reflect this crisis of purpose among humanistic intel-lectuals. On the one hand, it reflects the loss of public intellectuals, of those academicians who can actually intervene in the larger conversa-

tion that affects the destiny of large numbers of persons, such as the
issue of black underclass. On the other hand, it also reflects the fact
that we find our jobs more and more alienating as we are more and
more servicing an upper slice of a labor force that tends to put less and
less premium on humanistic studies. Pascal begins to displace French
as a language—Pascal computer language. Reading Plato and Aristotle
seemingly becomes ornamental and decorative rather than substantive
and engaging. It is nice to know a little Plato you can invoke at a cock-
tail party when you are off relaxing and not making money. But there
is no sense that what is at stake might be your very life, as Socrates and
many others believed. This is true at large because we live in a culture
in which the literary is in fact being marginalized vis-à-vis the audio
and the visual by means of the mass media. For those of us who are still
intellectuals of the book, it is nice to run into other people who are
reading the same books because there are not that many of us around
anymore. We might think that John Rawls is very important, as I think
he is, but we also see the degree to which Rawls finds himself as a
towering figure, the last liberal political theorist, as someone who has
to be translated in broader ways so that the relevance and pertinence
of what he has to say is translatable given the kind of business culture,
the business civilization of which we are a part. This is especially so in
the last twenty years, in which we have become a "hotel civilization," a
phrase Henry James invoked for the fusion of the security of the family
and the uncertainty of the market—both profoundly private institutions often distrustful of the common good and the public interest, but
more and more serving as the very model of what our culture looks
like. When we shift to the discourse on the underclass, we see in fact
that the culture of consumption, which is to say the culture of advanced
capitalist American society, evolves more and more around the market,
around buying and selling, around a process of commodification that
tends to undermine values, structures of meaning, in the name of the
expansion of buying and selling, in the name of the procuring of profit.

This is indeed more than a challenge—it is a highly dangerous situation. In a market culture in which commodification holds sway over
more and more spheres of human life, an addiction to stimulation becomes the requisite for the consumerism that helps keep the economy
going. Therefore, it tends to undermine community, links to history
and tradition, neighborhoods, even qualitative relations, since the very
notion of commitment becomes more and more contested and bodily
stimulation becomes a model for human relations. We see it in the employment of women's bodies in dehumanized ways in the advertising
industry. We see it in the television sit-coms that tend to evolve around

orgiastic intensity. Crack is quite exemplary in this regard. Crack is indeed the postmodern drug because it is the highest level of stimulation known to the human brain. It is ten times more powerful than orgasm, an expression of a culture that evolves around the addiction to stimulation. Stimulation becomes the end much more so than the means, yet the means is the very sphere in which human relations, community, and traditions are linked to human history, especially traditions of resistance.

Contemporary Discourse on the Underclass

What does this have to do with the black underclass? When we look at the black underclass we see a qualitative fissure in the history of people of African descent in this country. Between about 1964 and 1967 black neighborhoods underwent a qualitative transformation largely due to the invasion of a particular kind of commodification, namely, the buying and selling of a particular commodity—drugs. Whether or not this was conspiratorial, black communities undoubtedly have changed fundamentally. For the first time we have the disintegration of the *transclass character* of black communities in which different classes live together. The attempt to sustain the basic institutions of black civil society—family, church, fraternity, sorority, beauty shop, barber shop, shopkeeper, funeral parlor—that used to serve as the infrastructures for transmitting values and notions of self-respect and self-esteem still had some possibility of distribution across the black community.

The legacy of 243 vicious and pernicious years of slavery still has its impact on the black psyche. *Natal* alienation, the loss of ties at birth of ascending and descending generations—a loss to both predecessor and progeny—has certainly created an airborne people, a dangling people, a people who must forever attempt to acquire their self-identity and self-image in a positive way as they are bombarded with negative ones. To have lived for 243 years with no legal standing, no social status, no public work, and only economic value means that the issue of self-identity remains central. Marcus Garvey understood this very well. The issue of self-doubt, especially among the middle class, and issues of self-contempt, self-hatred, self-affliction, and self-flagellation among large numbers of black folk still remain crucial issues in black America.

You can imagine what the legacy of slavery and *Natal* alienation is when it intersects with a culture of consumption in which addiction to stimulation becomes the only means by which a vitality is preserved by a self in a society that promotes spectatorial passivity and evasive banality. The culture of consumption generates a passivity by means of spectatorial enactment. It generates a sense of deadening such that the self tries to preserve some sense of itself by engaging in some mode of therapeutic release. We get this in sports, in simulated sexuality, the disco culture, in music, and so forth. We engage in some ritualistic practice—going to Friday night parties, going to church on Sunday—for the self to feel as if it is alive, vital, and vibrant.

The legacy of slavery mediated with Jim Crowism, second-class citizenship, urbanization, all the different stages and phases that black people have been through from 1619 up to the present, are followed by the culture of consumption that begins to become more and more dominant between 1965 and the present. This has produced what I want to argue is the major challenge presented to black America, to black scholars, black intellectuals, black leaders, and black people: the highest level of forms of self-destruction known in black history. These demons that are at work, the demons of meaninglessness, of hopelessness, and a sense of nothingness, have conjoined with the institutional and structural marginalization of large number of black people, though not all (we should not overlook the black working middle class, even black prosperity among a selective slice of the black middle class, including a few of ourselves, owing to the struggle of those in the 1960s).

This level of self-destruction exists because for the first time there are now no longer viable institutions and structures in black America that can effectively transmit values such as hope, virtue, sacrifice, risk, and putting the needs of others higher or alongside one's own needs. In the past we've seen black colleges in which every Sunday they were forced to sit in those pews and Benjamin Mays would get up and say, "You must give service to the race," reminding these black, petit-bourgeois students that even as they went out into the world they had a cause, an obligation and a duty to do something beyond simply their own self-interest. What they did may have been narrow, myopic, and shortsighted, but the point is they had an institution that was transmitting that value. And it is not just the black school. We can talk about the black church, fraternities, and whole hosts of other institutions in black civil society. We no longer have these to the degree we did in the past, and they are being eroded slowly but surely. This is what is most frightening. This is why we get the exponential increase in black suicides between eighteen and thirty-five, unprecedented in black history. This is why we get escalating black homicides in which you get some of the most cold-hearted, mean-spirited dispositions and attitudes displayed by black people against other black people as well as nonblacks. It is a breakdown in the moral fabric.

Conservatives have made much of this point—Glenn Loury, Thomas Sowell, and a host of others have been saying there is something different about black America now, and they highlight the loss of values. But they understand loss of values as simply choices made by viduals, as if they are not shaped by the larger structural institutional realities of cultural consumption. Of course, these larger structures are affecting America as a whole, not just black America, but the negative consequences tend to be concentrated among those who have less access to financial and emotional resources.

Given this conjecture, the question becomes: How does one generate institutions and infrastructures? These institutions and infrastructures produced certain kinds of people—moral, virtuous people, not perfect people but persons who are willing to sacrifice and struggle. How do you sustain these institutions and infrastructures so that traditions of resistance can be sustained and if possible even expanded? So that when the hotter moments of American society emerge—those moments in which new progressive and prophetic possibilities surface—you have institutions and infrastructures that can come together to take advantage of them? If black people have learned anything in America it is that America is a profoundly conservative country, even given all of its commitments to experimentation and improvisation. By conservative I mean conservative in terms of its corporate capitalist structures, in terms of its unwillingness to give up its racism, sexism, and homophobia. Therefore, when you have a chance to push the movement forth you have to move quickly because the leaders and organizations will be crushed. The CIA and the FBI will move quickly and therefore you know it is not going to last that long. But in order to seize that kind of opportunity you have to have the ability to produce individuals who will sacrifice, who will live and die for the movement. These are not petty issues. Part of the problem in contemporary black America is that there is not a deep enough care, and thereby not a willingness to sacrifice. It may sound like I am making a moralist claim, but I am actually trying to make a systemic claim because it has to do with the relative paucity of institutions and infrastructures that can produce these kind of people and with the willingness of these people to actually sacrifice their time and energy to engage in a kind of struggle, as those who came before us had to do in order to produce us.

The Role of the Black Philosopher in Building Institutions

What has this to do with black philosophy? It has much to do with black philosophy. It means that we engage in institution building, as we have tried to do for the last sixteen years, so that we can at least keep each other in part accountable, even if we do not see each other as much as we like. This is very small, but very important. It means that we are keeping records of what we do, trying to sustain the vision, and trying to hold each other accountable in terms of our sacrifice. It means that we no longer feel as if the issues that once motivated us, issues of freedom and justice, are no longer salient in our own work. I am not talking about censorship or about indoctrination. I am talking about accountability. Accountability is mediated by means of discussion and dialogue—respectful discussion and dialogue. But it is accountability, nevertheless. Even as we reflect on the black underclass we can sustain our institutions to keep the discussion going and then to intervene into the larger discussion about the black underclass.

We have talked about the work of William Julius Wilson, keeping in mind that there has always been a black underclass since the end of slavery. What is significant now is its size, its social gravity, and the frightening and terrifying responses to it. Again, historical perspective is crucial. What are the ways in which the black underclass's position can be enhanced? On the one hand, I think Wilson is right that it is going to be a matter of public policy, that no private institution is willing and able to solve the problem of the black underclass. The only private institutions that have the resources to do so, namely, multinational corporations, hardly pay their taxes, so you cannot expect them to take on a major problem like the black underclass. And the notion of the black middle class—not Wilson's view—as the source of the panacea has to be the biggest hoax ever played on any emerging bourgeoisie in the history of the modern world. No middle class in the modern world has been cast as the source of the resolution of the problems of their ethnic or racial working class and underclass. They do not have the resources to do it. In addition, we have primarily a "lumpenbourgeosie," which is to say we have no serious economic or business class for the most part. Instead, our businesses tend to be locked within the lower echelons of the entrepreneurial sector of the economy, in which the multinational corporate sector is the major controller of resources. So to talk about black business in this way is ridiculous. Reginald Lewis, the leading black businessman in the country, and John H. Johnson, the second leading black businessman in the country, are not a part of the first five hundred of *Forbes*. So to look to these folk as the solution is comical.

The focus then becomes the public sphere, the contestation for power within the state, and hence black participation in politics. But in this very conservative moment it does not look good. The Democratic party is undergoing, as we know, a very slow but sure disintegration itself, especially given its association with black folk. So it becomes highly problematic to talk credibly about politics and policies. It is very clear that resources have to be in place to enhance the situation of the black underclass. People do not want to talk about money and resources, but it is the first step—not the only step—but it is the first step.

Without broader employment, without the child care requisite for the women who are the majority of the black underclass, without the manpower and womanpower problems there can be no serious talk about resolutions of the black underclass. In addition, as I noted, it is not just a matter of money, but a matter of values and sensibility, of morally latent ways of life and ways of struggle. A new kind of black leadership must emerge, a new kind of black organization and association—or set of organizations and associations—that can bring power and pressure to bear on the powers that be. One cannot talk about enhancing the plight of the black underclass without talking about politics, and to talk about politics is to talk about mobilization and organization. And yet to talk about organization and mobilization means to talk about the paucity of institutions and infrastructures.

This is why things become depressing at times. When you look around and see what is in place in the black community as it is undergoing this state of siege, you wonder what can be reinvigorated let alone created at an institutional level—not just an individual here, not just a book or an article there. These are important but they are limited. One has to talk organizationally. I would argue that Tommy Lott's discussion of rap music (see Chapter 5) is pertinent here: the degree to which there is institutional articulation of rap music so that power and pressure can be brought to bear as opposed to just the powerful critique mediated through radio. What kind of institutional translation is taking place? Very little. What are the conditions under which institutional translation can take place? This is a very difficult issue. Even the Jesse Jackson campaign is no answer to this because there are no serious infrastructures and institutions in the Rainbow Coalition. It is the coming together of persons every four years in a campaign. It is not a deep rooting of institutions and infrastructure in the black and other communities that can be sustained over time and space. Part of that has to do with Jackson's own institutional impatience. His refusal to engage in serious infrastructure building is part of the problem.

Presently I would argue that as black intellectuals and as black activists our reflections on the black underclass are significant because the kind of demystification that we engage in is important at the intellectual level. I want to affirm this quite emphatically because we live in an anti-intellectual culture and we boldly have to assert our right to engage in intellectual reflection without its having an overnight payoff. It might be linked to a larger project, but it may not have overnight payoff. Still, it must be done. If you are thinking as an intellectual who wants to have effectivity and efficacy further down the road, then you have to think about ways in which the kind of malaise that so much of black America finds itself can be met.

When we look around the black community, we see a set of prophetic churches and mosques, many of them patriarchal and deeply homophobic, but a link to a black freedom struggle that generates persons who are willing to live and die for struggle. They still produce persons who exude and exemplify what they exult and extol in terms of their values. We see some political organization, some neighborhood blocks or associations. These are very important. We see infrastructures in relation to sports, Big Brothers programs, little leagues. All these character-building activities that seem minuscule actually are very important in terms of helping produce certain kinds of persons who can indeed be willing to engage in struggle. But that is about it.

Even our black colleges more and more have been so fundamentally shaped by capitalist values that most of our students are graduating in business and communication. These students often find humanistic studies ornamental or decorative, something they have to take because it is part of a patch that old folks used to like. But they want to make money and therefore will zip through these classes and take business classes seriously, because they want to get into the middle class. That is not just black students, but students across the board. It is deeply shaping the values of a whole new generation to whom Malcolm X is "Malcolm the tenth" and Martin Luther King, Jr., is some kind of cultural icon that has no link whatsoever to everyday lives. What a challenge!

That is the impasse and the dilemma that I want to suggest. I do not have any easy way out other than this institution building, of which this conference is in many ways an instance, given the sixteen-year history of dialogue among black philosophers. There are other such institution-building efforts, but I hope that we are on the wave of such an institution-building activity regulated by an all-embracing moral vision, one that takes seriously class, gender, empire, sexual orientation, social analysis, historicist sensibility, the dedisciplinizing orientation, and worldliness, but also one that takes seriously praxis—which is to say, life commitment, which is to say, sacrificial commitment. I am not calling for martyrdom. I am just calling for sacrifice. But it is very important, because to be a member of the professional managerial class tends to mitigate against this very sense of commitment. Do you have to go against it? It means then that the rewards are less. It means that the status is indeed less, even if you are at a power elite institution such as Princeton. It means that the status has to have less value because what you are about dwarfs that.

In regard to this greater cause we can continue to produce persons who cultivate and build on these traditions of resistance so that when the hot moment comes—nobody can predict when the hot moment, our "December '55 moment," comes—these infrastructures and institutions can begin to come alive quickly before the repression sets in. And the repression and attacks will inevitably set in because this is America, and there is a lot at stake in the prosperity of America. Black people understand that. Yet it can be pushed, and progressive white comrades and feminist comrades will help push. Then we will be pushed back and the next generation will have to engage in their own challenge.

We hope the next generation of black philosophers will reflect on how they are going to deal with those human beings of African descent who are unemployed, underemployed, have inadequate health care, housing, education, and so on. The battle is perennial, yet each of us in our time must fight.

NOTE

Acknowledgment: This is a transcript of a speech given at the conference Meditations on Integration, held at the University of Delaware, June 1989.

ABOUT THE CONTRIBUTORS

ANITA L. ALLEN is associate professor of law at Georgetown University Law Center and Harvard Law School. She has published extensively on issues of privacy and the law, and on theory of legal rights. She is the author of *Uneasy Access: Privacy for Women in a Free Society*.

BERNARD R. BOXILL is professor of philosophy at the University of North Carolina at Chapel Hill. He has published extensively in the areas of ethics, social justice, and political theory regarding the black American experience. He is the author of *Blacks and Social Justice*.

LEONARD HARRIS is professor and chairperson of the African-American Studies Department at Purdue University. He has published scholarly articles on the history of blacks in philosophy and normative ethical theory. He is the editor of *Philosophy Born of Struggle* and *The Philosophy of Alaine Locke*.

FRANK M. KIRKLAND is associate professor of philosophy at Hunter College and the City University of New York Graduate Center. He has published a number of scholarly articles on Kant, Hegel, and Husserl. He has edited a collection of essays titled *Phenomenology—East and West*.

BILL E. LAWSON is assistant professor of philosophy at the University of Delaware. He has published articles on political obligations, crime victimization, and the social contract.

TOMMY LOTT is associate professor of philosophy at Stanford University and the University of Massachusetts, Boston. He has published scholarly articles in the areas of modern philosophy and cultural studies. He is currently editing a volume on slavery and social policy.

HOWARD MCGARY is associate professor of philosophy at Rutgers

University. He has published extensively in the areas of moral and social philosophy and African-American social and political thought. He is co-author (with Bill E. Lawson) of *Between Slavery and Freedom: Philosophy and American Slavery* (forthcoming).

ALBERT G. MOSLEY is professor of philosophy at Ohio University. He has published in the areas of logic, epistemology, and philosophy of art. He is the author of *An Introduction to Logic: From Everyday Life to Formal Systems*.

CORNEL WEST is professor of philosophy and chairperson of the African-American Studies Program at Princeton University. He has published extensively in the areas of religious thought, cultural diversity, and American philosophy. He is the author of *The American Evasion of Philosophy*; *Prophecy and Deliverance*; and *Prophetic Fragments*.

Index